CURING
the Dread of
DEATH

Theory, Research and Practice

Edited by
R.E. Menzies, R.G. Menzies & L. Iverach

First published 2018 by:
Australian Academic Press Group Pty. Ltd.
18 Victor Russell Drive
Samford Valley QLD 4520, Australia
www.australianacademicpress.com.au

Copyright © 2018 rests with the identifies authors for all contributions to this book.

Copying for educational purposes
The *Australian Copyright Act 1968* (Cwlth) allows a maximum of one chapter or 10% of this book, whichever is the greater, to be reproduced and/or communicated by any educational institution for its educational purposes provided that the educational institution (or the body that administers it) has given a remuneration notice to Copyright Agency Limited (CAL) under the Act.
For details of the CAL licence for educational institutions contact:
Copyright Agency Limited, 19/157 Liverpool Street, Sydney, NSW 2000.
E-mail info@copyright.com.au

Production and communication for other purposes
Except as permitted under the Act, for example a fair dealing for the purposes of study, research, criticism or review, no part of this book may be reproduced, stored in a retrieval system, or transmitted in any form or by any means electronic, mechanical, photocopying, recording or otherwise without prior written permission of the copyright holder.

Curing the Dread of Death: Theory, Research and Practice.

ISBN   9781925644111 (paperback)
ISBN   9781925644128 (ebook)

Disclaimer
Every effort has been made in preparing this work to provide information based on accepted standards and practice at the time of publication. The publisher and authors, however, makes no warranties of any kind of psychological outcome relating to use of this work and disclaim all responsibility or liability for direct or consequential damages resulting from any use of the material contained in this work.

Publisher: Stephen May
Copy Editor: Rhonda McPherson
Original cover art: Morgan Lawrence
Cover design: Luke Harris, Working Type Studio
Typesetting: Australian Academic Press
Printing: Lightning Source

Dedication

For Mum, Dad and Lachlan. Thank you for your endless love and support — REM.

For James William (Jim) Ovens, who showed me the art of dying — RGM.

For John and David, who have taught me to embrace the complexities of life with strength and tenderness — LI.

Contents

About the Editors...ix

List of Contributors..xi

Preface...xiii

Section 1: Theoretical Issues

Chapter 1

Impermanence and the human dilemma: Observations across the ages...................3

Rachel E. Menzies

> The opening chapter reviews the way in which various cultures have dealt with death from ancient times until the present. The role of death anxiety in myth and ritual, religion, art and literature are explored. It will be argued that communities across history have developed a range of ways to deny and conquer death.

Chapter 2

Fear of death: Nature, development and moderating factors.................................21

Ross G. Menzies and Rachel E. Menzies

> This chapter traces the natural history of death anxiety across the lifespan. The developmental literature will be reviewed to explore children's growing understanding of the construct of death across the first decade of life. The moderating factors of gender, age, religiosity, and health status are reviewed, as is the intriguing observation that death fears typically diminish in the last decades of life.

Chapter 3

Beyond the dread of death: Existentialism's embrace
of the meaninglessness of life...41

Gerard Kuperus

> Kuperus overviews the common threads in the philosophic positions of Sartre, Nietzsche, Camus, and related European philosophers of the late 19th century and early 20th century. The central existential concepts of absurdism, angst and responsibility will be introduced. It will be shown that existentialism emphasises the significance of living this life well, rather than fearing death.

Chapter 4

Love, death, and the quest for meaning 57

Mario Mikulincer

> Mikulincer applies attachment theory to explain the ways people experience and cope with the existential concerns of mortality and meaninglessness. The chapter reviews evidence that a sense of attachment security — a sense that the world is generally safe, other people are generally helpful, and I'm valuable and lovable — provides a psychological foundation for easing existential anxieties and constructing an authentic sense of continuity, coherence, meaning, connectedness, and autonomy.

Chapter 5

The death instinct and psychodynamic accounts of the wound of mortality 83

Ross G. Menzies and Rachel E. Menzies

> It is a broadly held view that Sigmund Freud dismissed death as being of little significance to our psychic struggles. While superficially true, this bland claim is an oversimplification of his theoretical position. Menzies and Menzies explore the contradictory nature of Freud's theorising on the death instinct and death anxiety, before examining modern psychoanalytic conceptions of our dynamic struggle with death.

Chapter 6

An intelligent design theory of the origins, evolution and function of religion: Toward an integration of existential and evolutionary perspectives 103

Tom Pyszczynski and Sharlynn Thompson

> In this chapter, an intelligent design theory of the origins and functions of religion is developed by integrating useful ideas from both evolutionary and existential perspectives. Pyszczynski and Thompson argue that integrating evolved cognitive proclivities emphasised by evolutionary theories with the emphasis on the motivational and emotional forces that bias these processes provides a more complete understanding of the origins and function of religion.

Chapter 7

Death anxiety and psychopathology 121

Lisa Iverach

> Lisa Iverach examines the evidence suggesting that death anxiety is a transdiagnostic construct that underpins the anxiety disorders, obsessive-compulsive disorder (OCD), panic and somatoform disorders, mood disorders and even eating disorders. It is argued that death anxiety must be tackled directly to improve long-term outcomes in mental health.

Section 2: Treatment Approaches

Chapter 8

Death in existential psychotherapies: A critical review 145

Joel Vos

> This chapter explores possible misinterpretations of the existential philosophers that have been made by the public, various writers, and even some developers of existential therapeutic schools. Reductionist and nonreductionist existential therapies are described in detail. Finally, an integrative existential-psychotherapeutic perspective on death will be suggested, with an overview of specific competencies and a review of empirical evidence.

Chapter 9

Cognitive and behavioural procedures for the treatment of death anxiety 167

Rachel E. Menzies

> This chapter provides a review of the central cognitive and behavioural procedures that have been trialled in the treatment of death anxiety in clinical and non-clinical populations.

Chapter 10

Death acceptance and the meaning-centred approach to end-of-life care 185

Paul T. P. Wong, David F. Carreno, and Beatriz Gongora Oliver

> No group more directly face death and impermanence than the terminally ill. Accordingly, end-of-life care may inform the treatment of death anxiety. The range of psychological approaches used in end-of-life care will be described and reviewed.

Chapter 11

Continuing bonds between the living and the dead in contemporary western societies: Implications for our understandings of death and the experience of death anxiety 203

Edith Steffen and Elaine Kasket

> Detachment from loved ones who have died is often considered to be a healthy grief response in western societies. However, in more collectivist cultures it is argued that continuing ties to loved ones who have died is an important part of grieving. This chapter will explore the application of continuing bonds as part of grief therapy.

Chapter 12

Treating low self-esteem: Cognitive behavioural therapies and
terror management theory..219

Peter J. Helm, Jennifer E. Duchschere and Jeff Greenberg

> Terror management theory proposes that high self-esteem buffers against death fears and existential dread. Individuals with low self-esteem have been shown to be particularly vulnerable to mortality priming in the laboratory. Accordingly, this chapter reviews the literature on various cognitive behavioural approaches to low self-esteem. Emphasis is placed on incorporating terror management theory (TMT) into cognitive behaviour therapy (CBT), acceptance and commitment therapy (ACT) and dialectical behaviour therapy (DBT) when dealing with self-esteem.

Chapter 13

Therapeutic interventions for the dread of death:
Personal and clinical reflections...239

Thomas Heidenreich und Alexander Noyon

> Drawing on material presented in earlier chapters, and European existential thinking, this chapter provides an overview of therapeutic interventions for dealing with and confronting the fear of death. Starting from a case example, the authors explore religious and philosophical approaches as well as ways of including therapeutic tools such as literature and music in the therapeutic context.

About the Editors

Rachel E. Menzies

Rachel Menzies completed her honours degree in psychology at the University of Sydney, taking out the Dick Thompson Thesis Prize for her work on the dread of death and its relationship to obsessive-compulsive disorder (OCD). She published her first paper on death fears in *Clinical Psychology Review* as an undergraduate student, and followed this by convening a symposium on the topic at the 8th World Congress of Behavioural and Cognitive Therapies in Melbourne in 2016. Her manuscript on death fears and OCD was the lead paper in the first edition of the *Australian Clinical Psychologist*. She was recently featured in *The Conversation Yearbook 2016*, a collection of the top 1% of 'standout articles from Australia's top thinkers' published by Melbourne University Press. In 2017, she gave her first invited plenary address, and an invited workshop, at the 47th Congress of the European Association for Behavioural and Cognitive Therapies (EABCT). Both presentations explored death anxiety, existential issues and their role in abnormal behaviour.

Ross G. Menzies

Professor Menzies completed his undergraduate, masters and doctoral degrees in psychology at the University of NSW. He is currently Professor of Psychology in the Graduate School of Health, University of Technology Sydney (UTS). In 1991, he was appointed founding Director of the Anxiety Disorders Clinic at the University of Sydney, a post which he held for over 20 years. He is the past New South Wales President, and twice National President, of the Australian Association for Cognitive and Behaviour Therapy (AACBT). He is the editor of Australia's national CBT journal, *Behaviour Change*, and has trained psychologists, psychiatrists and allied health workers in CBT around the globe. Professor Menzies is an active researcher with more than two decades of continuous funding from national competitive sources. He currently holds over A$7 million in research funding. He has produced eight books and more than 180 journal papers and book chapters, and was the President and Convenor of the 8th World Congress of Behavioural and Cognitive Therapies.

Lisa Iverach

Lisa has published several theoretical and experimental papers on the topic of death anxiety, including a comprehensive review regarding the role of death anxiety in psychopathology, which appeared in Clinical Psychology Review. She has also shared her knowledge of death anxiety at conferences and via several media interviews. During her exploration of death anxiety as a transdiagnostic factor, Lisa was a Research Fellow at the Centre for Emotional Health, Macquarie University, and a Senior Research Fellow in the Faculty of Health Sciences at the University of Sydney. In addition to her research on death anxiety, Lisa has published widely on the topic of social anxiety and speech disorders, and she has presented her research at national and international conferences. In order to embrace the inevitability of change in life, Lisa recently made a career transition into the government sector, and is now coordinating research projects with universities around Australia to understand the relationship between human behaviour and future transport (e.g., drones, electric cars, automated vehicles), which fascinates her just as much as death anxiety does.

List of Contributors

Carreno, David F., University of Almeria, Andalusia, Spain

Duchschere, Jennifer. E., The University of Arizona, Tucson, United States of America

Greenberg, Jeff, The University of Arizona, Tucson, United States of America

Heidenreich, Thomas, Hochschule Esslingen, Esslingen am Neckar, Germany

Helm, Peter J., The University of Arizona, Tucson, United States of America

Iverach, Lisa, The University of Sydney, New South Wales, Australia

Kasket, Elaine, Regent's University London, England

Kuperis, Gerard, University of San Francisco, California, United States of America

Menzies, Rachel E., The University of Sydney, New South Wales, Australia

Menzies, Ross G., University of Technology Sydney, New South Wales, Australia

Mikulincer, Mario, Interdisciplinary Center (IDC) Herzliya, Israel

Noyan, Alexander, Hochschule Mannheim, Germany

Oliver, Beatriz G., Torrecardenas Hospital, Almeria, Andalusia, Spain

Pyszczynski, Tom, University of Colorado, Colorado Springs, United States of America

Steffen, Edith M., University of Roehampton, London, England

Thompson, Sharlynn, University of Colorado, Colorado Springs, United States of America

Vos, Joel, University of Roehampton, London, England

Wong, Paul T.P., Meaning-Centerd Counselling Institute, North York, Ontario, Canada

Preface

The dread of death has appeared throughout recorded human history in art, literature, song, myth and ritual. In both ancient and modern societies, death has been personified in a variety of forms, such as the grim reaper, stalking the terrified living as a spectre to haunt us all. The awareness of our own mortality, arguably unique to humans, was famously described by William James as 'the worm at the core' of our existence. The lingering tension of death appears to pervade cultural and religious practices, such as the meditative handling of skull-shaped bracelets in Tibetan Buddhism, the decoration of family gravestones associated with Dia de Muertos (i.e., the day of the dead) in Mexico, and the wearing of a crucifix in various Christian denominations. Death is everywhere.

Rachel Menzies (Chapter 1) opens our book with an exploration of the many ways in which humans have come to grips with the presence of death across time. From *The Epic of Gilgamesh,* written over 4000 years ago, to the Fates of ancient Greece, mummification in Egypt, and Buddhist practices in Japan, Tibet and China, Menzies takes us on a tour of our attempts to respond to the finitude of life. She also describes the most recent trends in preserving our contact with the dead. For example, tattoo parlours have seen increasing requests for 'memorial tattoos', which use a combination of cremation ashes and ink to preserve a part of our lost loved one's inside our own skin. She explores those who seek comfort in computerised chatbots to imitate the personality of those who have departed (see also Steffen and Kasket, Chapter 11). Whether one sees these behaviours as maladaptive attempts to deny death, or adaptive efforts to extend the bonds to the deceased, will vary from reader to reader (and, as Steffen and Kasket point out, from culture to culture).

In Chapter 2, Rachel and Ross Menzies show us that the fear of death is slowly acquired across the early years of life. Various components of the death concept, such as the inevitability and irreversibility of death, appear to be mastered by children in stages between three and ten years of age. Interestingly, the growth in this awareness of mortality in children coincides with a rise in anxiety and phobic reactions to threatening objects, situations and activities. That is, awareness of the nature of death breeds exaggerated fear and avoidance of (perceived) possible encounters with it. Iverach (Chapter 7) takes this notion further, arguing that death anxiety is a transdiagnostic construct, underpinning a range of mental health problems including the anxiety and mood disorders. Recent research in clinical samples of psychiatric patients supports this claim, demonstrating relationships between fear of death and various markers of clinical severity, including overall distress, number of lifetime diagnoses and even number of psychiatric hospitalisations. Iverach persuades us that the majority of psychiatric conditions may be expressions of underlying death anxiety.

Other than potentially developing fears and psychiatric disorders, how do humans respond to the knowledge of the certainty of their death? Many of our contributors (see Chapters 2, 4, 6 and 12) argue that terror management theory (TMT) best accounts for the behavioural and emotional responses experienced in response to the construct of death. TMT proposes that broad cultural practices (e.g., seeking academic achievement, attaining wealth and professional success, forming strong political affiliations, extending the self through children and family) may serve as defensive mechanisms in the face of the terror of death. Considerable experimental research supports the claim that adherence to strongly held 'cultural worldviews' may serve to buffer against death fears. As Helm, Duchschere and Greenberg (Chapter 12) show us, this is achieved by building robust self-esteem — a sense of self that provides a virtual immortality in the face of death. Mikulincer (Chapter 4) expands the TMT position by showing that attachment security may similarly moderate the typical responses to death priming seen in 'mortality salience' research designs. Attachment security — a sense that the world is generally safe, other people are generally helpful, and that one is valuable and lovable — appears to provide a solid psychological basis for reducing death dread.

The 'cultural worldviews' described by TMT include religious belief, and the role of religion in mitigating dearth anxiety is explored at length by Pyszczynski and Thompson (Chapter 6). As these authors argue, religion transforms death from an unsolvable problem to a controllable one by providing a pathway to literal immortality through virtuous behaviour. Theoretically, the symbolic immortality achieved through adherence to other worldviews would seem unnecessary given strongly held religious beliefs. Unfortunately, as Pyszczynski and Thompson argue, using religious belief to deal with death anxiety comes at a cost, particularly at a national and international level. Strongly held religious belief often contributes to disdain and hostility, as well as violence toward other groups with different perspectives. Further, as Menzies and Menzies (Chapter 2) point out, some of the personal benefits of involvement in religious communities may be achieved through other activities that also involve ingroup identification, social networking and support. These authors briefly review the work of Haslam, Dingle, Chopik and others that have found profound benefits on mental health from such activities as choir singing, creative writing and increasing social networks more generally. In a similar vein, Kuperus (Chapter 3) questions the need for God in forming a positive view of life. His chapter focuses on atheist existentialists (Nietzsche, Sartre, and Camus) who all suggest — in different ways — that the lack of an afterlife can actually lead us to a greater celebration of life. Nietzsche, famous for declaring 'God is dead', suggests that we are inauthentic beings, shaped by the activities of the herd. The ultimate prescription that Nietzsche presents to us is to become who we truly are. Vos (Chapter 8) agrees, arguing that the existentialists are typically misunderstood — standing far more for life and creating meaning than wallowing with anxiety in the shadow of death.

Creating meaning is also at the centre of Wong, Carreno and Oliver's approach to death anxiety (Chapter 10). Rather than denial of death, these authors encourage death acceptance and have developed protocols that help patients connect with various sources of meaning in their lives. The therapist encourages patients to clarify their personal values and to live in the service of those values, in a manner that is not dissimilar to acceptance and commitment therapy (ACT). Vos (Chapter 8) picks up on many of these issues in his review of existential psychotherapies. The number of approaches within this broad philosophic framework is large, and Vos does a thorough job of exploring the differences between each major school or approach. Many of the popular approaches, like that of Irvin Yalom, are shown to combine TMT and the psychodynamic theory of defence mechanisms. These therapists claim that we defend ourselves existentially against the terror evoked by life's truths. Clients are encouraged to 'unpeel' their resistances to life, particularly death anxiety, which are seen to prevent complete living. Therapeutic techniques consist of staying with feelings, self-expression, free association, identifying emotions and fostering trust in the ability to experience and carry negative feelings.

Therapeutically, a range of other approaches is reviewed in this volume. Rachel Menzies (Chapter 9) explores the status of cognitive behaviour therapy (CBT), the gold standard in evidence-based psychotherapy for the anxiety disorders. She details the range of procedures on offer from the restructuring of catastrophic thinking (e.g., 'if I die before my children their lives will be ruined forever'), systematic desensitisation, graded exposure to death hierarchies, behavioural experiments and death education programs. Surprisingly few randomised trials of CBT for death anxiety exist, although the evidence for exposure-based procedures is encouraging. Helm, Duchschere and Greenberg (Chapter 12) explore the way in which CBT, acceptance and commitment therapy (ACT), and dialectical behaviour therapy (DBT) seek to address self-esteem, a known buffer against death anxiety. They show how each of these traditions can be better informed by the foundation stone of TMT, pointing the way forward to future improvements in standard psychotherapeutic offerings.

The treatment section of our volume finishes with Heidenreich and Noyon's personal and clinical reflections on working with the dread of death (Chapter 13). Bridging the gap between the European existentialist tradition and contemporary CBT, they emphasise a 'shared humanity' approach to death — an acknowledgement of the fact that both the therapist and patient must die. Death is not something that the wise counsellor will 'solve' for the client. Menzies and Menzies (Chapter 5) make similar observations in their review of contemporary psychodynamic practice. They congratulate the psychoanalytic revisionists, like Akhtar and Frommer, for chiding the therapist who places themselves above the death crisis. For, in reality, death is the great equaliser between client and clinician. Both remain equally ignorant of the actual experience of the event. Further, as argued by existential psychotherapists, the clinician (like the client) is just as vulnerable to the normal narcissism that lets one deny death.

As the reader can hopefully tell from this preface, our volume reviews the dread of death, and its management, from a broad range of perspectives with researchers and writers from a variety of cultures, academic traditions and disciplines across the globe. The fields covered are broad — including palliative care and grief, psychodynamic theory, social, developmental and clinical psychology, sociology and anthropology, counselling practice as well as history, art and philosophy. Throughout the volume, one message shines through: Death is not to be feared, but may hold the key to living a vital, authentic life. So many authors within the volume suggest that we cannot live fully without complete acceptance of the fragility and finiteness of life. The challenge is to discover pathways to death acceptance to enable a life of significance and meaning.

Rachel E. Menzies and Ross G. Menzies

Section 1: Theoretical Issues

Chapter 1

Impermanence and the human dilemma: Observations across the ages

Rachel E. Menzies

> I shall die, and shall I not then be as Enkidu?
> Sorrow has entered my heart! I am afraid of death.
>> The Epic of Gilgamesh (2100 BC)

As Gilgamesh's powerful 4000-year-old lament suggests, the dread of death has appeared since humans first started recording their history (Becker, 1973). William James famously described our awareness of our own inevitable death, arguably a uniquely human quality, as 'the worm at the core' of human existence (1902/1985, p. 119). Various cultures across history have shown ambitious and impressive attempts to deny and conquer death, from the ancient Egyptian practice of mummification, to the ongoing Day of the Dead festival in Mexico. To this end, myth, cultural practice, religion, literature, and art have all attempted to deal with the fear of our own mortality in a vast array of ways.

Death across the ages

Myth and ritual

While fears of ageing and mortality pervade a variety of cultural myths and rituals across the centuries, they are made particularly vivid in the mythology and rites of ancient Greece. The Greek gods themselves were defined by their immortality, frequently referred to as 'the deathless gods', and it was this enviable trait that separated them from humankind. The goddess of death and guardian of the underworld, Persephone, was often not referred to by name, for fear of attracting her attention. The Greek attitude towards mortality is particularly evident in the epithet attributed to this goddess of death: '*epaine*', or 'dread' (Mirto, 2012, p. 22).

Despite this dread, death was seen as largely inevitable, and the lifespan as something unchangeable and determined by fate — or, more accurately, the Fates. The Fates, a sisterly triad of 'all-terrible goddesses' (Pindar, as cited in Bowra, 1968, p. 100), were the divine personifications of destiny, consisting of Clotho, 'the spinner', who spun the thread of life and determined an individual's birth; Lachesis, 'the allotter', responsible for measuring the thread of life allotted to each human, and; Atropos, 'the inevitable', whose role involved choosing the manner and time of each individual's death and, finally, cutting the 'thin-spun' thread of their life with her 'abhorred shears' (Milton, 1853, p. 611). The role of the Fates in Greek myth suggests that death was viewed as a central part of being human, and an unavoidable condition of being alive. The goddess Athena herself is said to admit: 'The great leveller, Death: not even the gods can defend a man, not even one they love, that day when fate takes hold and lays him out at last' (Homer, Fagles, 1996, p. 115), while the goddess Aphrodite regretfully informs one of her mortal lovers: 'Old age will soon enfold you, remorseless, the same for everyone, for it stands one day at the side of all human beings, deadly, dispiriting — even the gods abhor it' (Homer, Cashford, 2003, p. 95).

Consistent with the Greek view of death as fearful yet inevitable, their mythology features notable examples of humans who have come close to cheating death, but have ultimately failed. Orpheus, arguably the most famous mythical musician, travelled to the underworld in an attempt to rescue his beloved and recently deceased wife, Eurydice. After Persephone had been charmed by his musical skills, the goddess agreed to allow Orpheus to return to earth with Eurydice, on the condition that he would not turn back to look at his wife on their walk out of the underworld. Orpheus failed to keep this promise, glancing back to check on his wife as they escaped, and she was forever confined to the realm of the dead. The myth of Tithonus further illustrates the tragedy that may ensue when humans pursue immortality. A goddess was believed to have fallen in love with the mortal Tithonus, and, wishing that he may stay with her forever, she begged Zeus to make her lover immortal. Although this wish was granted, the goddess forgot to ask Zeus for eternal youth. In a bitter twist, although Tithonus did indeed live eternally; 'hateful old age weighed him down completely so that he could neither move nor lift his limbs' (Homer, Cashford, 2003, p. 94). After experiencing the increasing cruelty of old age over his eternal lifespan, Tithonus was said to ultimately beg for death to overcome and release him.

While the myths of Greece give some sense of the ancients' dread of death, the rituals of the Eleusinian mystery festival serve as perhaps the most intriguing demonstration of the classical fixation on mortality. The Eleusinian Mysteries, which took place annually 14 miles outside of Athens, are the world's oldest known mystery festival, and easily the most famous (Clinton, 2007). Ostensibly, the festival invokes the mourning of the goddess Demeter for her young daughter, Persephone. Persephone was believed to have been abducted by Hades, the powerful god of the underworld, so that she may become his queen and rule alongside him in the afterlife. Travellers to Eleusis wishing to be initiated into the sacred rites would re-enact the distraught wanderings of Demeter as she searched for her stolen daughter, forming a fumbling, blindfolded procession, and thereby participating in the shared suffering of the two goddesses. This understanding of the rites has been pieced together by modern scholars with much difficulty, as the Mysteries' insistence on secrecy was maintained by the threat of death to anyone foolish enough to reveal the festival's rituals.

However, secrecy was characteristic of many mystery cults at the time. What was it about the Eleusinian Mysteries that attracted thousands of followers from within and outside of Greece? The ancient orator Isocrates puts it quite simply: by becoming an initiate in these rites, one was promised 'sweeter hopes concerning the end of life and eternity' (Johnston, 2009, p. 216). That is, the Mysteries of Eleusis guaranteed participants a better lot in the afterlife. This relationship between the Mysteries and death riddles the surviving ancient literature. A hymn attributed to the epic poet Homer, which forms the foundational understanding of the mythology underlying the Mysteries, claims:

> Blessed is the mortal on earth who has seen these rites, but the uninitiate who has not shared in them never has the same lot once dead in the dreary darkness. (Homer, Foley, 1994, p. 26)

By celebrating Persephone, wife of Hades, the initiate strengthened their relationship with the goddess of the underworld, and was therefore believed to be treated more favourably after death (Sourvinou-Inwood, 2003). Not only did participation guarantee a better fate for initiates in the afterlife, it also offered the initiates a practical preparation for their inevitable death. Plutarch makes a direct comparison between the ritual experiences of the initiates, and the journey in the afterlife, writing that the soul:

> suffers something like what those who participate in the great initiations suffer ... First of all there are wanderings and wearisome rushings about and certain journeys unending through the darkness ... But then one encounters an extraordinary light, and pure regions and meadows offer welcome ... in which now the completely initiated one, becoming free and set loose, enjoys the rite, crowned and consorts with holy and pure men. (Plutarch, Clinton, 2007, p. 354)

Participation in the Mysteries was thereby an enactment not only of Demeter's mourning for her missing daughter, but of the initiate's own death. The moment when the sanctuary doors were thrown open, revealing bright light, has been argued to deliberately resemble the moment of death (Clinton, 2007). In this way, the experience of the Mysteries may have been designed to prepare the initiate for their journey to the underworld, with the alternating darkness and light which characterised the rites representing the crossing of boundaries between this world and the next (Cole, 2003). After completing this symbolic enactment of one's own death, an Eleusinian initiate thereby earned a certain degree of authority on matters of death and dying. This is demonstrated in Aristophanes' ancient comedy *The Frogs*, which features a chorus of Eleusinian initiates, who guide the god Dionysos on his journey through the underworld. While other mortals are said to suffer in the 'weltering seas of filth and ever-rippling dung' (Ford, 2006, p. 313) of the underworld, the chorus of Eleusinian mystics are able to boast: 'For on us alone do the sun and the divine daylight shine, all of us who have been initiated' (Cole, 2003, p. 199). Even after death, it appears that those who had experienced the Mysteries were believed to receive a privileged and illuminated position in the gloomy land of the dead.

Similarly, in Aristophanes' *Peace*, one character nearing death attests: 'I must be initiated before I die', highlighting the importance of the Mysteries in an individual's views concerning their own mortality, and the need to experience the sacred rites before succumbing to death (Rogers, 1923, p. 37). Such benefits in the afterlife arguably explain the widespread popularity of the Mysteries at Eleusis. In fact, when Cicero, the renowned Roman politician and orator, reflected on all the wonders that had emerged from Athens, such as the Parthenon, the Olympics, the creation of theatre, and the invention of democracy, which did he believe to be the most significant? In his own words, 'Athens has produced many extraordinary and divine things but nothing better than those Mysteria ... Not only have we received a way of living with prosperity but also a way of dying with greater hope' (Clinton, 2007, p. 356).

While fewer written sources are available to illuminate the myths of ancient Egypt, their relationship with death is made profoundly evident in the Egyptian burial rites. Most notably, the ritual of mummification can be seen as a desperate attempt to preserve the body after death, and thus allow the deceased to continue their existence. The earliest known burials in Egypt occurred well before 3000 BC. Interestingly, these early burial pits were always found in the sand of the desert, rather than the soil of the valley, in order to make use of the natural preservation of the corpse offered by the sand, rather than allowing the body to rot in the soil (Spencer, 1982). This lengthy process, which typically lasted 70 days, involved a series of elaborate mortuary procedures as well as some revealing religious rites. The individual's brain was removed using a hook through the nostrils, and organs were removed by an incision in the flank, to be preserved separately. The interior of the body was anointed, the incision was stitched close, and the exterior was covered in natron, washed, and wrapped with linen. In order to recreate a plump and lifelike appearance, corpses were occasionally filled with sawdust or linen, artificial eyes were inserted, and patches of leather were sewn onto the skin to cover bedsores (Spencer, 1982). In addition, various burial spells were performed by priests, in order to prevent the corpse from decaying, being infested by maggots, producing foul odours and fluids, or showing any other indication that the body may in fact be deceased (Zandee, 1977). Finally, burial tombs were stocked with the finest cuts of beef, jars full of wine, bread, cosmetics, weapons, and even board games, to ensure that the deceased would be neither bored nor unfed when awakening in the afterlife.

The Egyptian mummification process represents one of the most vivid and determined efforts to deny our own mortality, through an ambitious and impressive attempt to completely preserve the body in as lifelike a form as possible. The awareness and fear of death pervaded not only Egyptian burial practices, but daily life. Egyptians would frequently carry an ankh amulet on their person, a symbol believed to confer on the wearer various powers associated with life and immortality (Hamilton-Paterson & Andrews, 1978). Further, the pharaoh was believed to be a divine and immortal incarnation of the previous leader, such that the death of a pharaoh was never devastating to the Egyptian people, because he was not understood to have truly died. In addition, Herodotus, regarded as the father of history in western literature, described the dinner-party behaviour of wealthy Egyptians in the 5th century BC:

> When the rich give a party and the meal is finished, a man carries round amongst the guests a wooden image of a corpse in a coffin, carved and painted to look as much like the real thing as possible, and anything from 18 inches to 3 foot long; he shows it to each guest in turn, and says: 'Look upon this body as you drink and enjoy yourself; for you will be just like it when you are dead. (Herodotus, De Sélincourt, 1996, p. 125)

While the mummification and burial rituals of the ancient Egyptians offer a quintessential example of the human attempt to conquer death throughout the ages, the deliberate destruction of the body may have in some cases served the same purpose. Among the Wari population of Brazil, funerary custom largely involved mortuary cannibalism, or the consumption of the deceased. Until the 1960s, Wari individuals typically disposed of their dead by eating the roasted brain, liver, heart, flesh, and occasionally consuming the ground bones. Elderly tribe members described such rituals as a means of coping with grief and the loss of a loved one. One participant in this ritual mortuary cannibalism stated that 'when we ate the body, we did not think longingly about the dead' (Conklin, 1995, p. 76). From the time of death, the distressed kin continuously hugged and cradled the corpse, which, until disposal, was never left to lie unaccompanied. One Wari member described observing a funeral in which the corpse was nearly destroyed by grieving attendants. This grief-induced possessiveness over the body appeared to reach such a level that a senior kinsman was forced to mandate that only one kinsman could hold the corpse at any one time. Although these physically destructive attempts to deal with death offer a stark contrast to the desperate preservative methods of the ancient Egyptians, rituals such as these provide a vivid picture of the diverse methods employed by human cultures across time in order to allay fears of death and impermanence.

Religion

According to theoretical accounts of early religion, most, if not all religious inspiration has derived from the dread of death (Malinowski, 1925). Throughout human history, religion has offered the promise of a literal immortality, through burial rites and ceremonies, communication with the deceased, and in the worship of spirits. While different religions have historically offered the guarantee of immortality in various ways, all religious traditions have attempted to address the search for meaning in life despite the inevitability of death (Lifton & Olson, 1974). Since the 4th century BC, religious cults have been founded on heroes who were believed to have cheated death or returned unscathed from the underworld, offering instructions to followers to help them in their eventual journey to the afterlife. It was among such cults that early Christianity arose, as one of many religious traditions at the time to be centred on a supernatural healer who had been resurrected from death (Becker, 1973).

Across the most widely practiced religions, the Abrahamic religions promise the direct continuance of life after death for the devout, and Hindu and Buddhist traditions heavily feature imagery of rebirth. However, while Islam, Christianity and Judaism arguably address the dread of death through a common promise of eternal life for adherents, the twin notions of the inevitability of death and the importance of accepting this are at the heart of Buddhism. Buddhist scriptures frequently encourage followers to contemplate the material and thus transient nature of the body. For instance, a series of ten 'meditations on impurity' are outlined in scriptures, and represent each stage of a human corpse's decomposition. One 5th century account of this practice encourages reflection on the human body as:

> A collection of over three hundred bones, jointed by one hundred and eighty joints, bound together by nine hundred sinews, plastered over with nine hundred pieces of flesh, enveloped in the moist inner skin, enclosed in the outer cuticle, with orifices here and there, constantly dribbling and trickling like a grease pot, inhabited by a community of worms, the home of disease, the basis of painful states, perpetually oozing from the nine orifices like a chronic open carbuncle ... there is no distinc-

tion between a king's body and an outcaste's in so far as its impure nauseating repulsiveness is concerned. (Buddhaghosa, 1991, p. 183)

Despite the emphasis on the impermanence of the human body, and the acknowledgment of the inevitability of decay that appears throughout Buddhism, bodily relics of the Buddha and of enlightened individuals, such as teeth and bones, have been collected, displayed in prominent temples, and worshipped with zeal across the ages. Such relics have been viewed as living entities, and even considered to be legal persons (Sharf, 1992). One lesser known Buddhist practice further highlights a desperate attempt to conquer death in contrast with the scriptural emphasis on accepting impermanence within the tradition. In Japan, some Buddhist monks died deliberately with the aim of living forever, in a practice known as self-mummification. Monks who achieved this difficult feat became a *sokushinbutsu*, or a 'living Buddha'. One such example is provided by Daijuku Bosatsu Shinnyokai Shonin in 1783, whose process of self-preservation and death was reportedly achieved after ten long years (Jerimiah, 2007). For the first three years, he was reported to have consumed a meagre diet of berries and twigs in order to reduce his body fat. For the next thousand days, he consumed simply pine bark and resin for the purposes of bodily preservation. In his final thousand days on earth, he consumed tea made from a poisonous substance often used to make lacquer. This deliberate consumption of toxins aimed to protect the body from being posthumously defiled by insects. Following this, he was buried alive, and meditated until his death. Oxygen was provided through a breathing tube in the walls of a stone room, and he rang a bell daily to signal to his followers that he was still alive. Once the bell no longer rang, the tomb was sealed. After three years, the tomb was re-opened, and his body had mummified.

Another historic example of the paradoxical attempts within Buddhism to conquer physical death while embracing impermanence is that of K b -Daishi, a Japanese monk and poet who founded the Shingon school of Buddhism. The poems of Kobo-Daishi are riddled with themes of transience, and frequently encourage the reader to reflect on mortality in order to gain inner peace. He encapsulates this notion of death acceptance as the key to happiness in his words: 'in order to attain serenity of mind ... consider that everyone's fate is to become a corpse', while another poem consists only of the line: 'When you tremble with worry, contemplate the truth that all elements of this world are nonsubstantial and impermanent'. At the centre of Shingon Buddhism was sacred Mount Koya, which features what remains today as the largest graveyard in Japan. In 835, Kobo-Daishi chose to be buried alive in a cave amidst the mountain's graveyard. However, he told his disciples that they need not grieve, because he would remain alive eternally in the cave (Miyata, 2006). Several years later, his followers opened the cave, and reported that his hair had grown nearly three feet long. Consistent with Kobo-Daishi's promise of an eternally living spirit, the monks on Mount Koya continue to prepare daily meals for their leader, who is believed to still be alive and meditating. The cave in which he is reported to reside is accessible only to the high priest, who enters the sacred space twice a day to serve the famous monk his required meals. Today, visitors to the cemetery can not only watch monks prepare these meals for Kobo-Daishi, they are also confronted with various legends centring on death. One particular well in the heart of the graveyard is a popular visiting spot for tourists, due to its reported ability to prophesise death. Local legend says that if you peer into the well and do not see your reflection, you will die within the next three years.

While Kobo-Daishi is believed to hold an eternal residency on Mount Koya after being buried alive, attempts for physical immortality within Buddhism have not always been so effective. As a result of the difficulty and length of the process, only approximately 20 individuals appear to have successfully self-mummified, and the act has since been declared illegal in Japan. However, the desire to maintain a perfectly preserved corpse, and the attempt to do so by deliberate self-imposed mummification, is by no means exclusive to Japan. Elsewhere in Asia, such as in Tibet and China, individuals whose bodies appear to have resisted decay or decomposition following their death had similarly been celebrated for their presumed spiritual attainment, or even worshipped as gods (Sharf, 1992). Despite this attempt to resist the natural process of decomposition through self-mummification, the display of such remains in temples may serve as a reminder to visitors of the inevitability of death. Further, the pervasiveness of such displays within Buddhism, as well as the worship of preserved bodily relics such as the corpses of saints within Catholicism, reflect the deeper struggle to confront mortality in the face of the scriptural emphasis on embracing impermanence.

Art and literature
The dread of death has played a significant role in literature and art throughout human history. As such, it is perhaps no surprise that the earliest surviving great work of literature, *The Epic of Gilgamesh*, centres on a young man's

struggle to understand death, and his pursuit of eternal life. Composed 4000 years ago, the epic poem tells the story of Gilgamesh, a Babylonian king, who mourns the death of his closest friend, Enkidu. In vivid and moving words, the king laments:

> My friend, whom I loved so dear …
> The doom of mortals overtook him.
> Six days I wept for him and seven nights.
> I did not surrender his body for burial,
> Until a maggot dropped from his nostril.
>
> Then I was afraid that I too would die,
> I grew fearful of death, and so wander the wild.
> What became of my friend was too much to bear …
> My friend, Enkidu, whom I loved, has turned to clay.
> Shall I not be like him, and also lie down,
> never to rise again, through all eternity?
> (George, 1999, pp. 77–78)

Gilgamesh's horror at his friend's death and decay, as well as his awareness of his own eventual fate, lead him on a lengthy quest to discover the secret of immortality. However, the king eventually learns that mortality is inevitable, and that humans are unable to outsmart death. In the words of an inn-keeper whom he meets on his journey:

> The eternal life you are seeking you shall not find.
> When the gods created mankind, they established death for mankind,
> And withheld eternal life for themselves. (Foster, 2001, p. 75)

While *The Epic of Gilgamesh* offers a glimpse into the pervasive fears of mortality in ancient Mesopotamia, the fear of death and desire for eternal life similarly riddles the later poetry of ancient Greece. The famous poetess Sappho, writing around 600 BC, paints a gloomy picture of death and the afterlife:

> When you lie dead
> No one will notice later or feel sad …
> Once lost in Hades' hall
> You will be homeless and invisible —
> Another shadow flittering back and forth
> With shadows of no worth. (Sappho, Poochigian, 2009, p. 17)

Her description of the dead as unseen shadows is eerie, yet clearly consistent with the classical Greek view of Hades, the name of which can be translated as 'invisible' (Mirto, 2012, p. 15). Sappho's poetry vividly demonstrates her reflection on her own impending death, and her laments over the loss of her youth:

> Stiffness has seized on these once supple limbs,
> And black braids with the passing years turned white.
> Age weighs heavily on me, and the knees
> Buckle that long ago, like fawns, pranced nimbly.
> I groan much, but to what end? Humans simply
> Cannot be ageless like divinities. (Sappho, Poochigian, 2009, p. 45)

Although Sappho's words reflect the ancient struggle to cope with the final stage of life, some later writers have attempted to offer consolation in the face of aging and death. In 44 BC, Cicero, the famous Roman orator, composed a short treatise encouraging the reader to embrace old age. Cicero describes the fear of death as one 'objection to growing old', acknowledging that this particular objection 'seems especially calculated to cause worry and distress to a man of my years' (Cicero, Freeman, 2016, p. 139). Despite this acknowledgment of the anxiety death has created among many of his peers, Cicero offers sage advice to readers that may fear their mortality:

> An actor does not need to remain on stage throughout a play. It is enough that he appears in the appropriate acts. Likewise, a wise man need not stay on the stage of this world until the audience applauds at the end. The time allotted to our lives may be short, but it is long enough to live honestly and decently ... Death comes to the young with force, but to the old when the time is right. To me there is great comfort in this idea, so that as death grows nearer, the more I feel like a traveler who at last sees the land of his home port after a long voyage. (pp. 145–149)

While Cicero acknowledges the inevitability of death, stating: 'We know that we cannot escape death — in fact, it may come for us this very day' (p. 155), he also emphasises the virtual immortality one can gain through the fame of one's deeds:

> To say a few boastful words about myself, as old men often will
> — do you think that I would have labored so hard day and night,
> at home and in wars abroad, if I believed that the end of this
> earthly life would mark the limit of my fame? (p. 169)

His words echo Sappho's similar claim 600 years earlier: 'I declare that later on, even in an age unlike our own, someone will remember who we are' (Sappho, Poochigian, 2009, p. 87). For the ancients, as for humans today, the pursuit of success, honor and glory during life can therefore be seen as one method of securing a sense of immortality in the face of death.

Themes of aging, death, and the desire for immortality can be seen to pervade ancient literature across a variety of cultures. By the Middle Ages, European literature reflected an increasing obsession with death and decay. In fact, an impressive array of genres had developed, explicitly inspired by and reflecting on death, including the *memento mori* ('remember that you will die') poetry, and *ars moriendi* (the art of dying) in the dramatic arts (Bús, 2008). The common thread underlying the diverse genres was the shared purpose of reminding the audience of the perishable and transient nature of all living things. This awareness and dread of death permeates English poetry as early as the tenth century. One verse from the period reminds its reader that:

> Soon comes Death, and none is spared
> ... Men and women all end so:
> Easy they come, and easy go. (Bús, 2008, p. 85)

One tale from the 15th Century echoes Dickens' *A Christmas Tale*, in its depiction of a corrupt ruler who changes his ways after glimpsing his father's corpse being feasted on by worms. After being repulsed by the fate of his father, and inevitably, all human beings, the ruler hangs a commissioned painting of the corpse on the wall of his bedroom as a perpetual reminder of this transience, and the futility of any worldly glory (Steel, 2013). The intentions and actions of this reformed ruler do not exist only in fabled form, and monastic cells at the time frequently displayed a human skull on each desk, to act as an unavoidable reminder of impermanence (Yalom, 2008). Worms frequently served as a symbol of decomposition and decay, and were in fact given a speaking part in one poem from the era which exemplified the *memento mori* genre: The *Disputation Between the Body and the Worms*. The *Disputation* features a memorable debate between a group of worms intent on devouring a woman's corpse, and the horrified corpse itself, which is unsurprisingly resistant to being eaten. When the corpse cites Biblical scripture claiming the dominion of humans over all others, the worms retort with 'that power lasts only while man has life; now your life is gone and you may not struggle with us' (Steel, 2013, p. 100). At the poem's conclusion, the horde of worms persuade the corpse to accept the fact that she is food for others, has always been so, and that neither her wealth nor her beauty will allow her to escape her fate. The poem is accompanied by an illustration of a corpse whose grave has been infested with worms and other insects, and a reminder that 'when you least expect it, death comes and overcomes you; when the grass is green, it is good to have death in mind' (p. 98).

From the 15th century, this increasing obsession with death is visually apparent in the artwork of the period, in the form of the *Danse Macabre* ('dance of death') and the 'vanitas' genre of still-life painting. The *Danse Macabre* genre of art was an allegory for the inevitability and universality of death, and featured Death personified, beckoning people from various social classes, ages, and sexes, into a dance. Kings, bishops, robbers, and children were all summoned into this unavoidable dance with Death, and the message of the genre is clear: Nobody escapes death, so be prepared. In a similar vein, vanitas artworks featured various symbols associated with death, including rotten fruit to suggest decay, bubbles to represent the transience of life and the swiftness with which death arrives, hourglasses, extinguished candles, and most explicitly, human skulls. Artworks adopting the vanitas style were intended to remind the viewer of the inevitability of death and the impermanence of earthly delights, and to encourage them to reflect on death and repent.

While the vanitas style peaked in the 16th century, the attempt to capture death on the canvas and reflect on the transience of life through art, has never ceased. Artists such as Vincent van Gogh, Gustav Klimt, Paul Cézanne and Andy Warhol have all created images of skulls, skeletons, or death personified. Salvador Dalí's paintings often featured a motif of swarming ants symbolising death and decay, to remind the viewer of their own mortality. Picasso's last well-known self-portrait was entitled *Self-Portrait Facing Death*, and depicts a man's face etched harshly with deep lines of age, staring at the viewer with wide, terrified eyes. In a profound example of mankind's struggle to cope with death, Edvard Munch completed a total of six paintings, and many more etchings and lithographs, under the title of *The Sick Child*. Each work depicts a singular moment before his sister's death of tuberculosis, featuring a young girl on her deathbed, accompanied by a grieving relative. Munch, who had nearly died from tuberculosis as a child, reportedly became obsessed with the image, and returned to it repeatedly over more than 40 years, creating numerous versions in order to express his feelings of loss and grief.

The dread of death in the present day

Across history, human societies have largely relied upon religion, myth, cultural rituals, literature and art in order to deal with the universal struggle with our own impermanence. However, modern technological developments are likely to revolutionise the way society deals with death. One increasingly popular movement is that of cryonics, involving the preservation of the deceased at low temperatures in the hope that they can be revived and restored to health in the future. Despite the passing of 2000 years, the process appears reminiscent of the ancient Egyptians' obsessive devotion to preservation of the corpse in order to ensure life after death. Over 1500 people in the United States have already made arrangements for cryonic preservation, at a cost of more than US$70,000 per body. While the science behind the cryogenics process may be dubious, the aim of the movement is not. The testimony of one cryonics registrant makes the goal clear:

> I have peace of mind knowing that no matter what happens in the future ... I am signed up (for cryonics) and there is that possibility I could wake up in the future.

On the website of one leading cryonics organisation, one couple describe cryonic preservation as 'a natural choice for us ... when you love life like we do'.

While cryonically preserved humans may seem like a thing of the future, the attempt to preserve and present the human body is clearly not new. In the 16th century, homes of wealthy Europeans would frequently feature human skulls inside cabinets of curiosities, and in the early 20th century, human remains were popular additions at World's Fairs across Northern America. However, despite these early origins, the fascination with human remains has not abated over the years. Body Worlds, an exhibition consisting of the skinless remains of humans, has attracted an audience of over 40 million people worldwide since its debut in 1995. As for the 25 individuals who have donated their entire bodies to be plastinated, posed, and displayed for millions of viewers, they may have found one path to virtual immortality.

While modern technology offers the promise of the preservation of one's own physical body, other methods have been less ambitious in attempts to preserve the memory of the deceased. In recent years, tattoo parlours have seen increasing requests for 'memorial tattoos', which use a combination of cremation ashes and ink in order to honour a deceased loved one and preserve a part of them inside one's own skin. Another service, named 'Save My Ink', offers to remove, preserve and frame the tattooed skin of the deceased, as a permanent reminder and heirloom for relatives left behind. For those with neither ashes nor tattoos to be remembered by, social media offers an alternative option. In 2015, Eugenia Kuyda used data from the text messages, Facebook and Twitter accounts of her deceased best friend, in order to create a computerised chatbot to imitate his personality. Although Kuyda described finding comfort in being able to receive and send text messages to the digital version of her departed friend, is a digital 'life after death' yet another way of denying the ultimate fate of ourselves and others?

Whilst technological advances may potentially hinder society's acceptance of mortality, the recent 'death positivity' trend offers a challenging alternative. This largely female-driven movement aims to increase society's awareness of and open discussion around death. Alongside this movement, the last decade has seen an increase in the popularity of the 'death café', an informal and not-for-profit gathering with the sole purpose of discussing mortality in an open and nonjudgemental setting, and challenging the taboo and secrecy around the topic of death. Death cafés bring together friends or strangers who discuss their thoughts about death and dying over cake and tea, and can be hosted at a member's house or a public café. The movement has spread to the United States, Australia, and Hong Kong, and over a thousand death cafes have been held across the globe. Another example of the trend towards death-positivity is the emergence of 'death doulas', or companions who support and assist the ill and their loved ones through the dying process. While the term 'doula' has traditionally referred to someone who supports a woman during pregnancy and birth, the notion of end-of-life doulas is gaining increasing popularity, with colleges established with the specific purpose of training doulas to deal with life and death. Today, the emergence of eco-friendly burial options, phone apps designed to help you plan your own funeral, and colouring books for adults solely featuring images of death, decomposition, and funeral rites, represent for many a step in the right direction, away from denial, avoidance and terror, and towards acceptance, peace, and an appreciation of life in the face of mortality.

References

Aristophanes. (1923). *Aristophanes: The peace. The birds. The frogs* (B.B. Rogers, Trans.), Michigan: Harvard University Press.

Aristophanes. (2006). *Aristophanes: Eleven plays*, (Ed. J. Ford), Special Edition Books.

Becker, E. (1973) *The denial of death*. New York, NY: The Free Press.

Bowra, C.M. (1968). *Landmarks in Greek literature*. London, England: Penguin.

Buddhaghosa. (1991). *The path of purification: Visuddhimagga* (B. Nanamoli, Trans.). Buddhist Publication Society.

Bús, E. (2008). 'Death's Echo' and 'Danse Macabre': Auden and the medieval tradition of death lyrics. *Hungarian Journal of English and American Studies, 14*(1), 83–93.

Cicero, M.T. (2016). *How to grow old: Ancient wisdom for the second half of life*. (P. Freeman, Trans.). Princeton, NJ: Princeton University Press.

Clinton, K. (2007). The mysteries of Demeter and Kore. In D. Ogden (Ed.), *A companion to Greek religion* (pp. 342–356). Oxford, England: Oxford University Press.

Cole, S.G. (2003). Landscapes of Dionysos and Elysian fields. In M. Cosmopoulos (Ed.), *Greek mysteries* (pp. 193–217). London, England: Routledge.

Conklin, B.A. (1995). 'Thus are our bodies, thus was our custom': Mortuary cannibalism in an Amazonian society. *American Ethnologist, 22*, 75–101.

Foley, H. (1994). *The Homeric hymn to Demeter: Translation, commentary and interpretative essays*. Princeton, NJ: Princeton University Press.

Foster, B.R. (2001). *The epic of Gilgamesh*. New York, NY: W.W. Norton.

George, A.W. (1999). *The epic of Gilgamesh*. London, England: Penguin.

Hamilton-Paterson, J., & Andrews, C. (1978). *Mummies: Death and life in ancient Egypt*. London, England: Collins.

Herodotus. (1996). *The histories* (A. De Sélincourt, Trans.). London, England: Penguin.

Homer. (2003). *The Homeric hymns* (J. Cashford, Trans.). London, England: Penguin.

James, W. (1985). *The varieties of religious experience*. Cambridge, MA: Harvard University Press. (Original work published 1902).

Jerimiah, K. (2007). Asceticism and the pursuit of death by warriors and monks. *Journal of Asian Martial Arts, 16*(2), 18–33.

Johnston, S. (2009). *Ancient religions*. Cambridge, MA: Harvard University Press.

Lifton, R.J., & Olson, E. (1974). Symbolic immortality. In *Living and dying*. London, England: Wildwood House.

Malinowski, B. (1925). *Magic, science and religion*. James Needham (Ed.). New York, NY: Macmillan.

Milton, J. (1853). Lycidas. In E. Brydges (Ed.), *The poetical works of John Milton* (pp. 604–620). Oxford, England: Oxford University.

Mirto, M.S. (2012). *Death in the Greek world: From Homer to the classical age* (A.M. Osborne, Trans.). Oklahoma, OK: University of Oklahoma Press.

Miyata, T. (2006). *A Henro pilgrimage guide to the 88 temples of Shikoku Island, Japan*. Sacramento, CA: Northern California Koyasan Temple.

Plutarch, as cited in Clinton, K. (2007). The Mysteries of Demeter and Kore. In D. Ogden (Ed.), *A companion to Greek religion*, Oxford, England: Blackwell.

Sappho. (2009). *Stung with love: Poems and fragments of Sappho* (A. Poochigian, Trans.). London, England: Penguin.

Sharf, R.H. (1992). The idolization of enlightenment: On the mummification of Ch'an masters in medieval China. *History of religions, 32*(1), 1–31.

Sourvinou-Inwood, C. (2003) Festivals and Mysteries: Aspects of Eleusinian Cult. In M. Cosmopoulos (Ed.), *Greek mysteries*, London, England: Routledge.

Spencer, A.J. (1982) *Life in ancient Egypt*. Penguin Books.

Steel, K. (2013). Abyss: Everything is food. *Postmedieval: A Journal of Medieval Cultural Studies, 4*, 93–104.

Yalom, I.D. (2008). *Staring at the sun: Overcoming the terror of death*. San Francisco, CA: Jossey-Bass.

Zandee, J. (1977). *Death as an enemy according to ancient Egyptian conceptions*. New York, NY: Arno Press.

Chapter 2

Fear of death: Nature, development and moderating factors

Ross G. Menzies and Rachel E. Menzies

How do we come to a mature view of death? Does it emerge in stages and, if so, what do these involve? Does anxiety arise as soon as a child can conceptualise death, or does it only appear with a fully developed, adult understanding of the concept? And what do we regard as an adult conception of death? Slaughter (2005) argues that the defining characteristic is to recognise death as a biological event caused by the failure of body systems. In contrast, young children may claim that the 'bogey man' or some other punishing agent is the cause of death. But would all adults pass Slaughter's (2005) test of death comprehension? After all, as Hoffman, Johnson, Foster, and Wright (2010) point out, adults can't agree on when life begins let alone why we take our last breath. Some will maintain that God has called a person home, and that God is the ultimate cause of death (and its creator, punishing us for the sins in the Garden of Eden). Clearly, death is a complex notion and religious and spiritual positions complicate the matter considerably.

This chapter traces the development of death fears across the lifespan. The literature will be reviewed to explore children's growing shift in their understanding of death across the first decade of life. Age and gender differences in death fears across adolescence and adulthood will be examined, as will factors that have been shown to moderate the intensity of death anxiety. The various maladaptive ways in which humans respond to death anxiety will then be briefly explored. Finally, advice for clinicians will be provided that emerges from this study of the natural history of the fear of death.

Early life

The earliest studies on children's conceptions of death were conducted by psychoanalytic researchers more than two decades before developmental psychologists displayed any interest in the topic. Although this may seem surprising, it must be remembered that Freud (1900, 1920, 1923) had made strong claims about children being essentially immune to the dread of death. Freud (1900) argued that children know nothing 'of freezing in the ice-cold grave, of the terrors of eternal nothingness' (p. 254), and that 'the fear of death has no meaning to a child' (p. 254; see further Chapter 5 in the present volume). For this reason, psychoanalytic researchers sought to investigate the emotional responses to death, mainly through open-ended interviews. Contrary to the Freudian hypothesis, these early studies (Anthony, 1940; Nagy, 1948; Von Hug-Helmuth, 1964) reveal an immature death concept that was typically associated with considerable fear and a range of avoidance strategies, principally denial.

> *Are you going to die Robert?*
>
> Robert: Well, yes. Everyone is gonna die.
>
> David: I won't die!
>
> Lily: I won't die either.

Like most preschool-aged children, these three-year olds reported by Hoffmann et al. (2010, p. 27–30) argue that death, if it does occur, may not apply to them. Further, death is something that happens only to the aged.

> Robert: Yes you can die. You, you, you'll most likely die at the age of like sixty, uh, three, or like sixty-four.
>
> David: No, I won't die.
>
> Robert: Or like sixty-eight.
>
> David: I won't die.

> Robert: You only, like, go up to zero.
>
> David: No. I won't die at all!
>
> Robert: And then zero, and then zero one.

Young children tend to see death as an altered state of living, like sleep or hibernation, and may claim that we transform into other substances or forms.

> Robert: Well it's like, well, it's like, um, well dying is like sleeping. (*Okay*) Except it's like, except you don't hear yourself snoring, except you're not snoring.
>
> *Right. And what happens to you then?*
>
> Lily: You turn into a stone.
>
> *You turn into a stone? Robert, what do you think happens then?*
>
> Robert: You're not in the stone, you like just, like you keep like, like you keep like for like, lying down, for like, all, like, all of the 'nother weeks.

While anxiety was the focus of these psychoanalytic researchers, those from the developmental, Piagetian tradition were far more interested in the way in which the concept of death is gradually acquired. In this regard, the data are surprisingly consistent. There is almost universal agreement that at least four components of the death concept are acquired in a sequential manner across development. These include, in order:

1. Irreversibility — the recognition that the dead cannot come back to life
2. Applicability — the understanding that death only happens to living things
3. Inevitability — the acknowledgement that living things must die eventually
4. Nonfunctionality — the understanding that death is characterised by bodily processes ceasing to function (e.g., speech, hearing, dreaming).

A child's understanding of the irreversibility of death occurs first, typically by age five or six years. Next, in the early years of school, the subcomponents of applicability, inevitability and nonfunctionality are acquired, usually by the age of seven to nine years (Slaughter, 2005). Some researchers add a final stage in the development of the death concept, referred to as 'causation' (i.e., the recognition that death is caused by the breakdown of bodily functions; Slaughter & Griffiths, 2007). This appears to be the last concept to be acquired, typically by around 10 years of age. However, as argued above, it is the present authors' view that this component is potentially confounded by religious and spiritual beliefs and is not necessary to understand the state of 'being dead'.

Of course, for the purposes of the present chapter, the critical question relates to when anxiety arises in this sequence. Fear of death has been documented in children as young as three years of age (Hoffman et al., 2010), suggesting that a complete understanding of the construct may not be required for fear to emerge. At least two explanations of this are logically possible. First, the inherently risk-averse nature of our species might make us wary of death even before we fully understand the concept. In fact, the child's lack of understanding might be a biological signal to be cautious (as with novel tastes, animals etc). Second, it is possible that only the concept of irreversibility is required for fear. That is, the recognition that the dead cannot come back to life may be sufficient to engender anxiety. Even if the child has not yet understood that all living things, and only living things, must die, the belief that *if* it happens there is no return may make it a terrifying possibility.

Fear of death appears to increase and dominate the worries of children across the period of five to 10 years of age, notably matching the developmental period in which the death concept is becoming complete. This has been established through childhood fear schedules, most notably the revised Fear Survey Schedule for Children (FSSC-R; Ollendick, 1983). Importantly, a recent version of the FSSC-R uses a fully pictorial format so that children as young as age four can complete it (the Koala Fear Questionnaire [KFQ]; Muris et al., 2003). This scale lists specific situations, activities or happenings (e.g., 'snakes', 'looking foolish', 'getting an injection from the nurse or doctor') and children are asked to rate the extent to which each item evokes fear. In young children the most common fears appear to involve animals, monsters, the dark and separation from parents (Gullone, 2000). Of course, these may be early derivatives of poorly articulated death anxiety. Marks (1987) and Iverach, Menzies and Menzies (2014) have argued that many specific fears and phobias appear to derive from the possibility that they could occasion death. It is surely obvious that separation from a guardian, or the presence of a monster, might increase the possibility of death.

More importantly however, considerable research on the FSSC-R has shown 'death and danger' to be one of five stable factors present on the scale. Notably, this factor emerges in the responses of children as young as age four to six on the KFQ. Further, by age seven to 10, items loading on the death factor are the most commonly endorsed fear items (Ollendick, 1983; Gullone, 2000). In sum, death anxiety is prominent in the first decade of life.

Adolescence

The death items on the FSSC-R remain the most commonly endorsed items throughout adolescence (see Gullone, 2000 for a comprehensive review). Further, these fears have been shown to be so prominent that they interfere with the lives of the majority of individuals in this developmental period. Ollendick and King (1994) explored daily interference with everyday activities of all FSSC-R items in 646 Australian adolescents. Sixty per cent of this large sample indicated that the common items of the death and danger subscale caused them considerable distress and interfered with their daily lives. This should not be surprising, as the development of formal logical thought (by around 12 years of age) increases the ability to contemplate our own death (Piaget, 1972). Further, as deductive reasoning and planning emerge in the period of formal operations (from 12 years of age onwards), the individual can better explore abstract concepts by manipulating ideas in their head. In this way, rumination about death and its consequences becomes possible.

Other aspects of adolescence may also contribute to the maintenance and growth of death anxiety. Compared to younger children, adolescents are more likely to have experienced death and loss in their lives (Ens & Bond, 2007). Further, with the emergence of abstract thought, the ability to internalise beliefs about a personal God increase. With these two factors in mind, Ens and Bond (2007) combined scales measuring religiosity, bereavement, and death anxiety into one questionnaire. Two hundred and twenty-six Canadian adolescents (aged 11 to 18 years) completed the measure. Showing how common the experience of loss is by this age, over 60% of the respondents reported a familial death (covering parents, siblings and grandparents). Surprisingly, Ens and Bond (2007) report no differences between the death anxiety levels of adolescents who had, or had not, experienced a familial death. Further, those who had experienced an immediate familial death (i.e., parents, siblings) did not differ in death anxiety from those who had experienced an extended familial death (i.e., grandparents). However, tempering any conclusion that could arise from these findings, there was a strong positive correlation between grief from bereavement and death anxiety ($r = .44$). In essence then, it appears that loss itself is not associated with heightened fear of death unless the adolescent has suffered substantial grief. A tempting explanation is that a painful experience of grief increases fear of future death, due to the sensitisation of death as a fear stimulus. Of course, the direction of causality in the relationship cannot be established from this correlational research design. It could simply be that children who are particularly sensitive to death (i.e., high in trait death anxiety) are those who will suffer grief in the face of any loss.

Notably, the relationships between religiosity and death anxiety were almost nonexistent in this study. Only the relationship between extrinsic-personal religiosity (e.g., 'I pray mainly to gain relief and protection') and death anxiety was significant ($r = .14$), and even this relationship accounted for little of the variance. No other religiosity scale score correlated significantly with death anxiety suggesting that religious belief does little for reducing death fears in this age group. As Firestone (1993) suggests, adolescence does not appear to be a period involving extensive contemplation on life, death and an afterlife, and so religiosity may not serve to buffer death fears.

Finally, female adolescents reported significantly greater fears of death than male adolescents. This is consistent with a large body of research in adulthood showing the same effect. It is an almost universal finding that women report more anxiety about death than do men (Davis, Martin, Wilee, & Voorhees, 1978; Iammarino, 1975; Lonetto & Templer, 1986; Sanders, Poole, & Rivero, 1980; Siscoe, Reimer, Yanovsky, Thomas-Dobson, & Templer, 1992; Thorson & Powell, 1988, 1993). Of course, this may simply be part of a greater picture of woman reporting more fears, phobias, and general anxiety than men. It has been suggested that these differences may be due to sex-role expectations that males are expected to repress fears (e.g., Dattel & Neimeyer, 1990).

Adulthood

What happens to death fears across adulthood? Do they increase or decrease, and what are the mediators of these effects? Interestingly, early theorists and researchers did not believe that death fears would significantly change across the adult years. As Lester (1967) put it, "Age will obviously affect attitudes until mental development is complete. Thereafter, it would seem that personality factors and life experiences are the important determinants" (p. 31). Early studies, limited by extremely restricted age ranges among participants, failed to find any age-related effects (e.g., Christ, 1961; Jeffers, Nichols, & Eisendorfer, 1961; Rhudick & Dibner, 1961; Swenson, 1961). However, in studies that have used well-established, reliable measures of death anxiety, and samples drawn across all periods of adulthood, age effects have generally been found. Kalish (1977), for example, drawing on large samples of white, black, Mexican and Japanese Americans, reported that 40% of the young, 25% of middle-aged, and 10% of the elderly expressed a fear of death. Similarly, Stevens, Cooper, and Thomas (1980) reported that individuals aged 60 to 83 years had lower scores on Templer's Death Anxiety Scale than individuals in any other normative age group (16–22 years, 23–39 years, and 40–59 years).

Several problems in this literature need to be acknowledged. First, as stated above, too many studies have used overly narrow age-ranges among their participants. Second, the vast majority of studies have used cross-sectional designs which make it difficult, if not impossible, to eliminate cohort effects. It is obvious that different age cohorts may have experienced death in completely different ways (e.g., exposure to different wars, outbreaks of different diseases, catastrophic world events). Further, as Kastenbaum (2000) points out, by old age certain types of individuals may have been eliminated (e.g., risk-takers), potentially biasing samples. Third, too few studies have controlled for physical health, a variable that may well account for variance in death anxiety scale scores.

A recent report from Chopik (2017) addressed these issues by conducting a large, longitudinal study of 9,815 adults over a four year period, controlling for health status. Consistent with the findings from the majority of recent studies, death anxiety declined across the test period. Further, greater social support at the start of the study predicted lower levels of death anxiety four years later. Chopik (2017) argued that close interpersonal relationships, extensive social networks and social support serve emotion regulation functions to decrease death anxiety across the lifespan. Mikulincer (2018) suggests that close relationships may give our lives meaning, and even extend life through the lives of children, grandchildren and friends. Close attachments have been shown to buffer death fears, even when reminded about death using deception in popular *mortality salience* research designs (Maxfield, John & Pyszczynski, 2014; Mikulincer & Florian, 2000; Smieja, Kalaska, & Adamczyk, 2006). According to attachment theory, the default defence against death awareness is attachment-system activation that results in attempts to attain care, safety and protection through others (see further Chapter 4 of the present volume).

Several theorists have proposed models that centre on acceptance and meaning-making in trying to explain the reduction in death anxiety across the lifespan. According to Wong, Reker, and Gesser's (1994) model, there are three different ways in which an individual can come to an acceptance of death (see further Chapter 10 in the present volume). The first, termed *neutral acceptance*, implies a stoic attitude to death. Death is a fact of life that is beyond one's control and is neither feared nor welcomed. As others have noted, such stoic attitudes appear to form a large part of the philosophic basis of contemporary cognitive behaviour therapy (CBT; Murguia & Diaz, 2015). *Approach acceptance* implies a belief in a positive afterlife. With better things to come, there is little to fear. *Escape acceptance* results from a decline in living conditions. In many ways, this is similar to Akhtar's (2010) hypothesis of the need to seek peace and rest. Put simply, a desire to die might be the result of the reduced autonomy and growing fatigue associated with ageing.

While acceptance of death has been shown to be inversely related to death anxiety in several reports, it is predominantly *neutral acceptance* that has been shown to reliably relate to death fears (see further Tomer & Eliason, 2000). Neimeyer, Wittkoski, and Moser (2004) suggest that the concept of meaning may explain the acceptance effect: 'Individuals who strongly endorse death acceptance are probably more able than others to see meaning in death by putting it into an overarching context' (p. 331). Alternatively, those capable of achieving acceptance may be individuals with high levels of *psychological flexibility*, readily shifting perspective and adapting to fluctuating situational demands. The construct of *psychological flexibility* has been shown to be associated with mental health status and predict outcomes in treatment studies across a variety of conditions (see Kashdan & Rottenberg, 2010 for a review).

Maladaptive responses to death anxiety: Denial in its various forms

Childhood denial of nonfunctionality and applicability

The most fundamental way that humans appear to respond to the death is denial. The individual refuses to acknowledge that death is real, or that it is beyond their control. Intriguingly, disputing the realities of death appears to begin in early childhood. In a sample of nine to 12 years old children Cotton and Range (1990) report that fear of death scores on the FSSC-R were negatively correlated with apparent understanding of the nonfunctionality component of death. The authors concluded that the participants were simply denying the truth of nonfunctionality as a defence against their fears, since this component of the death construct is typically understood many years earlier in development. Similarly, Orbach, Gross, Glaubman, and Berman (1986) found that 6-year-old to 11-year-old children who scored high on a general anxiety scale were less likely to endorse the applicability component of death. Again, rather than accept the unlikely conclusion that anxious children experience significant delays in cognitive development, the authors argued that they were simply defending against their fears through the use of denial.

In general, avoidance has been shown to be a poor response to fear with direct exposure to threats encouraged in behaviour therapy programs since the 1960s (Marks, 1987). Confronting the truth of death should theoretically be therapeutic and lead to lower death fears. This hypothesis is supported by the interview study of Slaughter and Griffiths (2007). Ninety children between the ages of four and eight had their understanding of death, fear of death, and general anxiety levels assessed. A regression analysis indicated that more mature death understanding was associated with lower levels of death fear, when age and general anxiety were controlled. These data provide support for the exposure principle. That is, directly discussing death and dying in biological terms may be confronting, but is likely to be a useful way of reducing fear of death in young children.

Religion and the denial of irreversibility

Religious belief appears to fundamentally challenge the irreversibility component of the death concept. Whether by moving to another place (e.g., heaven, afterlife) or living in another form (e.g., reincarnation), much religious practice rests on the idea that death is reversible i.e., I can live again. For this reason, the thanatocentric accounts of religion arose that essentially view religious belief as being motivated by fear. This position has had strong advocates across millennia (see further Chapter 6 of the present volume). For example, Petronius, the Roman author and courtier during the reign of Nero, tells us: *primus in orbe deos fecit timor* or 'it was fear that first made gods in the world' (cited in Jong et al. 2017, p. 2). Even more specifically, Feuerbach (1851/1967) argued that religion directly emerges from our dread of mortality: 'If man did not die, if he lived forever, if there were no such thing as death, there would be no religion' (p. 33).

Accordingly, involvement in organised religion has been seen as a coping or defence mechanism by many authors (Firestone, 1993; Yalom, 2008). It has been criticised as an avoidance strategy and a poor solution to anxiety (Yalom, 2008), despite the fact that it might reduce fear. An intrinsic religious orientation has been shown to be negatively associated with death anxiety in many adult studies (see Jong et al., 2017 for a recent review). Further, as inner conviction increases, death anxiety decreases (Cohen et al., 2005; Lester, 1967; Lonetto & Templer, 1986; Thorson & Powell, 1990). However, one needs to interpret these data with caution. As Jong et al. (2017) point out, most studies exploring the relationship between trait death anxiety and religiosity have involved participants drawn from the 'religious' population. In their meta-analysis and review of 100 articles exploring the relationship, only one article had a 'nonreligious' sample of greater than 50%. This is important, because thanatocentric theories of religion argue that the relationship between religious belief and death anxiety will be curvilinear, specifically negative quadratic (i.e., an inverted U-shaped curve). Terror Management Theory (TMT; Greenberg, Solomon, & Pyszczynski, 1987), for example, proposes that human awareness of death motivates us to seek immortality, whether literal or symbolic. Literal immortality is achieved through afterlife concepts (e.g., immortal souls, heaven, reincarnation), whereas symbolic immortality is achieved through lasting, culturally valued achievements that bolster self-esteem (e.g., wealth, academic or sporting achievements, ingroup memberships, parenting), and defending ingroup, cultural worldviews (see Chapter 6 of the present volume). Accordingly, Jong et al. (2017) argues that atheism might serve the same terror management function of reducing death fears as religion, given that atheism represents an ingroup worldview that can be defended. Committed atheists and strong religious believers may be expected to have the lowest fears of death, with the bulk of the population (lying somewhere between these anchors) being more likely to suffer. Jong et al. (2017) report that of the 11 studies that have explored possible curvilinear relationships between death anxiety and religiosity, 10 found evidence for the effect.

Psychopathology and the denial of uncontrollability

Could psychopathology, like religious belief, be another form of denial? Iverach et al. (2014) argued that the dread of death should be viewed as a transdiagnostic construct that may mediate a range of mental disorders (see further Chapter 7 in the present volume). They suggest that many disorders amount to individuals seeking to control death by avoidance, checking or safety behaviours. For example, body scanning, palpating of lymph nodes, requests for repeated medical tests and overuse of emergency services in the somatoform and panic disorders can be seen as a means of preventing death (Iverach et al., 2014). Similarly, the refusal to travel without security figures (e.g., a partner or close friend) in agoraphobia is intended to prevent death from sudden misadventure (Fleischer-Mann, 1995; Foa, Steketee, & Young, 1984; Marks, 1987). Further, as noted above, Marks (1987) argued that the majority of the specific phobias are associated with objects or situations that could result in death (e.g., heights, snakes, spiders, blood, water). All of this suggests that some individuals respond to death by refusing to accept that they can do nothing about it. They seek to control or prevent death through pathological avoidance and safety seeking.

In strong support of the notion that death fears mediate psychopathology, Menzies and Dar-Nimrod (2017) explored death anxiety (as measured by the Collett-Lester Fear of Death scale [CLFD]; Collett & Lester, 1969) in a large sample of individuals with obsessive-compulsive disorder (OCD; $n = 171$). Importantly, in addition to looking at the relationship between death anxiety and OCD, these authors explored lifetime markers of mental health. In a remarkably consistent set of findings, each CLFD subscale was also positively associated with: (1) OCD severity; (2) total number of lifetime mental health diagnoses, as measured by the lifetime version of the Anxiety and Related Disorders Interview Schedule, 5th edition (ADIS-5L; Brown & Barlow, 2014); (3) total number of lifetime, psychiatric hospitalisations; (4) total number of medications used; and (5) clinician ratings of ADIS-5L overall distress/impairment. Importantly, neuroticism scores did not account for the obtained relationships between mental health status and death anxiety. Further, the authors noted that mean scores on each of the four subscales of the CLFD were more than double those reported in studies of the general community. Taken together, these findings suggest that heightened death anxiety is associated with continuous mental health problems across the life-course as the individual seeks to control, avoid or conquer death in various ways. In sum, a variety of mental health disorders may be seen as complex and maladaptive manifestations of excessive death fears.

Clinical recommendations

What are the clinical recommendations that arise from the data presented in this chapter? In our view, three main points emerge.

First, in children, it is suggested that we talk directly in truthful terms about the biological facts of death. When should this be done? Answering children's questions about death with honesty and empathy should begin as soon as they are being asked (e.g., Lansdown & Goldman, 1988; O'Halloran & Altmeier, 1996; Shapiro, 1994; Slaughter & Griffiths, 2007; Webb, 1993). Exposure to the truths of death, according to both extant data and learning theory, should diminish fear. As Heidegger (1927) puts it, direct confrontation with mortality is 'one of the many ways to open the gates to existence' (p. 45).

Second, given the relationships between death anxiety and lifetime markers of poor mental health, it seems important to address death anxiety directly when treating a range of disorders. Iverach et al. (2014) argue that contemporary CBT generally fail to focus on death, and that this may contribute to the 'revolving door' of mental health problems that is so commonly seen in clinics around the world (p. 590). Menzies, Menzies, and Iverach (2015) point out that it is routine for individuals to be successfully treated for one anxiety-based condition, only to return with another. Menzies (2017) argues that CBT programs for anxiety, panic, OCD and somatoform disorders focus of reducing expectancies of proximal threats, but do little for longer term existential issues. For example, exposure programs for height phobia and compulsive washing aim to reduce expectancies of falling and disease respectively, but do not target the common element of death. Of course, exposure-based CBT could focus directly on death (e.g., imaginal exposure to looking at your own dead body) and some researchers have attempted this with positive results (see Chapter 9 of the present volume). However, Iverach et al. (2014) suggest that taking elements from existential psychotherapy, acceptance and commitment therapy (ACT), dignity therapy, and meaning-centred therapy might enhance treatment outcomes. These possibilities are explored in Section 2 of the present volume.

Finally, there is the thorny issue of religious practice. Is it to be recommended (given the relationship between high, intrinsic religious belief and low death anxiety) or avoided (given its apparent role as a means of denial, and the observation that committed atheism may also reduce death anxiety)? It must be remembered that in adults it is an *intrinsic* religiosity that has been associated with reduced death anxiety. The *inner* desire to spend time in prayer with one's God is not something that can really be encouraged or discouraged in treatment. To a large extent this desire is either present or absent in the individual. However, it must be acknowledged that individuals using religious belief to reduce death fears create a cost that all of us must bear. As Pyszczynski,

Vail, and Motyl (2010) persuasively argue, strongly held religious beliefs have a long and extensive history of contributing to bloody violence toward others. From a societal viewpoint, it seems easy to argue that religious practice is a maladaptive solution to death fears.

Some of the personal benefits of involvement in religious communities might be achieved through other activities that also involve ingroup identification, social networking and support. As discussed above, Chopik (2017) reports that increased social support is associated with reduced death anxiety across time. It is well established that social isolation is associated with a range of poor physical and mental health outcomes, and increasing social connectedness has been associated with improvements in mental and physical health in many reports (see further Jetten, Haslam, & Haslam, 2012). An interesting demonstration of these effects can be seen in research on choir singing groups and creative writing groups for the homeless and disadvantaged, conducted through the *School of Hard Knocks* and the University of Queensland (Dingle, Williams, Sharman, & Jetten, 2016). Participants in this study suffered with chronic mental health conditions including schizophrenia, bipolar disorder, recurrent depression, posttraumatic stress disorder, personality disorders and addiction. Twelve months after joining the choir or writing groups 44% of participants perceived their mental health to have improved and 46% reported their physical health to have improved (Dingle et al., 2016). Clearly, the benefits of ingroup identification and social support are not limited to religious groups.

Recently, Haslam, Cruwys, Haslam, Dingle and Chang (2016) have formalised this social identity approach to mental health with the development of their 'Groups 4 Health' program (G4H). Their five-module program is the first to specifically target the development of social group relationships to treat psychological distress. Reductions on measures of depression, general anxiety, stress, social anxiety, and loneliness were found at program completion and at 6-month follow-up. Measures of self-esteem and life satisfaction revealed significant improvements. Further, the treatment effects were mediated by participants increased identification with their G4H group (and other groups). While no measures of death anxiety were obtained, this work is consistent with the theoretical position of Mikulincer and colleagues regarding the importance of attachment in dealing with existential issues (see Chapter 4 in the present volume). As stated above, according to attachment theory, the default defence against death awareness is attachment-system activation and resulting attempts to attain care and protection through relationships. The laboratory demonstrations of the power of these effects is striking. Even preconscious reminders of death have been shown to activate the attachment system in lexical decision tasks (e.g., Mikulincer, Birnbaum, Woddis, & Nachmias, 2000). The benefits of secure, positive and supportive relationships seem clear.

Summary and concluding comments

As a child's understanding of death emerges and develops across the first decade of life, fear and anxiety to death-relevant stimuli increase. For most, these fears remain potent across adolescence, interfering with everyday activities. For many, however, death fears will slowly diminish across life with few apparent costs to the individual. In this regard, research has shown the value of attachments, social support, social identity and ingroup membership, bolstering cultural worldviews (see Chapter 6 of the present volume), and maintaining physical health. However, for some individuals, a lifelong struggle with complex mental health problems may arise from excessive death anxiety. In a futile attempt to control death, some will seek to prevent harm at all costs, resulting in a range of mental health disorders across childhood, adolescence and adulthood. While traditional CBT programs for the anxiety-related disorders reduce specific, proximal threats of death, they do little to address broader death fears that may underpin the psychiatric disorders experienced by these individuals. Novel approaches to death anxiety may be needed to stop this cycle of mental illness (see Section 2 of the present volume).

References

Akhtar, S. (2010). Freud's Todesangst and Ghalib's Ishrat-e-Qatar: Two perspectives on death. In S. Akhtar (Ed.), *The wound of mortality* (pp. 97-106). New York, NY: Aronson.

Anthony, S. (1940). *The child's discovery of death: A study in psychology.* New York, NY: Harcourt, Brace.

Brown, T.A., & Barlow, D.H. (2014). *Anxiety and Related Disorders Interview Schedule for DSM–5: Lifetime Version.* New York, NY: Oxford University Press.

Chopik, W.J. (2017). Death across the lifespan: Age-differences in death-related thoughts and anxiety. *Death Studies, 41,* 69–77.

Christ, P.E.I. (1961). Attitudes toward death among a group of acute geriatric psychiatric patients. *Journal of Gerontology, 16,* 56–59.

Cohen, A.B., Pierce, J.D., Chambers, J., Meade, R., Gorvine, B.J., & Koenig, H.G. (2005). Intrinsic and extrinsic religiosity, belief in the afterlife, death anxiety, and life satisfaction in young Catholics and Protestants. *Journal of Research in Personality, 39,* 307–324.

Collett, L., & Lester, D. (1969). The fear of death and dying. *Journal of Psychology, 72,* 179–181.

Cotton, C., & Range, L. (1990). Children's death concepts: Relationships to cognitive functioning, age, experience with death, fear of death and hopelessness. *Journal of Clinical Child Psychology, 19,* 123–127.

Dattel, A.R., & Neimeyer, R.A. (1990). Sex differences in death anxiety: Testing the emotional expressiveness hypothesis. *Death Studies, 14,* 1–11.

Davis, S.F., Martin, D.A., Wilee, C.T., & Voorhees, J.W. (1978). Relationship of fear of death and level of self-esteem in college students. *Psychological Reports, 42,* 419–422.

Dingle, G., Williams, E., Sharman, L., & Jetten, J. (2016). *School of hard knocks QLD: Final evaluation report.* School of Psychology, The University of Queensland.

Ens, C., & Bond, J. B. (2007). Death anxiety in adolescents: The contributions of bereavement and religiosity. *Omega, 55,* 169–184.

Feuerbach, L. (1967). *Lectures on the essence of religion.* (R. Manheim, Trans.). New York, NY: Harper & Row. (Original work published 1851).

Firestone, R.W. (1993). Individual defenses against death anxiety. *Death Studies, 17,* 497–515.

Fleischer-Mann, J. (1995). Exploration of attachment-separation, fear of death and separation anxiety in agoraphobia. *Dissertation Abstracts International, Section B: The Sciences and Engineering, 56,* 2370.

Foa, E.B., Steketee, G., & Young, M.C. (1984). Agoraphobia: Phenomenological aspects, associated characteristics, and theoretical considerations. *Clinical Psychology Review, 4,* 431–457.

Freud, S. (1900). The interpretation of dreams. *Standard Edition of the Complete Psychological Works of Sigmund Freud, 4,* 1-380. London: Hogarth Press

Freud, S. (1920). Beyond the pleasure principle. *Standard Edition of the Complete Psychological Works of Sigmund Freud, 18,* 1–64. London: Hogarth Press

Freud, S. (1923). The ego and the id. *Standard Edition of the Complete Psychological Works of Sigmund Freud, 19,* 1–66. London: Hogarth Press.

Greenberg, J., Solomon, S., & Pyszczynski, T. (1997). Terror management theory of self-esteem and cultural worldviews: Empirical assessments and conceptual refinements. In M. P. Zanna (Ed.), *Advances in experimental social psychology (Vol. 29, pp. 61–139).* San Diego, CA: Academic Press.

Gullone, E. (2000). The development of normal fear: A century of research. *Clinical Psychology Review, 20,* 429–451.

Haslam, C., Cruwys, T., Haslam, S.A., Dingle, G., & Chang, M. (2016). Groups 4 health: Evidence that a social identity intervention that builds and strengthens social group memberships improves mental health. *Journal of Affective Disorders, 194,* 188–195.

Heidegger, M. (1927). *Sein und zeit.* Frankfurt: Klostermann.

Hoffman, L., Johnson, E., Foster, M., & Wright, E. (2010). What happens when you die? Three-to-four-year-olds chatting about death. In S. Akhtar (Ed.), *The wound of mortality* (pp. 97–106). New York, NY: Aronson.

Iammarino, N.K. (1975). Relationship between death anxiety and demographic variables. *Psychological Reports, 31,* 262.

Iverach, L., Menzies, R.G. & Menzies, R.E. (2014). Death anxiety and its role in psychopathology: Reviewing the status of a transdiagnostic construct. *Clinical Psychology Review, 34,* 580–593.

Jeffers, F. C., Nichols, C. R., & Eisendorfer, C. (1961). Attitudes of older persons toward death. *Journal of Gerontology, 16,* 53–56.

Jetten, J., Haslam, C., & Haslam, S.A. (2012). (eds). *The social cure: Identity, health and well-being.* Hove, England: Psychology Press.

Jong, J., Ross, R., Philip, T., Chang, S., Simons, N., & Halberstadt, J. (2017). The religious correlates of death anxiety: a systematic review and meta-analysis. *Religion, Brain & Behavior.* doi: 10.1080/2153599X.2016.1238844.

Kalish, R.A. (1977). The role of age in death attitudes. *Death Education, 1,* 205–230.

Kashdan, T.B., & Rottenberg, J. (2010). Psychological flexibility as a fundamental aspect of health. *Clinical Psychology Review, 30,* 865–878.

Lansdown, R., & Goldman, A. (1988). The psychological care of children with malignant disease. *Journal of Child Psychology and Psychiatry, 29,* 555–567.

Lester, D. (1967). Experimental and correlational studies of the fear of death. *Psychological Bulletin, 67,* 27–36.

Lonetto, R., & Templer, D. I. (1986). *Death anxiety*. Washington, DC: Hemisphere.

Marks, I. (1987). *Fears, phobias, and rituals: Panic, anxiety, and their disorders*. New York, NY: Oxford University Press.

Maxfield, M., John, S., & Pyszczynski, T. (2014). A terror management perspective on the role of death-related anxiety in psychological dysfunction. *The Humanist Psychologist, 42*, 35–53.

Menzies, R.E. (2017). *Death anxiety, existential issues and abnormal behaviour*. Plenary address at the 47th Congress of the European Association for Behavioural and Cognitive Therapies (EABCT), 15 September, 2017, Ljubljana, Slovenia.

Menzies, R.E., Dar-Nimrod, I. (2017). Death anxiety and its relationship to obsessive-compulsive disorder. *Journal of Abnormal Psychology, 126*, 367–377.

Menzies, R.G., Menzies, R.E., & Iverach, L. (2015). The role of death fears in Obsessive Compulsive Disorder. *Australian Clinical Psychologist, 1*, 6–11.

Mikulincer, M. (2018). Love, death and the quest for meaning. In R.E. Menzies, R.G. Menzies & L. Iverach (Eds.), *Curing the dread of death: Theory, research and practice*. Brisbane, Queensland: Australian Academic Press.

Mikulincer, M., Birnbaum, G., Woddis, D., & Nachmias, O. (2000). Stress and accessibility of proximity-related thoughts: Exploring the normative and intraindividual components of attachment theory. *Journal of Personality and Social Psychology, 78*, 509–523.

Mikulincer, M., & Florian, V. (2000). Exploring individual differences in reactions to mortality salience: Does attachment style regulate terror management mechanisms? *Journal of Personality and Social Psychology, 79*, 260–273.

Murguia, E., & Diaz, K. (2015). The philosophic foundations of cognitive behavioural therapy: Stoicism, Buddhism, Taoism, and Existentialism. *Journal of Evidence-Based Psychotherapies, 15*, 37–50.

Muris, P. Meesters, C., Mayer, B. Bogie, N., Luijten, M., Geebelen, E., … Smit, C. (2003). The Koala Fear Questionnaire: A standardised self-report scale for assessing fears and fearfulness in pre-school and primary school children. *Behaviour Research and Therapy, 41*, 597–617.

Nagy, M. (1948). The child's theories concerning death. *Journal of Genetic Psychology, 73*, 3–27.

Neimeyer, R. A., Wittkowski, J., & Moser, R. P. (2004). Psychological research on death attitudes: An overview and evaluation. *Death Studies, 28*, 309–340.

O'Halloran, C., & Altmeier, E. (1996). Awareness of death among children: Does a lifethreatening illness alter the process of discovery? *Journal of Counselling and Development, 74*, 259–262.

Ollendick, T. (1983). Reliability and validity of the Revised Fear Survey Schedule for Children (FSSC-R). *Behaviour Research and Therapy, 21*, 685–692.

Ollendick, T.H., & King, N.J. (1994). Fears and their level of interference in adolescents. *Behaviour Research and Therapy, 32*, 635–638.

Orbach, I., Gross, Y., Glaubman, H., & Berman, D. (1986). Children's perception of various determinants of the death concept as a function of intelligence, age and anxiety. *Journal of Clinical Child Psychology, 15*, 120–126.

Piaget, J. (1972). Intellectual evolution from adolescence to adulthood. *Human Development, 15*, 1–12.

Pyszczynski, T., Vail, K.E., & Motyl, M.S. (2010). The cycle of righteous killing: Psychological forces in the prevention and promotion of peace. In T. Pick, A. Speckhard, & B. Jacuch (Eds.), *Homegrown terrorism: NATO Science for Peace and Security Series — E: Human and Societal Dynamics.* (pp. 227–243). Amsterdam, the Netherlands: IOS Press.

Rhudick, P.J. & Dibner, A.S. (1961). Age, personality and health correlates of death concern in normal aged individuals. *Journal of Gerontology, 16*, 44–49.

Sanders, J.F., Poole, T.E., & Rivero, W.T. (1980). Death anxiety among the elderly. *Psychological Reports, 46*, 53–54.

Shapiro, E. (1994). *Grief as a family process.* New York, NY: Guilford Press.

Siscoe, K., Reimer, W., Yanovsky, A., Thomas-Dobson, S., & Templer, D. (1992). Death depression versus death anxiety: Exploration of different correlates. *Psychological Reports, 71*, 1191–1194.

Slaughter, V. (2005). Young children's understanding of death. *Australian Psychologist, 40*, 179–186.

Slaughter, V., & Griffiths, M. (2007). Death understanding and fear of death in young children. *Clinical Child Psychology and Psychiatry, 12*, 525–535

mieja, M., Kalaska, M., & Adamczyk, M. (2006). Scared to death or scared to love? Terror management theory and close relationship seeking. *European Journal of Social Psychology, 36*, 279–296.

Stevens, S.J., Cooper, P.E., & Thomas, L.E. (1980). Age norms for the Templer's Death Anxiety Scale. *Psychological Reports, 46,* 205–206.

Swenson, W.M. (1961). Attitudes towards death in an aged population. *Journal of Gerontology, 16,* 49–52.

Thorson, J.A., & Powell, F.C. (1988). Elements of death anxiety and meanings of death. *Journal of Clinical Psychology, 44,* 691–701.

Thorson, J.A., & Powell, F.C. (1990). Meanings of death and intrinsic religiosity. *Journal of Clinical Psychology, 46,* 3797391.

Thorson, J.A., & Powell, F.C. (1993). Personality, death anxiety, and gender. *Bulletin of Psychonomic Society, 31,* 589–590.

Tomer, A., & Eliason, G. (2000). Beliefs about self, life, and death: Testing aspects of a comprehensive model of death anxiety and death attitudes. In A. Tomer (Ed.), *Death attitudes and the older adult (pp. 137-153).* Philadelphia, PA: Brunner-Routledge.

Von Hug-Helmuth, H. (1964). The child's concept of death. *Psychoanalytic Quarterly, 34,* 499–516.

Webb, N. (Ed.). (1993). *Helping bereaved children: A handbook for practitioners.* New York, NY: Guilford Press.

Wong, P.T., Reker, G.T., & Gesser, G. (1994). Death Attitude Profile — Revised. In R. A. Neimeyer (Ed.), *Death anxiety handbook* (pp. 121–148). New York, NY: Taylor & Francis.

Yalom, I. (2008). *Staring at the sun: Overcoming the terror of death.* San Francisco, CA: Jossey-Bass.

Chapter 3

Beyond the dread of death: Existentialism's embrace of the meaninglessness of life

Gerard Kuperus

> If eternal return is the heaviest of burdens, then our lives can stand out against it in all their splendid lightness.
> — The unbearable lightness of being, Milan Kundera (2014, p. 5)

In his work *Being and Time*, Heidegger presents his famous fundamental attunement of angst, or anxiety, which he describes as the anxiety about nothing, about not being any more: death. It is this anxiety about one's own finitude that throws one back onto oneself (see Heidegger, 2008, pp. 228–234). This dread of death is, for Heidegger, not a paralysing anxiety — at least, it does not have to be. We can move beyond the moment of crisis and rethink, what Heidegger calls our 'ownmost possibility', i.e., what I can be or can become (Heidegger, 2008, pp. 304–311). When I realise I am going to die, I can rethink my life and live my life differently, more authentically. Thus, the so-called dread of death, does not have to lead to a life of suffering and dread. Instead it can open up the possibility to embrace life.

Although, of all the existentialists, Heidegger and Kierkegaard are well-known for analysing dread or anxiety, this chapter focuses on three atheist existentialists: Nietzsche, Sartre, and Camus. All three provide alternative and quite interesting perspectives on death through the existentialist perspective that life is meaningless.

While these thinkers start with the basic insight that life is without meaning, it is exactly this insight that leads to the positive attitude that asks us to say 'Yes!' to life. Life is not about death and the afterlife (which for these thinkers does not exist). Life should be about enjoyment, becoming who you are, and living to the fullest.

Any initial reader of the existentialist philosophers is often intrigued *and* troubled by the meaninglessness of life, since it seems to indicate to them that anything goes. This is not a naïve interpretation, I believe, but rather one of the biggest questions existentialism has to answer. For if there is no meaning to life, how could anyone argue that anything (such as helping those in need, or using fewer fossil fuels) even matters? When we think, for example, about our planetary crisis, does it — from an existentialist perspective — matter whether we do anything to avert this crisis? If one pushed the nihilist angle to its logical extreme, one could end up with an interpretation of existentialism in which both death and life would also be meaningless. Yet, in the thinkers discussed in the following we find, instead, a strong emphasis on the necessity to create value, to take responsibility, and to create a life that is worthy of living. In relation to the dread of death, it is then argued that existentialism moves beyond dread by emphasising the significance of living over death. In other words, the lack of meaning provides the possibility to dedicate oneself to life or living.

Nietzsche and the affirmation of life

Any reader of Nietzsche will very quickly realise that anything he writes — before even considering what it all might even mean — is written in a peculiar way. Nietzsche's writing style (or styles) is (or are) very personal, powerful, and poetic. How Nietzsche expresses his thoughts does play a significant role and actually establishes a meaning; his styles break from the tradition of the history of western thinking, a tradition branded by Nietzsche as 'dogmatism'. This break or divorce from the tradition consists of at least three different motives.

Chapter 3 Beyond the dread of death: Existentialism's embrace of the meaninglessness of life

1. Nietzsche breaks with the rational tradition

Ever since Socrates saw his approaching death as a blessing in the sky since he would finally be released from the body and be able to think purely, the Western canon has emphasised reason as the solution. Most notably, the motto of the enlightenment was faith in reason, and, with a few exceptions, philosophy tends to emphasise reason and rationality. We can say that generally speaking the whole tradition is following this trend. Philosophy is then a logical endeavour, and this is evident in its style of rational arguments. Nietzsche breaks from this tradition by using a very emotional and dramatic style of writing. He attempts to break away from philosophy, which has been a 'misinterpretation of the body and a *misunderstanding of the body*' (Nietzsche, 1974, pp. 34–35). Nietzsche raises the question 'whether it was not sickness that inspired the philosopher' (Nietzsche, 1974, p. 34). The sickness is perhaps rationality, faith in reason itself. By ignoring the body and denying our urges and drives, philosophy has denied our true being, and this suppression, which we also find in the message of Christianity, certainly in Nietzsche's time, is what Nietzsche diagnoses as our sickness. Philosophers need their philosophy to deal with this illness and philosophy itself is regarded as 'a prop, a sedative, medicine, redemption, elevation, or self-alienation' (Nietzsche, 1974, p. 34). It is this illness and the philosophies that express it with which Nietzsche attempts to break. We have to become artists, he says on many occasions. 'As an aesthetic phenomenon existence is still *bearable* for us, and art furnishes us with eyes and hands and above all the good conscience to be *able* to turn ourselves into such a phenomenon' (Nietzsche, 1974, pp. 163–164). Nietzsche's writing itself can be regarded as a transfiguration of ourselves, and our existence, into an artistic phenomenon. The way in which Nietzsche expresses his thoughts is, thus, an essential part of his break with the tradition.

2. Relatedly, Nietzsche abandons philosophy as a discipline that seeks truth

Even more, he breaks with truth. What we call truth is not some absolute; truth is not already there, objectively given to us. Philosophers and the Christian tradition have created truths, which Nietzsche regards merely as perspectives. We now need more perspectives, Nietzsche argues. We need a multiplicity of perspectives, so that we can overcome the existing 'truths'. This is one of the reasons Nietzsche emphasises that we are artists, creating ourselves and creating new perspectives. We, first of all, create these through ourselves, as authors of truth (or perspectives). With this, truth (and philosophy) become personal and perspectival.

3. Nietzsche's philosophy famously breaks away from Christianity

While science and philosophy have fooled themselves into thinking they have liberated themselves from Christian doctrines, the values of this tradition cast its shadow on all our thinking, our existence, who we are, our so-called 'truths', and our values. It is still what Nietzsche calls, 'the age of moralities and religions' (Nietzsche, 1974, p. 74). It is a time in which it is believed that there is truth, and that there are absolute moral values. Famously, Nietzsche seeks to establish a re-evaluation of all values.

These three points (the break from rationality, truth, and values) form the core of Nietzsche's declaration of the meaninglessness of life. In short, all meaning is merely created by us. Beyond those fabrications of truth there are merely perspectives. Generally speaking, we fail to recognise this meaninglessness, partly by keeping ourselves busy and living lives that fail to reflect on meaning. Nietzsche starts *The gay science* with his explanation of this drive to our activities: 'Whether I contemplate men with benevolence or an evil eye, I always find them concerned with a *single* task, all of them and everyone one of them in particular: to do what is good for the preservation of the human race' (Nietzsche, 1974, p. 73). While Nietzsche might point here to sexual drives that lead to procreation, the task is much more complicated. First of all, the context of *The gay science* is set in a sober Christian morality that oppresses our most basic drives. Thus, in Nietzsche's time a preservation of the human species is a serious task that is set in a world determined through good and evil. A strict religious education, punishment, and living a life that oppresses any enjoyment are the ingredients that lead to this preservation of the species. It is a service to God, in which the individual is obliterated. The 'founders of moralities and religions' or those who 'believe they promote the interest of God or works as God's emissaries ... promote the life of the species, *by promoting the faith in life*' (Nietzsche, 1974, p. 74). It is this life that tells us there is a meaning to life, and this is where our tragedy — living a life without happiness, dedicated to a meaning that does not exist — begins. Nietzsche writes about God's agents: "Life is worth living' everyone of them shouts; 'there is something to life, there is something behind life, beneath it; beware!" (Nietzsche, 1974, p. 74). Within this morality, living is dedicated not to life, but to death: the redemption of our suffering is found in the afterlife, which for Nietzsche does not exist.

Chapter 3 Beyond the dread of death: Existentialism's embrace of the meaninglessness of life

Reflecting on Nietzsche's writing from our own standpoint in the 21st century, it might seem that we have stepped beyond religious beliefs and values. Churches in many parts of the Western world are struggling to attract regular attendees. However, empty churches do not mean that God is really dead today. Nietzsche already predicted that the transformation beyond Christianity is not an easy or quick task: 'After Buddha was dead, his shadow was still shown for centuries in a cave — a tremendous, gruesome shadow. God is dead; but given the way of men, there may still be caves for thousands of years in which his shadow will be shown. — And we — we still have to vanquish his shadow too!' (Nietzsche, 1974, p. 167). The caves and shadows are implicitly referring to the deceit experienced in Plato's cave and are, in Nietzsche's context, the values, beliefs, and supposed truths that we live in. They are found in, among other things, the natural sciences in the form of ideas concerning teleology, origin, and organisation. They are found in our constitutions, in laws, in customs. They are found in the ways we experience love and hatred. And so forth.

How can we move away from these Christian values and develop our own? In a typical Nietzschean move, it is recognising that the negative motto 'the species is everything, *one* is always none' (Nietzsche, 1974, p. 74) can itself turn us onto the path of laughter, happiness, or gay science. It encompasses for Nietzsche the 'ultimate liberation and irresponsibility' in which the 'comedy of existence' becomes conscious of itself (Nietzsche, 1974, p. 74). It is only at this point that we recognise our own situation as silly and comedic. It is the turning point in which we take the moralists less seriously, and can turn tragedy into comedy. This is the situation in which we recognise the meaninglessness of life. Two consequences are important to note. The first one is that meaninglessness does not lead to suffering (as it did for Schopenhauer, Nietzsche's great inspiration). Instead, it is the meaningful life dedicated to God that leads to suffering, since it is a life aimed at a (nonexistent) beyond that can only be obtained through an oppression of pleasure. Overcoming the illusion that life has a meaning in the form of an afterlife should release us from this suffering and allow us to enjoy life.

Secondly, for Nietzsche, meaninglessness does not force us to abandon the idea that there can be values. Instead, the lack of absolute values creates the possibility to create new values, our own values. In order to do this, we have to move from a life that stands in service of preserving the species to a life that makes the person into a someone (rather than a no one). Nietzsche expresses this through a few concepts, first of all, through his demand, or rather the demand on our conscience that 'You shall become who you are' (Nietzsche, 2001, p. 155). Our task, in a life that is ultimately without a prescribed meaning, is to let go of the values and truths that are not our own. Instead, we should create our own values. Much of Nietzsche's work is, arguably, dedicated to this self-realisation, the becoming of the self, famously expressed as the *Übermensch*, the beyond of our current human state. *Thus spoke Zarathustra* describes all the trials, errors, and small victories one can make along the way to overcoming one's self (which is in principle a self who is not who you are, but determined through a herd instinct). The process is first of all (indeed) a process, and not so much a state one will reach. The process consists of constantly re-evaluating all values, including the values that one (re)invents. As becomes clear in a work such as the *Genealogy of morals*, such re-evaluation involves the laborious task of tracing the history and lineage of our values. This means that we do not make some reactionary decision to steal simply on the basis that we want to reject all biblical values, including 'Thou shall not steal'. In fact, it might very well be the case that such a value is going to be part of one's future values. However, one would not accept it because the bible tells us to do so. One would accept it only on the basis of a personal evaluation of and reflection on stealing. Nevertheless, we might come to different insight regarding stealing and property. To provide an example, Nietzsche himself offers a provocative insight on 'even the most harmful' people who are perhaps really the most useful when it comes to the preservation of the species (Nietzsche, 1974, p. 73). Here, he goes beyond Socrates' description of the philosopher as a gadfly, the person who keeps annoying people with nagging questions: 'Hatred, the mischievous delight in the misfortunes of others, the lust to rob and dominate, and whatever else is called evil belongs to the most amazing economy of the preservation of the species. To be sure, this economy is not afraid of high prices, of squandering, and it is on the whole extremely foolish. Still it is *proven* that it has preserved our race so far' (Nietzsche, 1974, p. 73). This is a somewhat challenging passage to interpret, since it seems to celebrate the most harmful people. Yet, he seems to suggest that the fact that such people are essential to our economy indicates indeed how wasteful and foolish we are as a society. Nietzsche, arguably, does not ask us to celebrate murder and stealing, but rather points out the hypocrisy of our current morals in which we celebrate justice and rights while, in fact, those who thrive most, do so precisely because they have no sense of justice and righteousness.

Chapter 3 Beyond the dread of death: Existentialism's embrace of the meaninglessness of life

What the passage also shows is that the re-evaluation of all values is not only a tremendous task in terms of tracing the history of certain values, it is also a herculean task in terms of defining the values and beliefs we have, many of which we are not explicitly aware.

In this regard, we should also contextualise this discussion about values within Nietzsche's criticism of 'weak' values such as pity, since they are part of a slave morality, the morality that emphasises that being weak is in itself good. The slave morality, which Nietzsche traces back to the oppression of the Jews, results in a reactionary system of values in which 'the wretched alone are the good; the poor, impotent, lowly alone are the good; the suffering, deprived, sick, ugly alone are pious ... and you, the powerful and noble, are on the contrary the evil, the cruel, the lustful, the insatiable, the godless to all eternity' (Nietzsche 1989, p. 34). The slave morality is a reaction to the master morality, in which the powerful saw themselves as good, in opposition to the weak, the plebs. Both value systems, master and slave moralities, are problematic since they define good by what they themselves are not.

In challenging these values, Nietzsche does not simply reverse all the values we currently have. That would be merely another reactionary reassessment (and he does make very clear that both the slave and the master moralities are flawed precisely because they negatively define good, i.e., through the position they despise). Of course, for Nietzsche the *Übermensch* needs to move beyond reactionary values. In this process, one might indeed first discover that the *Übermensch* is not only good: s/he/they might also be evil. Moreover it means that we eventually have to step beyond those qualifications: Beyond Good and Evil!

To return now to death and the dread of death, we have already seen how Nietzsche emphasises life over death. We can explore this further through his eternal recurrence of the same, expressed (among others) in the following passage, called 'The greatest weight', from *The gay science*:

> What, if some day or night a demon were to steal after you into your loneliest loneliness and say to you: 'This life as you now live it and have lived it, you will have to live once more and innumerable times more; and there will be nothing new in it, but every pain and every joy and every thought and sigh and everything unutterably small or great in your life will have to return to you, an in the same succession and sequence — even this spider and this moonlight between the trees, and even this

moment and I myself. The eternal hourglass of existence is turned upside down again and again, and you with it, speck of dust! (Nietzsche, 1974, p. 273)

The passage might strike the novice reader of Nietzsche as odd: does he — instead of believing in a Judeo-Christian God and an afterlife — believe in some form of reincarnation? I do not believe Nietzsche introduces anything like that. Rather, he asks the reader to imagine every single moment of one's life as repeating over and over again, not because it actually does, but merely to emphasise the significance of every moment. The imperative is that one should always act in such a way that you would want to do it again and again. Even while I am a mote of dust, and what I do really does not matter in the context of a meaningless life, I should still care about it. Why? The key to answering this question lies exactly in the fact that the eternal recurrence of the same is nothing but a thought experiment; I will not have second chances. My life occurs only once, so I better live it in the best possible way, whatever that means. At least it means that it is *my* life, i.e., a life that I create as my own.

One of the interesting aspects of the eternal recurrence is that it puts us beyond death, first by denying death (everything will happen again and again) and secondly by recognising that things will not recur. The eternal recurrence is in that regard not so much about death, but rather about life — live it as if you want to have it reoccur again and again.

Sartre

We have seen now how for Nietzsche the discovery of the meaninglessness of life is a liberation, but one that comes with the demand to become who we are. Life is not about dying and death, but about living. To be thrown into the abyss, so to speak, means that we can end the oppressing values of our existence; yet, it does not 'let us off the hook'. We are given the tremendously difficult task to 'become who you are'. While Nietzsche describes this as a joyful or gay endeavour, Sartre focuses on the responsibility that we are facing in this new reality. He is the thinker who more than any other existentialist emphasises our ethical duties. For him, the very fact that there is no predetermined meaning to life — that all meaning is created by us — ultimately means that we are responsible for ourselves (for everything we do and fail to do) as well as for others.

Sartre describes existentialism as the idea that 'existence precedes essence' (Sartre, 1999, p. 34). We are absolutely free to determine ourselves. There is no predetermined path we are supposed to follow. I choose the path for myself and with that I 'choose myself'. Sartre recognises Nietzsche's idea of the herd mentality in which we do whatever everyone else is doing. Let's say I go to college, since all my friends go to college, my teachers have been preparing me for this step, and its very clearly the expectation of my parents, who have never even mentioned the possibility that I do anything else. For Sartre, this kind of pattern shows us exactly how we deal with our freedom: while we could choose to work and travel the world, build a cabin in the woods, or pursue some other dream, we typically do not do it, precisely because it would be our own choice, and thus our own responsibility. If I do choose my own actions and I, for example, run out of money in a remote part of China, if I break an arm, or if I fail to save money for my retirement, I can only blame one person: myself. Thus, Sartre writes, it is 'very distressing that God does not exist' since now 'everything is permissible' and one 'can't start making excuses for himself [sic]' (Sartre, 1999, p. 41). Interestingly, while we always seem to seek freedom, we are actually 'condemned to be free' (Sartre, 1999, p. 41). It is, in fact, one of two things we did not choose. The first thing we did not choose is that we are and, secondly, we did not choose to be free.

Sartre thus defines human existence as entirely free, even condemned to freedom. We are entirely responsible for ourselves. He even takes this a step further by arguing that in choosing ourselves, we choose everyone. Taking a personal example, he writes, 'if I want to marry, to have children; even if this marriage depends solely on my own circumstance or passion or wish, I am involving all humanity in monogamy and not merely myself' (Sartre, 1999, p. 37). Sartre's argument might make little sense within our contemporary ideas of freedom and individuality. Doesn't freedom mean precisely that we can do whatever we want, and wouldn't a meaningless world emphasise exactly such a notion of freedom? To put it differently: isn't Sartre a megalomaniac by assuming that the nature of his sexual relationships has any impact on the rest of humanity? It is helpful to understand that Sartre was highly influenced by Immanuel Kant and that his point here is in essence a Kantian one. He follows in particular Kant's categorical imperative which states that the maxims of our actions constitute universal laws. When we choose something for ourselves, we imply that this is the best choice for the rest of humanity, as well. Sartre puts it as follows: 'what would happen if everybody looked at things that way?' (Sartre, 1999, p. 38). He takes the example of the lie (an example used by Kant as well) and concludes that 'the act of lying implies that a universal value is conferred upon the lie' (Sartre, 1999, p. 38). The existentialist individual, for Sartre, is thus determined through responsibility: 'I am responsible for myself and for everyone else. I am creating a certain image of man of my own choosing. In choosing myself, I choose man' (Sartre, 1999, p. 37). Even our passions cannot be used as an excuse for our decisions; we are also responsible for our passions. 'We are alone and with no excuses' (Sartre, 1999, p. 41).

Sartre, thus, argues that there is an incredible responsibility in all of our actions. This strong sense of responsibility is often contextualised in the historical time Sartre was developing as an existentialist thinker. *The humanism of existentialism* was published in 1946 shortly after the defeat of the German occupation and the full scope of the Holocaust came to light. Sartre painfully realises that ethics is not only about what we do, but moreover about what we neglect to do. We cannot simply blame those who were part of the Third Reich, who actively rounded up, transported, processed, and killed a staggering number of six million people. Everyone who stood by silently, who did not act against this violence, should also be considered responsible. Sartre formulates his philosophy as the opposite of quietism, 'the attitude of people who say 'let others do what I can't do" (Sartre, 1999, p. 47). Sartre's idea that we are responsible, even if our options seem to be limited and even if we seem powerless, was a serious and confrontational reflection in the wake of the Holocaust. Today, the notion of quietism is no less relevant: genocides, racism, xenophobic actions, and acts against the planet itself might seem to be unpreventable by the individual. Yet, if we do not speak up and act against it, we are — in Sartre's thinking — responsible as well. There is no such thing as an innocent bystander. If we convince ourselves otherwise, for example, by stating that we cannot change anything about the violent world around us, we fall into the trap of bad faith, discussed in detail in *Being and nothingness*. We always have a choice, and if we choose not to act we are responsible for the consequences.

As Nietzsche, Sartre does not focus on death. The emphasis is life and living and in that regard Sartre's philosophy focuses on making the right choices in our lives. We are not to obsess about death. While Sartre's views regarding resistance and the use of violence are not without ambiguity and seem to have shifted over the course of his career, Sartre's thinking suggests that putting our own life on the line can be a viable choice. His philosophy is not determined through a dread of death, but has moved beyond it, to life. Death itself can be a choice.

Camus and the absurd

While Sartre can be called the most moralistic of all existential thinkers, Camus takes us in a seemingly different direction: the absurd. The human condition is absurd since we are constantly engaged in all kinds of activities with absolute dedication, even while everything in the end is meaningless. The tensions between dedication and meaninglessness could be called the absurd. Camus, famously, starts *The myth of Sisyphus* with stating that 'There is but one truly serious philosophical problem, and that is suicide' (Camus, 2016, p. 3). I will discuss here how his philosophy shows us that life can be worth living, precisely in its meaninglessness.

In our general usage of the term 'absurd' we use it to dismiss something (as in 'that is absurd'), and the logical argument called the *reductio ad absurdum* rejects something by showing that it leads to an absurd conclusion. On the basis of such everyday and logical uses of the word 'absurd', we might assume that Camus' philosophy suggests that meaninglessness leads to absurdity and that any kind of ethical demand is necessarily rejected. Perhaps surprisingly, Camus urges us to embrace the absurd and as we see in the following, his novel *The stranger* shows us exactly that meaningless should not lead to an attitude in which nothing matters. Camus' existentialism, or his philosophy of the absurd, tells us that first and foremost, we should not live indifferently.

Mersault, the main character of *The stranger*, is the kind of person we should not become. He has come to the insight that there is no meaning to life and on the basis of that insight, he decides that nothing really matters. Whether he marries or not, whether he loves, how to go about the funeral of his mother, or whether or not to pull the trigger — it simply does not matter. Throughout *The stranger* Mersault never makes a single decision. Things just happen to him. When he kills an Arab on the beach (a stranger, although the title of the novel plays on both the death of this stranger and the ultimate stranger, Mersault) it seems to be the result of the heat, the light of the sun, and the fiery breadth of the sea. Here is the somewhat lengthy passage:

> The sun was starting to burn my cheeks, and I could feel drops of sweat gathering in my eyebrows. That sun was the same as it had been the day I'd buried Maman, and like then, my forehead especially was hurting me, all the veins in it throbbing under the sun. It was this burning, which I couldn't stand anymore, that made me move forward. I knew that it was stupid, that I wouldn't get the sun off me by stepping forward. And this time, without

getting up, the Arab drew his knife and held it up to me in the sun. The light shot off the steel and it was like a long flashing blade cutting at my forehead. At the same instant the sweat in my eyebrows dripped down over my eyelids all at once and covered them with a warm, thick film. My eyes were blinded behind the curtain of tears and salt. All I could feel were the cymbals of sunlight crashing on my forehead and, indistinctly, the dazzling spear flying up from the knife in front of me. The scorching blade slashed at my eyelashes and stabbed at my stinging eyes. That's when everything began to reel. The sea carried up a thick, fiery breath. It seemed to me as if the sky split open from one end to the other to rain down fire. My whole being tensed and I squeeze my hand around the revolver. The trigger gave. (Camus, 2006, p. 59)

It is Mersault's last act in freedom, before being imprisoned, and yet nothing seems free about the act. He did not deliberately choose to pull the trigger and kill another human being. Circumstances — the sun and the sea that conglomerate on this day, on the beach, hitting him in the eyes — make him act. It is only after this act (which somehow is not an act) and imprisonment that he becomes aware of the fact that he lost what he never exercised: his freedom.

Mersault could be seen as the quintessential example of how we should not live our lives; we should not take for granted the fact that we are free nor should we live our lives as if none of our choices matter. Camus does indeed find that life is without meaning, but that does not mean nothing matters. I should live my life well, and enjoy what I do with it. Famously, Sisyphus, in his repetitive and endless task, is still happy: 'Each atom of that stone, each mineral flake of that night filled mountain, in itself forms a world. The struggle itself toward the heights is enough to fill a man's heart. One must imagine Sisyphus happy' (Camus, 2016, p. 24). Even in a seemingly futile task, it is ultimately one's attitude toward the world that determines our well-being.

Furthermore, *The Stranger* also carries a political message. Situated in Algeria, Mersault as a Frenchman is also in this sense a stranger. While Mersault treats the whole world with indifference and does not necessarily kill the Arab out of any racist tendencies (after all, he does not commit himself to anything) his trial shows us another awful aspect of colonialism. Camus — himself an Algerian — portrays how Mersault is not so much judged on the basis of killing an Arab, but more on the basis of his character flaws that become apparent by the way he treated his mother — putting her in a home — and his disrespectful behaviour during her funeral. Camus' implicit criticism of French politics is found in the form of the plot that suggests that he might have gotten away with killing an Arab, if he had been a good son.

We then return to the question of whether or not the lack of meaning and absolute values in this life allows for treating others poorly and for horrible chapters of human history, such as colonialism. By describing Mersault's life as one without passion — a life not lived — Camus, first of all, tells us that we should not live a life in which we are indifferent and lack any kind of dedication. He builds a political message on this insight: a meaningless life does not imply that one can barge into any country, take over, and set up a regime that imposes new values and oppresses the old. Existentialism is a philosophy of freedom and that freedom allows for an expression of the individual. Colonialism is the destruction of the possibility of such an expression.

Of course, Mersault is sentenced to death. He is in that situation Dostoyevsky experienced in his mock death sentence. In *The idiot*, Dostoyevsky reflects on this experience: 'What if I didn't have to die! … I would turn every minute into an age, nothing would be wasted, every minute would be accounted for' (Dostoyevsky, 2008, p. 64). This is not necessarily a dread of death; it is rather a re-evaluation of life. It is the realisation that we should make every moment of our lives count, even if there is no meaning to it all. The most oppressing part, for Dosteyevsky, is the time of his life that has been wasted. Mersault seems to realise this, or perhaps Camus wants us to realise that if we live a life in which we merely let things happen, we are not living life to the fullest. It is death that can make us recognise this point.

Conclusion: Beyond the dread of death

The movement of existentialism is often associated with the dread of death. Figures like Kierkegaard and Heidegger are well known for their respective analyses of death. Yet both argue that our lives should not be determined by a dread of death. Their views are consistent with the thinkers discussed in this chapter — we should focus on living, on making the right choices during this life, and to creating ourselves in an authentic way.

In this chapter I have particularly focused on atheist existentialists (Nietzsche, Sartre, and Camus) who all suggest — in different ways — that the death of God and the lack of an afterlife do not have to lead us to dread death, but rather to celebrate life. Nietzsche, known for declaring the death of God, suggests that we are inauthentic beings, determined through the herd. We are not ourselves, and the ultimate prescription Nietzsche presents to us is to become who you are. We are mistaken if we follow those who tell us there is something beyond this life. This life is it, and we better make something of it. Sartre accepts Nietzsche's ideas insofar as they point to a lack of a higher being, and a lack of meaning to life. Yet, precisely in this lack of meaning, Sartre emphasises our responsibilities. His philosophy thus also emphasises the significance of living this life well, rather than fearing death. Lastly, we have seen that Camus presents us with the case of Mersault, who represents the ultimate failure: someone who does not make choices and who does not embrace life, until he is confronted by death. His anguish does not so much represent a dread of death, but rather the ultimate confrontation with the fact that his life has been wasted and that he has no second chances. Arguably, death is the release from this anguish.

Existentialism emphasises living, over death. By focusing on living a good life; that is, by celebrating life, and by making the right choices that would make one's life worth living again and again (even while it only happens once), we can overcome the dread of death. Angst about dying is not an existentialist state of being — at least not a permanent one. The emphasis is, after all, existence. The dread of death is part of a culture that believes in an afterlife to compensate for the fact that life is finite. Existentialism does not need this belief since it emphasises and celebrates life. In that celebration, existentialism steps beyond the dread of death and — in Kundera's words — 'our lives can stand out against it [the eternal return] in all their splendid lightness' (Kundera, 2014, p. 5). For Kundera and the existentialists discussed in this chapter, our lives are not merely lightness. We are burdened not by death but by life itself.

References

Camus, A. (2006). *The stranger.* New York, NY: A.A. Knopf.

Camus, A. (2016). *The myth of Sisyphus, and other essays.* New York, NY: Vintage Books.

Dostoyevsky, F. (2008). *The Idiot.* New York, NY: Oxford University Press.

Heidegger, M. (2008). *Being and time.* New York, NY: Harper Collins.

Kundera, M. (2014). *The unbearable lightness of being.* London, England: Faber and Faber.

Nietzsche, F.M. (1974). *The gay science: With a prelude in rhymes and an appendix of songs.* New York, NY: Vintage Books.

Nietzsche, F.M. (1989). *On the genealogy of morals: Ecce homo.* New York, NY: Vintage.

Nietzsche, F.M. (2001). *The gay science.* Cambridge, England: Cambridge University Press.

Sartre, J.P. (1999). The humanism of existentialism. In *Essays in Existentialism.* Secaucus, NJ: Carol Publishing Group.

Chapter 4

Love, death, and the quest for meaning

Mario Mikulincer

Attachment theory (e.g., Bowlby, 1973, 1980, 1982, 1988), which was originally formulated to describe and explain infant-parent emotional bonding, has been applied, first, to the study of adolescent and adult romantic relationships and then to the study of emotion regulation and coping with stressful and traumatic events. In the present chapter I present an attachment perspective on coping with existential concerns of mortality and meaninglessness. According to attachment theory, the sense of attachment security — a felt sense, rooted in one's history of close relationships, that the world is generally safe, other people are generally helpful when called upon, and I, as a unique individual, am valuable and lovable, thanks to being valued and loved by others — provides a psychological foundation for easing existential anxieties and constructing an authentic sense of continuity, coherence, and meaning.

We begin by presenting a brief overview of attachment theory and Mikulincer and Shaver's (2003, 2016) theoretical model of the activation and functioning of the attachment behavioural system in adulthood. I then review studies showing that a heightened awareness of one's finitude and life meaninglessness drive people to move toward protective others or activate mental representations of security providers in order to bolster feelings of safety and security and thereby reduce existential anxiety. I also review studies indicating that the availability of a loving and supportive external or internalised figure and the resulting sense of security are effective antidotes to mortality concerns and can provide a solid platform for feeling a meaning in life. In addition, I present empirical evidence on the ways individual differences in attachment security shape the experience of, and coping with, concerns about mortality and meaninglessness.

Attachment theory: Basic concepts

The main construct in Bowlby's (1982) attachment theory is the *attachment behavioural system*, an innate psychobiological system that motivates people to seek proximity to protective others (*attachment figures*) in times of need. When these attachment behaviours assure proximity to a responsive and supportive attachment figure, they contribute to a general sense of 'felt security' (Sroufe & Waters, 1977), which makes exploration, learning, and participation in social relationships easier and more successful. Although the attachment system is most crucial in the early years of life, because of human infants' extreme immaturity and dependence on others, Bowlby (1988) claimed that it is active throughout life and is manifested in thoughts and behaviours related to proximity- and support-seeking and in the resulting sense of security. This idea has now been bolstered by experimental studies showing that even minimal symbolic threats automatically activate mental representations of a person's attachment figures (e.g., Mikulincer, Gillath, & Shaver, 2002) and by neuropsychological research indicating that the human brain evolved to function within the context of social relationships (see Coan, 2016, for a review).

Bowlby (1973) also described important individual differences in attachment-system functioning. In his view, although all human beings are born with a capacity to seek proximity, safety, and help with the regulation of negative emotions in times of need, important individual differences arise as a function of the reactions of one's relationship partners to bids for proximity and support and the incorporation of such reactions into mental representations of self and others (what Bowlby, 1973, called *working models of self and relationships*). Interactions with attachment figures who are available, sensitive, and supportive in times of need facilitate the smooth, normative functioning of the attachment system, promote a sense of connectedness and security, and contribute to positive working models of self and others. As a result, a person feels generally secure and efficacious and can explore the physical and social environment curiously, learn diverse skills, develop cognitively and emotionally, enjoy life's challenges, and deal constructively with negative emotions and stressful life events (Mikulincer & Shaver, 2016). However, when a person's attachment figures are not reliably available and supportive, a pervasive, dispositional sense of security is not attained, worries about one's social value and about others' intentions are strengthened, and strategies of affect regulation other than confident proximity seeking and effective self-regulation are adopted (what Main, 1990, called *secondary attachment strategies*, characterised by *anxiety* or defensive *avoidance*).

In social-psychological studies of adolescents and adults, tests of attachment theory have focused on a person's *attachment orientation* — the systematic pattern of relational expectations, emotions, and behaviour that results from a particular history of attachment experiences (Fraley & Shaver, 2000). Hundreds of attachment studies (reviewed by Mikulincer & Shaver, 2016) have found that attachment orientations can be conceptualised and measured along two orthogonal dimensions of attachment-related *anxiety* and *avoidance*. Attachment *anxiety* reflects the degree to which a person worries that relationship partners will not be available in times of need and is afraid of being rejected or abandoned. Attachment-related *avoidance* reflects the extent to which a person distrusts relationship partners' goodwill and strives to maintain independence and emotional distance from partners. People who score low on both dimensions are said to be secure with respect to attachment. The two dimensions can be measured with reliable and valid self-report scales, such as the Experience in Close Relationships scale (ECR, Brennan, Clark, & Shaver, 1998), and are associated in theoretically predictable ways with many aspects of psychological, relational, and social functioning (see Mikulincer & Shaver, 2016, for a review).

Although a person's attachment style is often conceptualised as a single global orientation toward close relationships (i.e., a stable trait), and is often measured as such (e.g., Brennan et al., 1998), a person's attachment security is rooted in a complex cognitive and affective network that includes many different episodic, context-related, and relationship-specific, as well as fairly general, attachment representations (Collins & Read, 1994; Mikulincer & Shaver, 2016). In fact, research shows that a person's sense of attachment security can change depending on natural or experimentally induced contexts and recent experiences (e.g., Baldwin, Keelan, Fehr, Enns, & Koh Rangarajoo, 1996). Moreover, the experimental priming of mental representations of security providers or security-enhancing interactions (what Mikulincer & Shaver, 2007, called *security priming*) can momentarily instill a sense of security and even dispositionally insecurely attached people can enjoy the psychological benefits of felt security.

Mikulincer and Shaver (2016) proposed that a person's location in the two-dimensional space defined by attachment anxiety and avoidance reflects both his or her sense of attachment security and the ways in which he or she deals with threats and stressors. Those who score low on these dimensions are likely to feel confident concerning their relationship partner's good intentions and their own self-worth (e.g., Baldwin et al., 1996; Collins & Read, 1990; Mickelson, Kessler, & Shaver, 1997). Moreover, they rely on more effective affect-regulation strategies and enjoy higher levels of psychological well-being than people who score high on either avoidance or anxiety. Specifically, more secure individuals generally appraise stressful events in less threatening terms (e.g., Mikulincer & Florian, 1995), and possess more optimistic expectations about being able to cope effectively (e.g., Berant, Mikulincer, & Florian, 2001). They also tend to cope more effectively with stressful events by relying on others' support and adopting problem-focused strategies rather than less effective emotion-focused defences, such as denial, suppression, or extreme, dysregulated expression of emotions combined with demands for help (e.g., Mikulincer & Florian, 1998; Simpson, Rholes, & Nelligan, 1992). More secure individuals also experience more frequent and prolonged bouts of positive affect and are more resilient in times of stress (e.g., Berant et al., 2001; Mickelson et al., 1997).

People who score high on measures of either attachment anxiety or avoidance differ from their more secure peers in using less effective coping strategies, and they differ from each other in adopting different affect-regulation strategies that Cassidy and Kobak (1988) called 'hyperactivating' or 'deactivating' (of their attachment behavioural system). Those who score high on attachment anxiety typically adopt *hyperactivating attachment strategies* — energetic attempts to achieve proximity, support, and love combined with a lack of confidence that these resources will be adequately provided, and with feelings of intense sadness or anger when what is wanted is in fact not provided. Hyperactivation of the attachment system includes increased vigilance to threat-related cues and quick detection of real or imagined cues of attachment-figure unavailability. As a result, the attachment system is chronically activated, psychological pain related to attachment-figure unavailability is frequent, and doubts about the chances of achieving relief from anxiety and a reliable sense of security are heightened (Mikulincer & Shaver, 2016).

In contrast, people who score relatively high on attachment-related avoidance tend to adopt *attachment-system deactivating strategies*, manifested in distancing themselves from stimuli and occasions that activate the attachment system and preferring to handle distress alone. These strategies involve dismissal of threat- and attachment-related cues, suppression of threat- and attachment-related thoughts and emotions, and repression of threat- and attachment-related memories. These tendencies are reinforced by adopting a self-reliant stance that decreases dependence on others and discourages acknowledgement of personal faults, weaknesses, or needs.

In short, each attachment strategy has a major regulatory goal (insisting on proximity to an attachment figure or on self-reliance), which goes along with particular cognitive and affective phenomena shape the experience, regulation, and expression of distress and other negative emotions (Mikulincer & Shaver, 2016). Moreover, these strategies affect the ways in which people experience and cope with threatening events, including concerns about mortality and meaningless — the focus of the following sections of this chapter.

Existential concerns as triggers of attachment-system activation

According to attachment theory, the attachment system was 'designed', or selected, by evolution as a regulatory device for dealing with all kinds of threats, including existential concerns about mortality and meaninglessness. As a result, real or symbolic threats to a person's sense of continued existence and inner coherence can automatically drive him or her to seek proximity to a security-enhancing figure or activate inner representations of security providers, and then obtain protection and restore felt security (Mikulincer & Shaver, 2016). This means that existential concerns can be viewed as triggers of attachment behaviours and cognitions and that felt security can be an effective shield against these concerns. In contrast, lack of available, responsive, and sensitive attachment figures may cause people to feel overwhelmed and terrified by worries about mortality and life meaninglessness or to search for other forms of defence against these worries while relying on external and cultural sources of self-worth.

Death awareness

Awareness of one's mortality is a major cause of existential anxiety that automatically activates psychological defences (e.g., Pyszczynski, Sullivan, & Greenberg, 2015). According to attachment theory, the default defence against death awareness is attachment-system activation and resulting attempts to attain care, protection, and safety. In an early study of the mental accessibility of security-enhancing representations, Mikulincer, Birnbaum, Woddis, and Nachmias (2000, Study 3) found that preconscious reminders of death can automatically activate the attachment system. Participants were subliminally exposed to the word 'death' or a neutral word for 22 milliseconds in each of several trials and then they were asked to decide whether a string of letters was a word or not (lexical decision task). These strings included words related to attachment security (e.g., love, hug, closeness), attachment-unrelated positive words, neutral words, and nonwords. Findings indicated that the death prime, compared to the neutral prime, increased the mental availability of words related to attachment security (as indicated by faster reaction times in the lexical decision task). The word 'death' had no effect on the mental availability of attachment-unrelated positive or neutral words.

There is also evidence that conscious death reminders increase proximity-seeking behaviours and cognitions. For example, Mikulincer and Florian (2000, Study 5) found that a mortality salience induction led to higher reports of desire for intimacy in romantic bonds (as assessed by Sharabany's, 1994, intimacy scale) than a neutral induction. In a series of three experiments, Taubman-Ben-Ari, Findler, and Mikulincer (2002) reinforced this initial finding by examining the impact of making mortality salient on relational strivings and beliefs. In Study 1, Taubman-Ben-Ari et al. (2002) found that a mortality salience induction led participants to report higher willingness to initiate social interactions with a hypothetical same-sex target than a neutral condition. In the next two experiments, Taubman-Ben-Ari et al. (2002) focused on cognitive factors that have been found to facilitate the formation of close relationships — confidence on one's interpersonal skills (Buhrmester, Furman, Wittenberg, & Reis, 1988) — and to inhibit the formation of these relationships — rejection sensitivity (e.g., Downey & Feldman, 1996). Death awareness biased cognitive judgements and expectations in ways that favor close relationships. Specifically, making mortality salient, as compared to a neutral condition, led to higher appraisals of interpersonal skills and reduced expectations of being rejected by a partner. Overall, these findings imply that mortality salience promotes a positive orientation towards social interactions and interpersonal relationships.

In two subsequent studies, Mikulincer, Florian, and Hirschberger (2004) examined the effects of mortality salience on a person's attitudes towards romantic relationships. In the first study, they focused on Lee's (1977) styles of romantic love and examined the impact of mortality salience on a person's preference for different love styles. As compared to a neutral condition, making mortality salient heightened preference for love styles that can maintain and enhance the quality and stability of love relationships (i.e., eros and agape styles). In the second study, they assessed participants' preferences for romantic partners with different love styles. Findings were consistent with predictions from attachment theory: As compared to a physical pain condition, making mortality salient heightened preference for partners who held eros or agape styles — the two styles that contribute to satisfactory relationships — and lowered preference for partners who held a ludus style — a style that can endanger a bond's stability.

In another study, Florian, Mikulincer, and Hirschberger (2002, Study 1) examined the effects of mortality salience on the sense of commitment in romantic relationships. Specifically, participants were asked to write about either their own death or a neutral topic (watching TV). Following a distracter task, all participants then rated the extent to which they were committed to their romantic partner (e.g., 'I am completely devoted to my partner') as well as their moral commitment to marriage (e.g., 'Marriages are supposed to last forever'). Participants in the mortality salience condition reported greater psychological commitment to their romantic partner than participants in the neutral condition. However, there was no significant effect of mortality salience on moral commitment. Florian et al. (2002) concluded that death reminders increase the sense of love and closeness to a romantic partner but not marriage-related moral duties.

It is important to note that the above reviewed finding do not necessarily mean that death reminders trigger attachment-system activation. In fact, proximity seeking can serve purposes other than protection and security, such as encouraging sexual intercourse and hence reproduction. To demonstrate attachment-system activation, it is necessary to show that proximity seeking serves a protective function. This demonstration can be accomplished in two ways. First, if felt security buffers a person from the terror of death awareness, seeking proximity to a security-enhancing figure following mortality salience should reduce the need for other terror management defences, such as cultural worldview validation or self-esteem enhancement. Second, if felt security shields people from death anxiety, interference with proximity seeking should increase concerns about death.

In two studies, Florian et al. (2002) provided evidence for the protective function of felt security following mortality salience. In one study (Florian et al., 2002, Study 2), people were randomly assigned to a mortality salience or a neutral condition and then randomly divided into two subgroups based on a manipulation of romantic commitment. Participants in the commitment condition were asked to describe emotions associated with committing themselves to a romantic partner. Participants in the no commitment condition were asked similar questions about a neutral topic (listening to the radio). All of them then rated the severity of punishment that was appropriate for various social transgressions, which was meant to assess a common worldview defence — punishing people who transgress social norms (Rosenblatt, Greenberg, Solomon, Pyszczynski, & Lyon, 1989). The results showed that mortality salience (as compared with the neutral condition) increased participants' harsh judgements of purported social transgressions in the no commitment condition, but it had no effect on punishment severity when romantic commitment had been made salient. That is, asking people to think about their commitment to a romantic bond reduced the use of other defences against the threat of death.

In another study (Florian et al., 2002, Study 3), participants were randomly divided into three conditions according to the kinds of thoughts that were made salient (problems in a romantic relationship, academic problems, neutral topics). All participants then completed Greenberg, Pyszczynski, Solomon, Simon, and Breus's (1994) word-completion task, which measures the implicit accessibility of death-related thoughts. Findings showed that participants in the 'problems in romantic relationship' condition produced more death-related words than participants in the 'academic problems' and neutral conditions. That is, thinking about difficulties in close relationships heightens death-thought accessibility, implying that interfering with closeness to a security-enhancing partner can elicit death concerns.

Studies also have shown that proximity seeking to security-enhancing figures and the resulting sense of security can override the need for other defences against death awareness. Hirschberger, Florian, and Mikulincer (2003) asked whether death awareness can still drive people to seek proximity to a relationship partner even when this partner's complaints or criticisms can threaten their self-esteem. Participants were assigned to a mortality salience or a control condition and were asked to imagine having dinner at their partner's parents' home and then receiving one of three kinds of evaluations from their partner — either admiration ('I'm very proud of you. You were so friendly and nice tonight'), a complaint ('Tonight you seemed to be really withdrawn, and you didn't even offer to help my mother'), or a criticism ('As usual, you were totally self-absorbed all evening and didn't help my mother. You are an egotist! What kind of a person are you?'). They were then asked to rate their willingness to engage in emotionally intimate interactions with their partner.

Participants who had been exposed to a mortality salience induction were more interested in emotional intimacy than participants in the neutral condition. Moreover, whereas in the neutral condition a partner's admiration led to a stronger desire for intimacy than a partner's complaint or criticism, this difference was not significant in the mortality salience condition. In fact, death reminders increased the desire for emotional intimacy even after a partner complained or criticised, implying that death awareness makes people willing to pay the price of diminished self-esteem to maintain emotional closeness with a romantic partner. A similar finding was reported by Wisman and Koole's (2003), who observed that a mortality salience induction heightened preference for sitting close to other people in a group discussion, rather than sitting alone, even if this seating preference required exposing their worldviews to potential attack (they knew that other participants would disagree with their beliefs).

Overall, findings from these studies indicate that felt security is a shield against existential threats and makes people less inclined to try to validate their beliefs or enhance their self-esteem following death reminders. Reliance on worldview defences or self-esteem inflation may be more probable when proximity seeking fails to restore security and then to accomplish its protective function.

Concerns about life's meaning

The perception of coherence and meaning in life is crucial for maintaining emotional balance (e.g., King, 2012; Park & Edmonson, 2012), and people often react defensively when their sense of meaning is threatened by life circumstances (e.g., Kruglanski, Gelfman, & Gunaratna, 2012; Park & Edmonson,

2012). From an attachment perspective, we would expect threats to one's sense of meaning, like any other serious threat to one's welfare, to trigger a search for comfort, love, and reassurance from attachment figures.

Adult attachment researchers have not focused specifically on meaninglessness and its effects on attachment-system activation. However, Shaver and Mikulincer (2012) reported a study examining the influence of meaninglessness on proximity seeking. Participants were randomly assigned to one of three meaning-related conditions (high meaning condition, low meaning condition, neutral condition), according to King, Hicks, and Abdelkhalik's procedure (2009, Study 3), and were then asked to complete Sharabany's (1994) Intimacy Scale assessing their desire for closeness in relationships. Participants in the high-meaning and low-meaning conditions wrote a brief essay about how the statement 'Human life is purposeful and meaningful' might be viewed as either true or untrue, respectively. Participants in the control condition wrote an essay on a neutral topic (shopping at a drugstore). Those in the low-meaning condition reported a stronger desire for romantic intimacy than those in the high-meaning or the neutral control condition. There was not a significant difference between the latter two conditions. Thus, raising the possibility of life's meaninglessness led to an increased wish for closeness and intimacy — the motivational signature of attachment-system activation.

Attachment-related differences in experiencing and managing existential concerns

According to Mikulincer and Shaver (2016), individual differences in attachment orientations are directly manifested in the way people regulate negative emotions. Avoidant attachment has been found to be associated with attempts to block or inhibit any emotional state that is incongruent with the goal of keeping the attachment system deactivated (Mikulincer & Shaver, 2016). These inhibitory efforts are directed mainly at fear, anxiety, anger, sadness, shame, guilt, and distress, because these emotions are associated with threats and feelings of vulnerability that can automatically reactivate proximity seeking. In addition, anger often implies emotional involvement or investment in a relationship, and such involvement is incongruent with avoidant people's preference for independence and self-reliance (Cassidy, 1994). Avoidant individuals also attempt to block or inhibit emotional reactions to potential or actual threats to attachment-figure availability (rejection, betrayal, separation, loss), because such threats are direct triggers of attachment-system activation.

Avoidant deactivating strategies cause people to avoid noticing their own emotional reactions. Avoidant individuals often deny or suppress emotion-related thoughts and memories, divert attention from emotion-related material, suppress emotion-related action tendencies, or inhibit or mask verbal and nonverbal expressions of emotion (Mikulincer & Shaver, 2016). By averting the conscious experience and expression of unpleasant emotions, avoidant individuals make it less likely that emotional experiences will be integrated into their cognitive structures, what Bowlby (1980) described as 'defensive exclusion' and the creation of 'segregated mental systems'.

Unlike secure and avoidant people, who tend to view negative emotions as goal-incongruent states that should either be managed effectively or suppressed, anxiously attached individuals tend to perceive these emotions as congruent with attachment goals, and they may seek to sustain and even exaggerate them. Attachment-anxious people are guided by an unfulfilled wish to cause attachment figures to pay more attention and provide more reliable protection and support (Cassidy & Kobak, 1988; Mikulincer & Shaver, 2016). Therefore, they tend to exaggerate the presence and seriousness of threats and to over-emphasise their sense of helplessness and vulnerability, because signs of weakness and neediness can sometimes elicit attachment figures' attention and care (Cassidy & Berlin, 1994).

How is anxious hyperactivation sustained? One method is to exaggerate the appraisal process, perceptually heightening the threatening aspects of even fairly benign events, hold pessimistic beliefs about one's ability to manage distress, and attribute threat-related events to uncontrollable causes or global personal inadequacies (Mikulincer & Shaver, 2016). Another method is to attend to internal indicators of distress (Cassidy & Kobak, 1988). This includes hypervigilant attention to the physiological aspects of emotional states, heightened recall of threat-related experiences, and rumination on real and potential threats (Shaver & Mikulincer, 2014). Another hyperactivating strategy is to intensify negative emotions by favouring an approach, counter-phobic orientation toward threatening situations or making self-defeating decisions and taking ineffective actions that are likely to end in failure. All of these strategies create a self-amplifying cycle of distress even after a threat objectively recedes.

The experience and management of death concerns

There is extensive evidence that attachment-related differences in emotion regulation are manifested in the experience and management of death concerns. For example, a number of studies conducted in my laboratory focused on attachment-style differences in the strength of death anxiety, assessed in terms of overt fear of death (Florian & Mikulincer, 1998; Mikulincer, Florian, & Tolmacz, 1990), unconscious expressions of this fear (responses to projective TAT cards; Mikulincer et al., 1990), or the accessibility of death-related thoughts (the number of death-related words produced in a word completion task; Mikulincer & Florian, 2000; Mikulincer, Florian, Birnbaum, & Malishkevich, 2002). Findings consistently indicated that people scoring relatively high on attachment anxiety tend to intensify death concerns and thoughts. Specifically, attachment anxiety is associated with heightened fear of death at both conscious and unconscious levels, as well as heightened accessibility of death-related thoughts, even when no death reminder is present. In contrast, people scoring relatively high on avoidant attachment tend to suppress overt death concerns and exhibit dissociation between their conscious reports and unconscious indexes of death anxiety. Avoidance is related to both low levels of self-reported fear of death and heightened death-related anxiety assessed with a projective measure.

Attachment-related differences have also been found in people's construal of death concerns (Florian & Mikulincer, 1998; Mikulincer et al., 1990). Anxiously attached people tend to attribute these worries to the loss of social identity after death (e.g., 'People will forget me'), whereas avoidant people tend to attribute them to the unknown nature of the hereafter (e.g., 'uncertainty about what to expect'). On the one hand, people scoring relatively high on attachment anxiety tend to hyperactivate worries about rejection and abandonment, viewing death as yet another relational setting in which they can be abandoned or forgotten. On the another hand, people scoring relatively high on avoidant attachment work to sustain self-reliance and strong personal control and then worry mainly about the uncertain and unknown aspects of death that can threaten their sense of control.

Studies have also consistently shown that attachment orientations shape the ways people manage death concerns. According to terror management theory (e.g., Pyszczynski et al., 2015), human beings' knowledge that they are destined to die makes it necessary for them to engage in self-promotion, defend their cultural worldviews, and deny their animal nature. Many studies have shown that experimentally induced death reminders lead to more negative reactions to the human body, moral (i.e., worldview) transgressors, and members of outgroups (see Pyszczynski et al., 2015, for a review).

Although worldview validation has been assumed to be a normative defence against universal existential threats (Pyszczynski et al., 2015), this response is more characteristic of insecure than of secure people. For example, experimentally induced death reminders produced more severe judgements and punishments of moral transgressors, greater willingness to die for a cause, and more support for a conservative president candidate only among insecurely attached people, either anxious or avoidant (Caspi-Berkowitz, 2003; Mikulincer & Florian, 2000; Weise et al., 2008). Securely attached people were less affected by death reminders. Moreover, the experimental priming of attachment security buffered the effects of mortality salience on increased support for violent measures against terrorists (Weise et al., 2008) and increased support for the war in Iraq and harsh foreign policy toward North Korea (Gillath & Hart, 2010).

Other studies also found that insecurely attached people reacted to mortality salience with increased adherence to culturally consensual beliefs about romantic bonds (Smith & Masey, 2012) and a heightened self-enhancing tendency of naming their children after themselves (Vicary, 2011). Moreover, Anglin (2014) reported that people scoring relatively high on both anxiety and avoidance dimensions reacted to death reminders with an exacerbation of their habitual relational ambivalence — heightened strivings to repair troubled relationships and lowered expectations for improving such relationships.

Some of the studies reveal ways in which more secure people react to death reminders. Mikulincer and Florian (2000) found that secure people reacted to mortality salience with an increased sense of symbolic immortality — a constructive, transformational strategy that, while not solving the unsolvable problem of death, leads people to invest in their children's care and to engage in creative, growth-oriented activities whose products live on after death. Secure people also reacted to mortality salience with heightened attachment needs — a more intense desire for intimacy in close relationships (Mikulincer & Florian, 2000; Smith & Masey, 2012), heightened reliance on a romantic partner in times of need (Cox et al., 2008), and greater willingness to engage in social interactions (Taubman Ben-Ari et al., 2002). In addition, Yaakobi, Mikulincer, and Shaver (2014) found that parenthood can serve as a buffer against mortality salience mainly among more secure people. Mortality salience led to more vivid and accessible parenthood-related cognitions, parenthood-related thoughts buffered the effects of mortality salience on death-thought accessibility, and thinking about infertility led to heightened death-thought accessibility mainly among participants who scored relatively low on attachment-related avoidance but not among highly avoidant people.

Caspi-Berkowitz (2003) also found that secure people reacted to death reminders by strengthening their desire to care for others. In her study, participants read hypothetical scenarios in which a relationship partner was in danger of death and they were asked about their willingness to endanger their own life to save their partner's life. More secure people reacted to death reminders (as compared with a neutral condition) with heightened willingness to sacrifice themselves. Insecure people were generally averse to self-sacrifice and reacted to death reminders with less willingness to save others' lives. It's notable that insecure individuals, who seem more ready than secure ones to die for their cultural worldviews, are more reluctant to sacrifice themselves for a particular relationship partner.

These studies imply that, even when faced with their mortality, secure people maintain felt security. They heighten their sense of social connectedness and symbolically transform the threat of death into an opportunity to contribute to others and grow personally. This makes it seem that being part of a loving and accepting social network is a vehicle for self-transcendence. It promotes a sense of symbolic immortality, making it less necessary to validate one's worldview and promote oneself and one's own group.

Defensive, distorting reactions to mortality seem to result from recurrent failures of attachment figures to accomplish their protective, supportive, anxiety-buffering functions. As a result, insecure people lack a sense of continuity with and connection to the world, and are unable to rely on a solid psychological foundation that sustains vitality in the face of mortality. Instead, they cling to particular cultural worldviews and derogate alternative views in an attempt to enhance their impoverished self-concepts and achieve a stronger sense of value and meaning.

The experience of meaning in life

Adult attachment researchers have not yet examined whether people differing in attachment orientation also differ in their experience of meaning in life. However, there is good evidence that feelings of closeness and social support (which are core aspects of felt security) are associated with a heightened sense of life's meaning (e.g., Hicks & King, 2009; Steger, Kashdan, Sullivan, & Lorentz, 2008). Similarly, Lambert et al. (2010) reported that perceived closeness to family members and support from them was associated with greater meaning in life among young adults. Moreover, implicit priming of relational closeness increased the perception of life's meaning when participants were in a bad mood (Hicks & King, 2009). In contrast, experimental manipulations of rejection, social exclusion, and loneliness, which elicit attachment insecurities, reduce people's sense that life is meaningful (e.g., Hicks, Schlegel, & King, 2010; Stillman et al., 2009).

In an experimental study of security priming, Mikulincer and Shaver (2005) examined the attachment basis of meaning in life. Participants who had previously completed a self-report attachment measure were primed with representations of either a security provider or a person who did not serve attachment functions. They then completed a self-report measure of the extent to which they perceived the world as understandable and life as 'making sense' (Antonovsky, 1987). Lower scores on attachment anxiety and avoidance (i.e., greater attachment security) were associated with higher levels of meaning and coherence in life. Moreover, as compared to neutral priming, security priming increased the sense of meaning and coherence even among dispositionally insecure participants.

Attachment orientations can also affect perceptions of life's meaning by contributing to other thoughts, beliefs, and feelings that bolster the sense of meaning. One such belief concerns the purpose and direction of one's life — that is, believing that one has a stable, valued, and congruent set of ambitions and goals, combined with the belief that one is able to accomplish these goals (Emmons, 2005). Attachment insecurities have been shown to bias the formation and organisation of these personal goals (Mikulincer & Shaver, 2007). Attachment anxiety is associated with pessimistic appraisal of goal pursuit (lower ratings of success and higher ratings of difficulty in goal pursuit) and relatively high inter-goal conflict (i.e., the extent to which being successful in one area of striving had a harmful effect on another striving). Avoidant attachment is associated with low commitment to goal pursuit and lower levels of abstraction (higher-level organisation) in framing personal goals. Moreover, both forms of insecure attachment are associated with reduced goal integration (i.e., the extent to which two strivings were perceived as parts of a single broader purpose in life). In other words, both attachment anxiety and avoidance seem to prevent people from perceiving different goal strivings as coherently integrated into an overall sense of purpose and direction.

Another meaning system that can be affected by attachment orientation is self-identity — the set of personal qualities, traits, values, and beliefs that provides a person with an inner sense of sameness and continuity (Erikson, 1968; Marcia, 1980). Several studies have shown that adolescents' secure attachment to parents is associated with higher scores on identity achievement and lower scores on identity diffusion (e.g., Abubakar et al., 2013; MacKinnon & Marcia, 2002). Studies assessing self-reports of attachment orientations in close relationships also found that attachment insecurities were associated with less identity achievement and more identity diffusion (e.g., Ávila, Cabral, & Matos, 2012; Doumen et al., 2012). In a meta-analysis of 14 studies, Årseth, Kroger, Martinussen, and Marcia (2009) concluded that more secure people are more likely to report identity achievement and less likely to report diffuse identity.. These findings have been replicated in longitudinal studies showing that attachment orientations predict identity formation 18 or 24 months later (Ávila et al., 2012; Zimmermann & Becker-Stoll, 2002).

A third meaning system that can be affected by attachment orientations is a religious approach to life. One of the most common and powerful meaning systems, present throughout recorded history, is religion (e.g., Zinnbauer & Pargament, 2005). According to Hood, Hill, and Williamson (2005), religions are well-suited to provide a powerful source of meaning in life, because all religions provide people with answers to questions about human nature, stories about the purposeful creation of the world, expectations about an afterlife, guidelines for selecting and pursuing goals, ways to distinguish good from evil, and rewards for proper behaviour as well as severe punishments for bad behaviour. Research confirms that religiousness is related to meaning in life (e.g., Steger & Frazier, 2005; Tomer & Eliason, 2000), with intrinsic spirituality being more strongly related than socially oriented, extrinsic religiousness (e.g., Francis & Hills, 2008).

Adult attachment studies have found that people who report greater attachment security to parents or romantic partners are more likely to report having a personal relationship with God and to believe in a personal God (e.g., Granqvist, 1998; Granqvist & Hagekull, 2000). In addition, attachment security has been associated with a more intrinsic (autonomous) religious orientation (e.g., Kirkpatrick & Shaver, 1990), greater commitment to religious beliefs and practices (e.g., Byrd & Boe, 2001; Saroglou, Pichon, Trompette,

Verschueren, & Dernelle, 2005), and higher scores on a measure of mature spirituality (Freeze & DiTommaso, 2014; Hart, Limke, & Budd, 2010). Studies also found that more secure believers reported more satisfaction with regard to their religious beliefs and practices (e.g., Hamilton, Martin, & Martin, 2012) and are more likely to rely on various forms of religious coping, such as praying and seeking spiritual support (e.g., Chou, Esplin, & Ranquist, 2013; Pollard, Riggs, & Hook, 2014).

Concluding remarks

Although existential concerns can be overwhelming and terrifying, it would be a mistake to conclude that human beings can deal with them only by erecting psychologically distorting and socially damaging defences. A host of studies show that people who have developed a solid sense of attachment security can deal effectively with the fact of mortality and the need for meaning. Moreover, they deal with these threats while remaining relatively open, creative, optimistic, honest, generous, and well connected socially (e.g., Gillath, Sesko, Shaver, & Chun, 2010; Mikulincer, Shaver, & Rom, 2011). Overall, a coherent body of research indicates that people who are treated well by others, beginning early in life, find life engaging, enjoyable, and meaningful and can deal with the fact of death by contributing to others and to grow personally.

References

Abubakar, A., Alonso-Arbiol, I., Van de Vijver, F.J., Murugami, M., Mazrui, L., & Arasa, J. (2013). Attachment and psychological well-being among adolescents with and without disabilities in Kenya: The mediating role of identity formation. *Journal of Adolescence, 36*, 849–857.

Anglin, S.M. (2014). From avoidance to approach: The effects of mortality salience and attachment on the motivation torepairtroubled relationships. *Personality and Individual Differences, 66*, 86–91.

Antonovsky, A. (1987). The salutogenic perspective: Toward a new view of health and illness. *Advances, 4*, 47–55.

Årseth, A.K., Kroger, J., Martinussen, M., & Marcia, J.E. (2009). Meta-analytic studies of identity status and the relational issues of attachment and intimacy. *Identity, 9*, 1–32.

Ávila, M., Cabral, J., & Matos, P.M. (2012). Identity in university students: The role of parental and romantic attachment. *Journal of Adolescence, 35*, 133–142.

Baldwin, M.W., Keelan, J.P.R., Fehr, B., Enns, V., & Koh Rangarajoo, E. (1996). Social-cognitive conceptualization of attachment working models: Availability and accessibility effects. *Journal of Personality and Social Psychology, 71*, 94–109.

Berant, E., Mikulincer, M., & Florian, V. (2001). Attachment style and mental health: A 1-year follow-up study of mothers of infants with congenital heart disease. *Personality and Social Psychology Bulletin, 27*, 956–968.

Bowlby, J. (1973). *Attachment and loss: Vol. 2. Separation: Anxiety and anger.* New York, NY: Basic Books.

Bowlby, J. (1980). *Attachment and loss: Vol. 3. Sadness and depression.* New York, NY: Basic Books.

Bowlby, J. (1982). *Attachment and loss: Vol. 1. Attachment* (2nd ed.). New York, NY: Basic Books.

Bowlby, J. (1988). *A secure base: Clinical applications of attachment theory.* London, England: Routledge.

Brennan, K.A., Clark, C.L., & Shaver, P.R. (1998). Self-report measurement of adult attachment: An integrative overview. In J.A. Simpson & W.S. Rholes (Eds.), *Attachment theory and close relationships* (pp. 46–76). New York, NY: Guilford.

Buhrmester, D., Furman, W., Wittenberg, M.T., & Reis, H.T. (1988). Five domains of interpersonal competence in peer relationships. *Journal of Personality and Social Psychology, 55*, 991–1008.

Byrd, K.R., & Boe, A. (2001). The correspondence between attachment dimensions and prayer in college students. *International Journal for the Psychology of Religion, 11*, 9–24.

Caspi-Berkowitz, N. (2003). *Mortality salience effects on the willingness to sacrifice one's life: The moderating role of attachment orientations.* Unpublished doctoral dissertation, Bar-Ilan University, Ramat Gan, Israel.

Cassidy, J. (1994). Emotion regulation: Influences of attachment relationships. *Monographs of the Society for Research in Child Development, 59*, 228–283.

Cassidy, J., & Berlin, L.J. (1994). The insecure/ambivalent pattern of attachment: Theory and research. *Child Development, 65*, 971–981.

Cassidy, J., & Kobak, R.R. (1988). Avoidance and its relationship with other defensive processes. In J. Belsky & T. Nezworski (Eds.), *Clinical implications of attachment* (pp. 300–323). Hillsdale, NJ: Erlbaum.

Chou, H.G., Esplin, J., & Ranquist, S. (2013). Childhood attachment to parents and frequency of prayer during the college years. *Mental Health, Religion & Culture, 16,* 863–875.

Coan, J.A. (2016). Toward a neuroscience of attachment. In J. Cassidy & P.R. Shaver (Eds.), *Handbook of attachment: Theory, research, and clinical applications* (3rd edition, pp. 242–271). New York, NY: Guilford.

Collins, N.L., & Read, S.J. (1990). Adult attachment, working models, and relationship quality in dating couples. *Journal of Personality and Social Psychology, 58,* 644–663.

Collins, N.L., & Read, S.J. (1994). Cognitive representations of attachment: The structure and function of working models. In K. Bartholomew & D. Perlman (Eds.), *Advances in personal relationships: Attachment processes in adulthood* (Vol. 5, pp. 53–92). London, England: Jessica Kingsley.

Cox, C.R., Arndt, J., Pyszczynski, T., Greenberg, J., Abdollahi, A, & Solomon, S. (2008). Terror management and adults' attachment to their parents: The safe haven remains. *Journal of Personality and Social Psychology, 94,* 696–717.

Doumen, S., Smits, I., Luyckx, K., Duriez, B., Vanhalst, J., Verschueren, K., & Goossens, L. (2012). Identity and perceived peer relationship quality in emerging adulthood: The mediating role of attachment-related emotions. *Journal of Adolescence, 35,* 1417–1425.

Downey, G., & Feldman, S.I. (1996). Implications of rejection sensitivity for intimate relationships. *Journal of Personality and Social Psychology, 70,* 1327–1343.

Emmons, R.A. (2005). Striving for the sacred: Personal goals, life meaning, and religion. *Journal of Social Issues, 4,* 731–745.

Erikson, E.H. (1968). *Identity: Youth and crisis.* New York, NY: Norton.

Florian, V., & Mikulincer, M. (1998). Symbolic immortality and the management of the terror of death: The moderating role of attachment style. *Journal of Personality and Social Psychology, 74,* 725–734.

Florian, V., Mikulincer, M., & Hirschberger, G. (2002). The anxiety buffering function of close relationships: Evidence that relationship commitment acts as a terror management mechanism. *Journal of Personality and Social Psychology, 82,* 527–542.

Fraley, R.C., & Shaver, P.R. (2000). Adult romantic attachment: Theoretical developments, emerging controversies, and unanswered questions. *Review of General Psychology, 4,* 132–154.

Francis, L.J., & Hills, P.R. (2008). The development of the Meaning in Life Index (MILI) and its relationship with personality and religious behaviours and beliefs among UK undergraduate students. *Mental Health, Religion & Culture, 11,* 211–220.

Freeze, T.A., & DiTommaso, E. (2014). An examination of attachment, religiousness, spirituality and well-being in a Baptist faith sample. *Mental Health, Religion & Culture, 17,* 690–702.

Gillath, O., & Hart, J. (2010). The effects of psychological security and insecurity on political attitudes and leadership preferences. *European Journal of Social Psychology, 40,* 122–134.

Gillath, O., Sesko, A.K., Shaver, P.R., & Chun, D.S. (2010). Attachment, authenticity, and honesty: Dispositional and experimentally induced security can reduce self- and other-deception. *Journal of Personality and Social Psychology, 98,* 841–855.

Granqvist, P. (1998). Religiousness and perceived childhood attachment: On the question of compensation or correspondence. *Journal for the Scientific Study of Religion, 37,* 350–367.

Granqvist, P., & Hagekull, B. (2000). Religiosity, adult attachment, and why 'singles' are more religious. *International Journal for the Psychology of Religion, 10,* 111–123.

Greenberg, J., Pyszczynski, T., Solomon, S., Simon, L., & Breus, M. (1994). The role of consciousness and accessibility of death related thoughts in mortality salience effects. *Journal of Personality and Social Psychology, 67,* 627–637.

Hamilton, S., Martin, M., & Martin, D. (2012). A statistical investigation of the relationship between personal attachment style and satisfaction with evangelical church membership. *Journal of Religion and Health, 51,* 1306–1316.

Hart, J.T., Limke, A., & Budd, P.R. (2010). Attachment and faith development. *Journal of Psychology and Theology, 38,* 122–128.

Hicks, J.A., & King, L.A. (2009). Positive mood and social relatedness as information about meaning in life. *Journal of Positive Psychology, 4,* 471–482.

Hicks, J.A., Schlegel, R.J., & King, L.A. (2010). Social threats, happiness, and the dynamics of meaning in life judgments. *Personality and Social Psychology Bulletin, 36,* 1305–1317.

Hirschberger, G., Florian, V., & Mikulincer, M. (2003). Strivings for romantic intimacy following partner complaint or partner criticism: A terror management perspective. *Journal of Social and Personal Relationships, 20,* 675–687.

Hood, R.W., Jr., Hill, P.C., & Williamson, W.P. (2005). *The psychology of religious fundamentalism.* New York, NY: Guilford.

King, L.A., Hicks, J.A., & Abdelkhalik, J. (2009). Death, life, scarcity, and value: An alternative perspective on the meaning of death. *Psychological Science, 20,* 1459–1462.

Kirkpatrick, L.A., & Shaver, P.R. (1990). Attachment theory and religion: Childhood attachments, religious beliefs, and conversion. *Journal for the Scientific Study of Religion, 29,* 315–334.

Kruglanski, A, W., Gelfand, M.; & Gunaratna, R. (2012). Terrorism as means to an end: How political violence bestows significance. In P.R. Shaver & M. Mikulincer (eds.), *The social psychology of meaning, mortality, and choice* (pp. 203–212). Washington, DC: American Psychological Association.

Lambert, N.M., Stillman, T.F., Baumeister, R.F., Fincham, F.D., Hicks, J.A., & Graham, S.M. (2010). Family as a salient source of meaning in young adulthood. *Journal of Positive Psychology, 5,* 367–375.

Lee, J.A. (1977). A typology of styles of loving. *Personality and Social Psychology Bulletin, 3,* 173–182.

MacKinnon, J.L., & Marcia, J.E. (2002). Concurring patterns of women's identity status, styles, and understanding of children's development. *International Journal of Behavioral Development, 26,* 70–80.

Main, M. (1990). Cross-cultural studies of attachment organization: Recent studies, changing methodologies, and the concept of conditional strategies. *Human Development, 33,* 48–61.

Marcia, J.E. (1980). Identity in adolescence. In J. Adelson (Ed.), *Handbook of adolescent psychology* (pp. 154–187). New York, NY: Wiley.

Mickelson, K.D., Kessler, R.C., & Shaver, P.R. (1997). Adult attachment in a nationally representative sample. *Journal of Personality and Social Psychology, 73,* 1092–1106.

Mikulincer, M., Birnbaum, G., Woddis, D., & Nachmias, O. (2000). Stress and accessibility of proximity-related thoughts: Exploring the normative and intraindividual components of attachment theory. *Journal of Personality and Social Psychology, 78,* 509–523.

Mikulincer, M., & Florian, V. (1995). Appraisal of and coping with a real-life stressful situation: The contribution of attachment styles. *Personality and Social Psychology Bulletin, 21,* 406–414.

Mikulincer, M., & Florian, V. (1998). The relationship between adult attachment styles and emotional and cognitive reactions to stressful events. In J.A. Simpson & W.S. Rholes (Eds.,) *Attachment theory and close relationships* (pp. 143–165). New York, NY: Guilford.

Mikulincer, M., & Florian, V. (2000). Exploring individual differences in reactions to mortality salience: Does attachment style regulate terror management mechanisms? *Journal of Personality and Social Psychology, 79,* 260–273.

Mikulincer, M., Florian, V., Birnbaum, G., & Malishkevich, S. (2002). The death-anxiety buffering function of close relationships: Exploring the effects of separation reminders on death-thought accessibility. *Personality and Social Psychology Bulletin, 28,* 287–299.

Mikulincer, M., Florian, V., & Hirschberger, G. (2004). The terror of death and the quest for love — An existential perspective on close relationships. In J. Greenberg, S.L. Koole, & T. Pyszczynski (Eds.), *Handbook of Experimental Existential Psychology* (pp. 287–304). New York, NY: Guilford.

Mikulincer, M., Florian, V., & Tolmacz, R. (1990). Attachment styles and fear of personal death: A case study of affect regulation. *Journal of Personality and Social Psychology, 58,* 273–280.

Mikulincer, M., Gillath, O., & Shaver, P.R. (2002). Activation of the attachment system in adulthood: Threat-related primes increase the accessibility of mental representations of attachment figures. *Journal of Personality and Social Psychology, 83,* 881–895.

Mikulincer, M., & Shaver, P.R. (2003). The attachment behavioral system in adulthood: Activation, psychodynamics, and interpersonal processes. In M.P. Zanna (Ed.), *Advances in experimental social psychology* (Vol. 35, pp. 53–152). New York, NY: Academic Press.

Mikulincer, M., & Shaver, P.R. (2005). Mental representations of attachment security: Theoretical foundation for a positive social psychology. In M.W.

Baldwin (Ed.), *Interpersonal cognition* (pp. 233–266). New York, NY: Guilford.

Mikulincer, M., & Shaver, P.R. (2007). Contributions of attachment theory and research to motivation science. In J. Shah & W. Gardner (Eds.), *Handbook of motivation science* (pp. 201–216). New York, NY: Guilford.

Mikulincer, M., & Shaver, P.R. (2016). *Attachment in adulthood: Structure, dynamics, and change* (2nd edition). New York, NY: Guilford.

Mikulincer, M., Shaver, P.R., & Rom, E. (2011). The effects of implicit and explicit security priming on creative problem solving. *Cognition and Emotion, 25,* 519–531.

Park, C.L., & Edmonson, D. (2012). Religion as a source of meaning. In P.R. Shaver & M. Mikulincer (eds.), *The social psychology of meaning, mortality, and choice* (pp. 145–162). Washington, DC: American Psychological Association.

Pollard, S.E., Riggs, S.A., & Hook, J.N. (2014). Mutual influences in adult romantic attachment, religious coping, and marital adjustment. *Journal of Family Psychology, 28,* 615–624.

Pyszczynski, T., Sullivan, D., & Greenberg, J. (2015). Experimental existential psychology: Living in the shadow of the facts of life. In M. Mikulincer, P.R. Shaver, E. Borgida, & J.A. Bargh (Eds.), *APA handbook of personality and social psychology, Vol. 1. Attitudes and social cognition* (pp. 279–308). Washington, DC: American Psychological Association.

Rosenblatt, A., Greenberg, J., Solomon, S., Pyszczynski, T., & Lyon, D. (1989). Evidence for terror management theory I: The effects of mortality salience on reactions to those who violate or uphold cultural values. *Journal of Personality and Social Psychology, 57,* 681–690.

Saroglou, V., Pichon, I., Trompette, L., Verschueren, M., & Dernelle, R. (2005). Prosocial behavior and religion: New evidence based on projective measures and peer ratings. *Journal for the Scientific Study of Religion, 44,* 323–348.

Sharabany, R. (1994). Intimacy friendship scale: Conceptual underpinnings, psychometric properties, and construct validity. *Journal of Social and Personal Relationships, 11,* 449–469.

Shaver, P.R., & Mikulincer, M. (2012). An attachment perspective on coping with existential concerns. In P.R. Shaver & M. Mikulincer (Eds.), *The social psychology of meaning, mortality, and choice* (pp. 291–307). Washington, DC: American Psychological Association.

Shaver, P.R., & Mikulincer, M. (2014). Adult attachment and the emotion regulation. In J.J. Gross (Ed.), *Handbook of emotion regulation* (2nd edition, pp. 237–250). New York, NY: Guilford.

Simpson, J.A., Rholes, W.S., & Nelligan, J.S. (1992). Support seeking and support giving within couples in an anxiety-provoking situation: The role of attachment styles. *Journal of Personality and Social Psychology, 62*, 434–446.

Smith, R., & Massey, E. (2012). Aspects of love: The effect of mortality salience and attachment style on romantic beliefs. *Omega: Journal of Death and Dying, 66*, 135–151.

Sroufe, L.A., & Waters, E. (1977). Attachment as an organizational construct. *Child Development, 48*, 1184–1199.

Steger, M.F., & Frazier, P. (2005). Meaning in life: One link in the chain from religion to well-being. *Journal of Counseling Psychology, 4*, 574–582.

Steger, M.F., Kashdan, T.B., Sullivan, B.A., & Lorentz, D. (2008). Understanding the search for meaning in life: Personality, cognitive style, and the dynamic between seeking and experiencing meaning. *Journal of Research in Personality, 42*, 660–678.

Stillman, T.S., Baumeister, R.F., Lambert, N.M., Crescioni, A.W., DeWall, C.N., & Fincham, F.D. (2009). Alone and without purpose: Life loses meaning following social exclusion. *Journal of Experimental Social Psychology, 45*, 686–694.

Taubman-Ben-Ari, O., Findler, L., & Mikulincer, M. (2002). The effects of mortality salience on relationship strivings and beliefs: The moderating role of attachment style. *British Journal of Social Psychology, 41*, 419–441.

Tomer, A., & Eliason, G. (2000). Beliefs about self, life, and death: Testing aspects of a comprehensive model of death anxiety and death attitudes. In A. Tomer (Ed.), *Death attitudes and the older adult* (pp. 137–153). Philadelphia, PA: Brunner-Routledge.

Vicary, A. (2011). Mortality salience and namesaking: Does thinking about death make people want to name their children after themselves? *Journal of Research in Personality, 45*, 138–141.

Weise, D.R., Pyszczynski, T., Cox, C.R., Arndt, J., Greenberg, J., & Solomon, S. (2008). Interpersonal politics: The role of terror management and attachment processes in shaping political preferences. *Psychological Science, 19*, 148–155.

Wisman, A., & Koole, S.L. (2003). Hiding in the crowd: Can mortality salience promote affiliation with others who oppose one's worldview. *Journal of Personality and Social Psychology, 84*, 511–527.

Yaakobi, E., Mikulincer, M., & Shaver, P.R. (2014). Parenthood as a terror management mechanism: The moderating role of attachment orientations. *Personality and Social Psychology Bulletin, 40*, 762–774.

Zimmermann, P., & Becker-Stoll, F. (2002). Stability of attachment representations during adolescence: The influence of ego-identity status. *Journal of Adolescence, 25*, 107–124.

Zinnbauer, B.J., & Pargament, K.I. (2005). Religiousness and spirituality. In R.F. Paloutzian & C.L. Park (Eds.), *Handbook of the psychology of religion and spirituality* (pp. 21–42). New York, NY: Guilford.

Chapter 5

The death instinct and psychodynamic accounts of the wound of mortality

Ross G. Menzies and Rachel E. Menzies

Psychoanalytic theory and research are often ignored or belittled within mainstream, contemporary psychology. This is despite the undeniable contributions to many fields of enquiry that psychodynamic researchers have made. For example, they were the first to report on children's understanding of death, a topic generally ignored in developmental psychology at the time. This chapter reviews psychodynamic accounts of death and death anxiety beginning with the complex theoretical position of Sigmund Freud. The broadly held view that Freud dismissed death as being of little significance to our psychic struggles will be rebutted as an oversimplification of the ambiguity of Freud's thinking. As others have suggested, it will be argued that Freud's personal dealings with death and loss across his life partly explain the complex relationship he formed with all matters relating to death. Finally, modern re-conceptions of our dynamic struggle with our own mortality will be presented.

Freud and death

The death instinct

Though it is fair to criticise Freud for promulgating nonfalsifiable (and often contradictory) theoretical positions, it must be acknowledged that he was a fine and detailed observer of human behaviour. Like Piaget, he could identify common patterns in behaviour from relatively few individuals and could build elaborate models from these observations. He noticed his clients returning again and again to painful memories or encounters rather than the happier moments of their lives (Frommer, 2016). Of course, it is now well established that depressed individuals do display attention and memory biases toward dark, emotional material (Bradley, Mogg, & Millar, 1996). For Freud (1920), this observation suggested that a self-destructive 'daemonic force' lay deep in the psyche. Opposing the operation of the pleasure principle, this force became known as the death instinct. Its aim was to return the living machine to its previous inorganic state, according to the 'Nirvana principle' — a desired release from the cycle of defensive bodily action and the necessary acts of self-care associated with survival. Freud (1920) essentially suggested that all organic matter seeks to return to nothingness. In a position that seems at odds with Darwinian natural selection, Freud (1920) saw complex defensive acts of the body (e.g., tissue repair) as an irritation to the central self-destructive urge.

The death instinct, according to Freud, was an obvious threat to all individuals from birth. Accordingly, it must be deflected outward by the ego and (to a lesser extent) the libido (Freud, 1940). It is said to be responsible for such varied phenomena as masochism, noncompliance in therapy, outward violence and a range of other, self-destructive behaviours (Akhtar, 2010). By 1940, in reference to the life and death instincts, Freud emphasised that the 'concurrent and mutually opposing action of the two basic instincts gives rise to the whole phenomena of life' (Freud, 1940, p. 149). In sum, the death instinct had found its home at the centre of Freudian thinking.

Surprisingly, the significance given the death instinct did not import value to the role of death anxiety. The latter concept had been dealt a huge blow in Freud's early writings on death and youth. Famously, Freud (1900) had proposed that children know nothing 'of freezing in the ice-cold grave, of the terrors of eternal nothingness' (p. 254), and that 'the fear of death has no meaning to a child' (p. 254). These claims were not effectively explored for many decades. However, as Slaughter (2005) notes, it was psychoanalytic researchers who were the first to explore childrens concept of death. To their credit, long before developmental and cognitive psychologists recognised the importance of the topic, dynamic researchers sought to discover what young children know of death. Nagy (1948) reported that many 3-year-old to 5-year-old children deny that death is a regular and final process. Some children took until nine years of age to see death as an inevitable happening. Further, many children misunderstood fundamental truths about death. Many felt that the permanent separation of the dead from the living was due to the distance between heaven and earth, or because coffins are nailed shut. Others felt that death was simply a permanent sleeping state (Anthony, 1940; Nagy, 1948). Finally, many did not understand the biological causation of death (e.g., heart or breathing having stopped). They often argued that a 'bogey man' or some other punishing agent was the cause of death (Nagy, 1948; Von Hug-Hellmuth, 1964).

More recent research has clarified the developmental issues involved in acquiring an accurate understanding of death and dying. Kane (1979) reports that as many as 42% of 4-year-olds understand the universality of death. Speece and Brent (1984) conclude that most individuals understand the irreversible and nonfunctional nature of death, along with its universality, by seven years of age. However, Slaughter (2005) points out that the biological causation of death still escapes many children, even at this point in their development (see Chapter 2 of the present volume for an elaborated discussion of these issues).

Of course, demonstrating that young children are aware of death (even if they often fail to completely grasp its causation), is not a direct challenge to Freud's central claim. Most importantly, Freud argued that there was no display of *fear* of death in the young. However, by the 1940s, psychoanalytic researchers had begun to question this proposition. Slaughter (2005), summarising early open-ended interview studies (e.g., Anthony, 1940; Nagy, 1948; Von Hug-Hellmuth, 1964), concluded that the analysts had shown children to find death an emotionally charged issue involving substantial sadness and fear. The open-ended research paradigm is, of course, easy to attack. It is a particularly uncontrolled method, making the obtained data difficult to interpret. Having said this, the interview transcripts themselves do seem to show anxiety and avoidance quite transparently. The following is an edited section of an interview with three pre-school children reported by Hoffmann, Johnson, Foster, and Wright (2010). The children, none of whom had turned four years of age, had been overheard by a child-care worker when they were spontaneously talking about death at lunch time in their pre-school. A recording on the topic was later made with parental consent, and the full unedited transcript printed (see Hoffmann et al., 2010, pp. 27–33).

What do you worry about?

(Lily raises her hand)

Lily: My cousin's pet goldfish.

You worry about that?

(Lily nods)

Why?

Lily: Because its dead!

It's dead? You worry about that?

Lily: Yep and it's for real, for real. (Yeah). It really is.

Robert: Well, my brother thinks his mum and dad are gonna die, at a very shortly longly but they're gonna die at very long, long-long, long, long time. Right?

Lily: But David's not gonna die, right?

David: No-mm (David shakes his head no).

Robert: Of course, he will.

David: No, we won't.

Robert: Yes, you can die.

David: I won't die!

Robert: Yes you will.

David: No, I won't.

Robert: Yes you can die. You, you, you'll most likely die at the age of like sixty, uh, three, or like sixty-four.

David: No, I won't die.

Robert: Or like sixty-eight.

Chapter 5 The death instinct and psychodynamic accounts of the wound of mortality

David: I won't die.

Robert: You only, like, go up to zero.

David: No. I won't die at all!

Robert: And then zero, and then zero one.

David: I won't die at all!

Robert: And zero one and zero two.

David: I won't die at all I said, Robert! Why won't-I di-I won' die.

Are you going to die Robert?

Robert: Well, yes. Everyone is gonna die.

David: I won't die!

Later, in the same interview, David raises heaven with the interviewer and Lily expresses her fears of her mother dying.

Heaven?

David: In the sky.

Do you ever hear of heaven?

David: Know what? Wheely died.

Who's Wheely?

David: She's my dog's grammy. She's in the sky.

She's an old dog?

David: Yeah, she died.

She's in the sky?

David: Yeah (regretful tone).

How did she get up there?

David: ... (laughs) I don't know. (Uh-huh) she's in cat heaven (okay) ... in the sky.

> Lily: Sometimes I'm worried about my mom dying. I, I, I, wish I could hug her when, when we die.

Okay

> David: Know what? [Dog's name]'s gonna go to doggy heaven in the sky.

You want to go to doggy heaven? You wouldn't mind dying if you went to doggy heaven? Is that right?

> David: I won't die

You're never, never gonna die?

> David shakes his head 'no' vigorously.

Finally, David expresses his worries about his mother, and the other children relate their fears.

> David: You know what? When, when me and mummy in the forest, um, um, um, I'm afraid she's gonna die in the forest?

How could somebody die in the forest? What would happen to them in the forest?

> Robert: They could die like animals. The animals ... yeah ... could bite off their skin.

Yeah ... right. What other things could make somebody die? Lily?

> Lily: Um, when, um, when I'm in the woods, I fe-, I fear that animals are around me, but they are, but I, but I hear their footsteps coming, coming towards me behind my back, coming, following me and they get louder and louder and louder and then they bite me. And that's where I got the, and that's where I got the bites.

Yea, well, what other bad things could happen to you? David?

> David: Mmm ... mmm ...

Chapter 5 The death instinct and psychodynamic accounts of the wound of mortality

Robert: I know! Well like, my brother is like, he thinks he's like, he thinks our mum and dad will die. My brother.

He thinks that, yeah.

Robert: But I don't think so. He thinks they'll die at a short age, but I think they'll die at a long age.

Is he worried about that?

Robert: Yeah ... why does he like fight about like a long, long time ago?

Hmm. Why is he worried?

Robert: Like a long, long time ago?

That's right. That's right. He doesn't really know that, right? You don't know about that. You don't really know about that, right?

Robert: Yeah, because he would like get like you get bigger, you get bigger, then you get stronger and then older and then like you like are very old and then after that you die.

But your parents are not very old, are they?

Robert: No. They're too young!

They're too young to die, right?

Robert: Yeah

(Hoffmann et al., 2010, pp. 27–33)

Psychodynamic reviewers of the transcript see the work of the defence mechanisms at play (see further, Parens, 2010). They propose that David uses denial ('I won't die') and reaction formation (i.e., when he laughs at the interviewer) throughout. They also argue that primary narcissism is responsible for each child insisting that they are right in their personal views on death. Though we could take issue with each of these propositions it would seem perverse, despite the uncontrolled (and at times) leading nature of the interview, to claim that no fear or anxiety are on display (Hoffman et al., 2010). Other reviewers of the same transcript (e.g., Parens, 2010) agree. Plainly, fear of death is present in this, and many other interviews with children that have been recorded since the 1940s. Freud's off-hand dismissal of death fears in the young was simply incorrect. In fact, it seems so far from the truth that Parens (2010) suggests it may have been a reflection of Freud's own defence mechanisms at work.

Freud further claimed that the unconscious 'does not believe in its own death; it behaves as if it were immortal' (1915, p. 296). Unfortunately, this declaration would dominate psychoanalytic thinking for the next 50 years, with many seemingly unaware of the contradictions arsing from Freud's own theorising. If the unconscious is the seat of the instincts, then the death instinct must sit squarely in this location of the psychic hardware. Noted by Akhtar (2010), Melanie Klein (1948/1975) puts it most clearly:

> If we assume the existence of a death instinct, we must also assume that in the deepest layers of the mind there is a response to this instinct in the form of fear of annihilation of life ... The layers arising from the inner working of the death instinct is the first cause of anxiety. (p. 29)

How could Freud identify the death instinct in 1920, but still give the fear of death little place in his thinking over the decades that followed? Three years later, in 1923, he further minimised the fear of death by claiming that it was simply analogous to the fear of castration (Freud, 1923). Akhtar (2010) notes that each of Freud's declarations, given his status within psychoanalytic circles, would be championed by others for many years. For example, as late as 1964 McClelland suggests that the fact that the reaper is represented as a man with a scythe supports Freud's claim that fear of death and castration are one and the same.

Freud's contention that death is relatively unimportant psychically seems to depend of a series of other claims. First, he argues that the mind can't understand or contemplate death because we've never experienced anything like it (Freud, 1926). This is a particularly bizarre proposition, given Freud's knowledge of Greek mythology. Thanatos (the personification of death) and Hypnos (the personification of sleep) are said to be twin brothers living next to each other in the underworld. The relationship between death and sleep is an obvious one, and has been noted many times. Both involve a loss of consciousness, the latter state being craved and experienced by most individuals

Chapter 5 The death instinct and psychodynamic accounts of the wound of mortality

on a nightly basis! In addition, many individuals have lost consciousness in other ways, such as fainting, head trauma, or fits. To suggest that the experience of death is so foreign that we cannot engage with it is akin to suggesting that virgins cannot contemplate sexual behaviour, and that sexual matters cannot influence human behaviour prior to first coitus. Intriguingly, Freud proposes quite the opposite in the domain of sexuality. It is said to influence the psyche from the first year of life.

This is not to dispute the broader point that humans seem to respond to death as if it happens to other people. In this regard, Freud, Becker, Yalom and others speak with one voice. There appears to be a tendency, as Becker (1973) famously puts it, to live in 'denial of death'. Yalom (2008) points to the great works from literature to support the proposition. In Tolstoy's (1886) novella 'The death of Ivan Ilyich', the protagonist displays the problem well:

> All his life the syllogism he had learned from Kiesewetter's logic — Julius Caesar is a man, men are mortal, therefore Caesar is mortal — had always seemed to him to be true only when it applied to Caesar, certainly not to him. There was Caesar the man, and man in general, and it was fair enough for them, but he wasn't Caesar the man and he wasn't man in general, he had always been a special being, totally different from all others, he had been Vanya with his mama and his papa, with Vitya and Volodya, with his toys, and the carriage-driver, then little Katya, Vanya with all the delights, sorrows and rapture of childhood, boyhood and youth. Did Caesar have anything to do with the smell of that little striped leather ball that Vanya had loved so much? Was it Caesar who had kissed his mother's hand like that, and was it for Caesar that the silken folds of his mother's dress had rustled the way it did? (p. 61)

But Freud's claim that we cannot imagine death is a very different proposition, based on shaky theoretical (and no empirical) ground. Any undergraduate psychology student familiar with stimulus generalisation would know that humans learn about stimuli, events and activities from similar activities in their past. Imagining death, given our regular loss of consciousness, should not be beyond us.

A second argument appears to be that whenever we try to imagine ourselves dead, we are inevitably still present as spectators (Freud, 1915). Again, the point seems poorly made. Put simply, the same could be said for almost any human behaviour, event or situation. Asked to imagine ourselves in a sexual encounter we may well picture the scene as an observer, watching the action. Further, even events that have occurred may be encoded in memory from an observer (rather than first-person, field) perspective. In fact, considerable research suggests that most situations involving anxiety and trauma are remembered by humans from an observer viewpoint (Hackman, Clark & McManus, 2000).

Explanations of Freud's minimisation of death anxiety

Why did Freud reject death anxiety as a prime driver of psychic struggles? Razinsky (2013) argues that he saw death dread as already well handled by philosophy. He suggests that Freud purposely avoided this direct competition with the grand thinkers of stoicism, phenomenology and existentialism and decided to focus on the base, bodily drives of sex and aggression instead. In other words, according to Razinsky (2013), it was a strategic decision to promote a new way of looking at man.

Another explanation relates to Freud's own life experiences and his personal battles with death and guilt. Breger (2000) described Freud as a man riddled with death fears from early childhood. Wallace (1978) notes that Freud expressed guilt over death wishes toward his father in his youth. In this regard, Akhtar (2010) points to Wahl's (1965) observation that such thoughts in childhood are particularly distressing to the young:

> These destructive hating thoughts are doubly frightening since the child not only fears the loss of his parents through the operation of his death wishes, but also, since he reasons by the law of Talion (to think a thing is to do a thing; to do a thing is to endure an equal and similar punishment to the self), he becomes fearful of his own death. (p. 140).

Breger (2000) and others describe Freud as having been plagued by fears of death since he was a small boy. The departure of his nanny, to whom he was deeply attached, and the death of his younger brother Julius appear to have had a profound effect on him (Parens, 2010). Later in life, the spectre of death would visit again. Not long after his sons had served in the Great War, he lost his daughter Sophie in 1920, followed by his grandson Heinerle in 1923. Later, he would live under the shadow of death with his own cancer diagnosis. Eissler (1978) and Akhtar (2010) note that letters from Freud in this period reveal a growing loss of attachments to the world. Breger (2000) essentially argues that

Freud was a man failing to cope with his own mortality and that his theories are a deep reflection of his own struggles. Could he be an example of Yalom's (2008) notion of refusing to 'stare at the sun'? That is, is Freud's minimising of death fear simply an avoidance strategy — 'if I don't think about it, it isn't real'? Similarly, Frommer (2016) asks whether, in declaring the unconscious incapable of imagining its own demise, Freud universalised a personal failure of imagination. Kogan (2010), echoing the earlier thoughts of Schur (1972), goes further in accusing the entire psychiatric community of falling victim to avoidance of death. The death anxiety of psychoanalysts themselves is proposed as an explanation for how little has been written on the topic by these therapists. The same, of course, could be claimed about other brands of psychotherapy. Iverach, Menzies, and Menzies (2014) have noted how little has been written about the topic within the cognitive behavioural tradition.

The Freudian clinical approach

As we have seen then, In Freud's theoretical writing there is a diminishing of death's importance, or as Razinsky (2013) puts it, 'a kind of disbelief in death, an unwillingness to recognise death as a possibly influential psychic factor' (p. 2). Most disturbing about Freud's theoretical bias against death is the impact it had on the development of dynamic clinical work. For if death is unimaginable to the unconscious, then it follows that death anxiety must be a derivative of something else. According to Freud, when clients are describing fear of death this must be masking more base fears. This position has remained unchanged in mainstream psychoanalytic circles. As recently as 2010, Coen (2010) states, 'in psychoanalysis we analyse fears of dying most effectively as expressions and derivatives of something else' (p. 104). The list of 'something else' is a long one. The supposed 'primary' anxieties typically include loss of attachment, abandonment, separation, castration and annihilation (Coen, 2010; Piven, 2003).

As Frommer (2016) points out, this approach to death anxiety robs it of its more legitimate place of importance in human struggles. Further, the distinctions between fear of death and some of the 'primary' anxieties seem dubious. This is most obvious in the case of annihilation anxiety which refers to the overwhelming terror of destruction of the self. Supposed derivatives of annihilation anxiety include fears of being mutilated, suffocated, drowned, invaded, or of evaporating or fading away. As others have noted, many of these fears are expressed by individuals with magical and aggressive beliefs in obsessive-compulsive disorder (see further Einstein & Menzies, 2004; Menzies, Menzies, & Iverach, 2015).

To arbitrarily state, with no empirical basis, that death anxiety is a derivative of annihilation anxiety is out of step with the evidence-based approaches in the rest of psychology. Further, superficially it seems pedantic and absurd. It is similar to suggesting that individuals with spider phobia are really afraid of puncture wounds and poison, rather than spiders. Destruction of the self occurs with the death of the individual. It may be the reason that some individuals don't want to die, but to suggest that it means they are not afraid of death seems obdurate. The range of reasons that individuals fear death is long, as any close inspection of popular death anxiety scales will reveal. For example, Hoelter's (1979) Multidimensional Fear of Death scale includes items on the dying process, the decay of the body, meeting one's maker, entombment in the grave, burning in cremation, never interacting with family again, the loss of others, pain, violent endings, fear of cancer and more. Obviously, individuals will vary in the items they endorse. Nevertheless, the scale has high internal consistency and appears to measure an overarching construct — fear of death.

The clinical approach of the analytic revisionists

Akhtar (2011) implores his analytic colleagues 'to sometimes — courageously — take the talk of death on its manifest level' and 'consider the possibility that when patients speak about death, this may in fact pertain to their actual mortality' (p. 113). Why is such a frank discussion seen as courageous in world of psychoanalysis? Frommer (2016) argues that the culture of psychoanalysis seeks to protect the patient and analyst from the vulnerability of admitting there is no solution to mortality. The present authors agree, and we would argue further that this protection began with Freud himself, a man who seemed unable to deal effectively with the losses in his life and death more broadly.

Akhtar (2010), Yalom (2008) and other revisionists give death anxiety centre stage in psychodynamic work. It is a driver of psychopathology, and should not be given secondary status to other fears. Further, like Becker and the existential social psychologists associated with terror management theory (TMT), it explains much of our everyday behaviour. Akhtar (2010) sees positive health behaviours, beliefs in heaven, reincarnation and the continuation of our soul, our fascination with near-death and after-life phenomenon and many other activities as culturally dealing with our fear. He states:

> We wax poetic about death. We paint scenes of dying, write
> stories and screenplays, make movies about terminal illness, and

stage operas involving death. Injecting imagination and pleasure into what seems morbid and frightening allows us a good night's sleep. The horrid witch of mortality becomes the maudlin muse of our creativity. (p. 1).

The role of religion and fantasy

Kogan (2010), Guzder (2010) and Yalom (2008) argue that the role of religion is essentially the denial of death, although only the latter author is particularly critical of such an approach to solving the existential crisis. Kogan (2010) sees positives to religious belief. He highlights the benefits of community, and the idea of 'eternal presence' as a means of dealing with the separation fears related to death. Guzder (2010) argues that religion, across cultures, seeks to provide morning rituals that are critical in providing concrete demonstrations of the event of death. So, for some, religion may provide the ultimate defence against mortality. Blacher (1983) and others see fantasy in the same vein, noting the overlap between fantasy and religion. Blacher (1983) interviewed individuals who had been resuscitated after cardiac arrest. Notable in these interviews were fantasies of 'rebirth' (e.g., coming back as a child) and 'resurrection', which seemed to serve the same purpose — reducing anxiety in the face of death. Following the death of a pet, adult explanations will do much to shape children's dealings with death as a construct (Kogan, 2010). For example, in our earlier transcript it is surely unlikely that David developed his view of 'doggy heaven' without the input of an adult. Whether such fantasies are helpful or harmful remains an empirical question.

Death and peace

Akhtar (2010) raises the possibility that the death instinct might not always give rise to anxiety. He describes it as a potential 'loyal and reliable guide to our final destination' (p. 5). He argues, consistent with Freud's (1920) original conception, that humans have a strong desire to lose 'ego-boundaries' — that is, to lose the self. In a similar vein, Stone (1971) argued that man has an urging to return to an earlier neonatal state when gratification was automatic through the umbilical cord. This is a time when the 'self' is a confusing notion given our oneness with mother. Stone's (1971) ideas echo the earlier position of Jacobson (1964) who proposed that across the life-course we maintain a constant desire for the original linkage to mother.

While these dynamic possibilities are speculative (and may seem preposterous to those outside of the enclave of psychodynamic research), one need not embrace them to be drawn to Akhtar's (2010) 'seeking peace' hypothesis. Put simply, the desire to die might be the result of the reduced autonomy and growing fatigue associated with ageing. Madow (1997) highlights the pains of ageing as similar to returning to an infantile state. Our brains shrink, we lose our capacities to walk and talk, may require nappies, eat soft food, and become intolerant to temperature changes. Who can fear death given these difficulties of living? Not surprisingly, these observations perhaps explain the decline in death anxiety seen across the life-course (see further Chopik, 2017). Of course, as Akhtar (2010) points out, this conception eliminates the need for an 'instinct' associated with the desire to die. In a related vein, Akhtar (1994; 2010) argues that as we age, we development a growing detachment from the modern world that we find ourselves in. In our dotage, forming a critical stance of the world that we now fail to understand may be helpful in promoting complete acceptance of death.

Death and reunion with the cosmos

Another strategy encouraged by Akhtar (2010) relates to the notion of a desire to reunite with the cosmos by giving up the individual self. Death provides the ultimate freedom to return to the stardust of the universe. It is an argument that derives from Freud's original death instinct but can also be found in Urdu and Persian poetry, various Buddhist writings, and European existentialism. Ghalib, the great 18th century Urdu poet writes: 'just the way the beginning sunlight at the time of dawn relieves the candle from the continued necessity to burn, the arrival of death cures all problems of life' (quoted in Akhtar, 2010, p 10). In this and similar couplets, Akhtar (2010) recognises a positive stance on death with four defining characteristics. Death is (1) an expected event and a part of life; (2) to be accepted with peaceful waiting; (3) associated with a combination of relief and joy; (4) a merger with a force larger than the self. In essence, Akhtar (2010) is calling for 'death acceptance' and suggests that this may be achieved by living a meaningful, emotionally rich life. In many ways, his position reminds us of contemporary acceptance and commitment therapy (ACT). Hayes, Strosahl, and Wilson (1999) and others from this tradition argue that peace and tranquillity can be found through living a values-based existence. Menzies (2016) sees more merit in these values-based aspects of ACT than traditional elements of cognitive behaviour therapy (CBT) in dealing with the inevitable loss of self. From these perspectives, the intensity of the fear of death may have much to do with how one has lived, rather than how one will die.

The small deaths of everyday living

Another therapeutic possibility centres in the observation that along life's path we experience a range of small changes or losses that can be regarded as deaths. Akhtar (2005) describes an incident that captures the essence of 'deaths while living':

> One day while I was getting a haircut, my eyes went to the clumps of the previous customer's hair on the floor. And once Tony began cutting my hair, I could see similar samples of my own — now quite gray — hair on the floor. The sight made me ask whether the hair that had been cut from my head still belonged to me. It somehow did not seem to, yet to say that I did not feel any affinity or sense of ownership toward it would also be called a lie. More significantly, I became aware that, due to the decisive intervention of a pair of scissors, what was a part of me moments ago had become an inanimate thing, cold and, frankly, a bit distasteful to behold. (p. 182)

Other 'deaths' can be highlighted. Where are the friends we left behind? Where is the 'me' we see in early photos? Where is the child that loved football when I was young? It is true, after all, that we are ever-changing and, in this sense, the self becomes a nonsense. We are an ongoing series of deaths or losses. Akhtar (2005, 2010) suggests that in these small deaths we have an opportunity to develop the right attitude to death. We have an opportunity to practice a Zen life of detachment, even from the self. At the very least, paying attention to these deaths should provide valuable exposure to the loss of self that may serve to normalise death. Again, whether mindful attention on such experiences proves therapeutic remains an empirical question.

Final thoughts

Psychoanalytic workers were among the first to explore the emergence of our understanding of death across development. Unfortunately, the dismissive attitude of their founding father relegated the fear of death to the periphery of human intrapsychic struggles. At best, the fear of death was seen as deriving from more central, primary fears that were the chosen focus of the analysts work. More recently however, several revisionists have pointed to the inconsistencies in the Freudian position. New avenues for treatment have emerged and falsifiable research questions have been generated. It is hoped that a more productive research period will arise from the theoretical work of Akhtar and other contemporary psychoanalytic workers.

Facing death and finding a solution to the psychic problems that come from the loss of self is something that each of us must confront. But in this regard, the therapist (of any theoretical persuasion) has a double problem in her work. First, she may have (foolishly) placed herself in the seat of wise counsellor, the solver of problems. She may seek to appear above the death crisis — a professional guide through the existential issues that the client brings. Yet, in reality, death is the great equaliser between client and clinician. Both remain equally ignorant of the actual experience of the event. Second, like all of us, she suffers from the normal narcissism that lets one deny death. In this, we agree with Becker (1973) who describes our innate narcissistic tendencies as a necessary madness that 'protects us from the greater clinical madness of having to fully apprehend our own mortality in an ongoing way' (p. 360). Modern psychodynamic writers are to be congratulated in calling for clinicians to honour the 'shared humanity' that we have with our clients. Frommer (2016) puts it well in critiquing his own sessions with a young woman struggling to come to grips with the death of her father. He writes:

> Yet when I think back to these moments with her, I feel a discomfort about our interchange. It's more about what I didn't say than what I did. I didn't tell her how difficult it is to make sense of death for me as well. I did not formulate out loud how her struggle with her father's disappearance is the human struggle with death we all share, and I did not offer a sufficient space in the treatment for us to live her bewilderment together. In short, I failed to join her in her confusion by becoming a 'like subject' but instead remained a more distant, still-knowing object, even in my not knowing. (p. 375)

References

Akhtar, S. (1994). Object constancy and adult psychopathology. *The International Journal of Psychoanalysis, 75,* 441–455.

Akhtar, S. (2005). *Objects of our desire.* New York, NY: Harmony Press.

Akhtar, S. (2010). Freud's Todesangst and Ghalib's Ishrat-e-Qatar: Two perspectives on death. In S. Akhtar (Ed.), *The wound of mortality* (pp. 97–106). New York, NY: Aronson.

Akhtar, S. (2011). *Matters of life and death: Psychoanalytic reflections.* London, England: Karnac Books.

Anthony, S. (1940). *The child's discovery of death: A study in psychology.* New York, NY: Harcourt, Brace.

Blacher, R.S. (1983). Death, resurrection, and rebirth: Observations in cardiac surgery. *Psychoanalytic Quarterly, 52,* 56–72.

Becker, E. (1973). *The denial of death.* New York, NY: Free Press.

Bradley, B., Mogg, K., & Millar, N. (1996). Implicit memory bias in clinical and nonclinical depression. *Behaviour Research and Therapy.* 34, 11–12.

Breger, L. (2000). *Freud: Darkness in the midst of vision.* New York, NY: Wiley.

Chopik, W.J. (2017). Death across the lifespan: Age-differences in death-related thoughts and anxiety. *Death Studies. 41,* 69–77.

Coen, S.J. (2010). The dead self must be reborn. In S. Akhtar (Ed.), *The wound of mortality.* (pp. 97–106). New York, NY: Aronson.

Einstein, D.A. & Menzies, R.G. (2004). The presence of magical thinking in obsessive compulsive disorder. *Behaviour Research and Therapy, 42,* 539–549.

Eissler, K. (1978). *Sigmund Freud: His life in pictures and words.* New York, NY: Harcourt.

Freud, S. (1900). The interpretation of dreams. *Standard Edition of the Complete Psychological Works of Sigmund Freud, 4,* 1–380. London: Hogarth Press.

Freud, S. (1915). Thoughts for the times on war and death. *Standard Edition of the Complete Psychological Works of Sigmund Freud, 14,* 273–300. London: Hogarth Press.

Freud, S. (1920). Beyond the pleasure principle. *Standard Edition of the Complete Psychological Works of Sigmund Freud, 18,* 1–64. London: Hogarth Press.

Freud, S. (1923). The ego and the id. *Standard Edition of the Complete Psychological Works of Sigmund Freud, 19,* 1–66. London: Hogarth Press.

Freud, S. (1926). Inhibitions, symptoms and anxiety. *Standard Edition of the Complete Psychological Works of Sigmund Freud, 20,* 87–174. London: Hogarth Press.

Freud, S. (1940). An outline of psychoanalysis. *Standard Edition of the Complete Psychological Works of Sigmund Freud, 23,* 139–207. London: Hogarth Press.

Frommer, M.S. (2016) Death is nothing at all: On contemplating nonexistence. A relational psychoanalytic engagement of the fear of death. *Psychoanalytic Dialogues, 26*, 373–390.

Guzder, J. (2010). Symbolic death, east and west. In S. Akhtar (Ed.), *The wound of mortality* (pp. 51–70). New York, NY: Aronson.

Hackman, A., Clark, D.M., & McManus, F. (2000). Recurrent images and early memories in social phobia. *Behaviour Research and Therapy, 2000*, 601–610.

Hayes, S.C., Strosahl, K.D., & Wilson, K.G. (1999). *Acceptance and commitment therapy: An experiential approach to behaviour change.* New York, NY: Guildford Press.

Hoelter, J.W. (1979). Multidimensional treatment of fear of death. *Journal of Consulting and Clinical Psychology, 47*, 996–999.

Hoffman, L., Johnson, E., Foster, M., & Wright, E. (2010). What happens when you die? Three-to-four-year-olds chatting about death. In S. Akhtar (Ed.), *The wound of mortality* (pp. 97–106). New York, NY: Aronson.

Iverach, L., Menzies, R.G. & Menzies, R.E. (2014). Death anxiety and its role in psychopathology: Reviewing the status of a transdiagnostic construct. *Clinical Psychology Review, 34*, 580–593.

Jacobson, E. (1964). *The self and the object world.* New York, NY: International Universities Press.

Kane, B. (1979). Children's concepts of death. *Journal of Genetic Psychology, 134*, 141–153.

Klein, M. (1948). The theory of anxiety and guilt. In *Envy and gratitude and other works 1946–1963.* (pp. 25–42, [1975]). New York, NY: Free Press.

Kogan, I. (2010). Fear of death: Analyst and patient in the same boat. In S. Akhtar (Ed.), *The wound of mortality* (pp. 79–96). New York, NY: Aronson.

Madow, L. (1997). On the way to a second symbiosis. In Akhtar, S., & Kramer, S (Eds). *The seasons of life: Separation-individuation perspectives* (pp. 155–170). Northvale, NJ: Aronson.

Menzies, R.G. (2016). *The dread of death, existentialism, and ACT: Achieving meaningful, long-term change for people in pain.* Invited presentation at the 2016 ANZ ACBS Annual Conference, RMIT, Melbourne, November 6, 2016.

Menzies, R.G., Menzies, R.E., & Iverach, L. (2015). The role of death fears in Obsessive Compulsive Disorder. *Australian Clinical Psychologist, 1*, 6–11.

Nagy, M. (1948). The child's theories concerning death. *Journal of Genetic Psychology, 73,* 3–27.

Parens, H. (2010). Children's understanding of death. In S. Akhtar (Ed.), *The wound of mortality* (pp. 37–50). New York, NY: Aronson.

Piven, J. (2003). Introduction. *The Psychoanalytic Review, 90,* 395–402.

Razinsky, L. (2013). *Freud, psychoanalysis and death.* New York, NY: Cambridge University Press.

Schur, M. (1972). *Freud: Living and dying.* New York, NY: International Universities Press.

Slaughter, V. (2005). Young children's understanding of death. *Australian Psychologist, 40,* 179–186.

Speece, M.W., & Brent, S.B. (1984). Children's understanding of death: A review of three components of a death concept. *Child Development, 55,* 1671–1686.

Stone, L. (1971). Reflections on the psychoanalytic concept of aggression. *Psychoanalytic Quarterly, 40,* 195–244.

Tolstoy. L. (1886). *The death of Ivan Ilyich.* London, England: Penguin.

Von Hug-Helmuth, H. (1964). The child's concept of death. *Psychoanalytic Quarterly, 34,* 499–516.

Wahl, C.W. (1965). New dimensions in psychosomatic medicine. *The American Journal of the Medical Sciences, 249,* 115.

Wallace, E.R. (1978). Freud's father conflict: The history of a dynamic. *Psychiatry: Interpersonal and biological processes, 41,* 33–56.

Yalom, I. (2008). *Staring at the sun: Overcoming the terror of death.* San Francisco, CA: Jossey-Bass.

Chapter 6

An intelligent design theory of the origins, evolution and function of religion: Toward an integration of existential and evolutionary perspectives

Tom Pyszczynski and Sharlynn Thompson

> If God has made us in his image, we have returned him the favor.
> — Notebooks, Voltaire (c. 1735 to c. 1750)

> God did not, as the Bible says, make man in His image; on the contrary, man ... made God in his image.
> — Lectures on the Essence of Religion, Ludwig Feuerbach (1851)

> In the beginning, Man created God, and in his image created he him.
> — Aqualung, Ian Anderson (1971)

The idea that humankind created gods in their own image is not new. It was famously suggested by Voltaire in the 18th century, Feuerbach in the 19th century, and Ian Anderson, of the rock band Jethro Tull, in 1971. The notion goes back much further than that — Roman philosopher Caecilius Statius implied this when he said 'fear made the first gods in the world' (Statius, 2003/1992 CE, line 661). The idea that humankind created gods is also the cornerstone of most scientific theories of the origins and function of religion. Evolutionary theories generally view religion as reflecting the appropriation of mechanisms that evolved for other purposes to solve more recent adaptive challenges, especially those involved in maintaining social order in groups, to facilitate the survival of the genes of individual group members (e.g., Boyer, 2004; Norenzayan et al. 2016). Cultures that are especially effective in preserving and extending their worldviews prosper because this facilitates the survival of individuals and their genes. Existential theories, on the other hand, focus primarily on the internal psychological experience of the individual, emphasising the emotional security and protection from anxiety that belief in higher powers capable of granting immortality provide (e.g., Becker, 1973; Solomon, Greenberg, & Pyszczynski, 1991). These individual psychological experiences then affect the appeal of religious ideas, which affect the extent to which they are accepted by groups and become part of the local cultural worldview.

Though evolutionary and existential perspectives are sometimes viewed as competing explanations for the origins and functions of religion and morality, and some evolutionary theorists dismiss the idea that the problem of death played an important role in the origins of religion (e.g., Atran, 2004; Boyer, 2001), we view them as complementary, with each adding insights needed to provide a comprehensive understanding. Evolutionary perspectives provide compelling explanations of the primitive building blocks of religious thought and experience and the long-term success of cultures with effective religious belief systems, but they are less able to explain the emergence, appeal to individuals, and spreading within groups of the core beliefs and values of religions, nor the psychological functions that religious belief serves for contemporary believers. Existential perspectives offer reasonable explanations of the forces that motivated the emergence and spread of religious beliefs and values, and those that continue to motivate individual commitment to them, but devote scant attention to the primitive pre-linguistic precursors of religion which were likely the building blocks from which more cognitively complex early humans created the beliefs and values that form the basis of ancient and modern religion, nor have they devoted sufficient attention to the role that such belief systems play on a broader social level.

In this chapter, we propose an 'intelligent design theory' of the origins and functions of religion by integrating useful ideas from both evolutionary and existential perspectives. Intelligent design theories of the origins of *humankind* are clearly inconsistent with modern evolutionary thinking. However, we argue that a focus on the use of human intelligence, and the forces that affect how it was used by individuals to shape their understanding of the world, adds useful insights that fill in the gaps and address issues given scant attention in the most influential contemporary evolutionary theories of religion. Integrating the emphasis on evolved cognitive proclivities emphasised by evolutionary theories of religion with the emphasis on the motivational and emotional forces that bias these processes will provide a more complete understanding of the origins and function of religion.

While recognising the diversity of thinking within both evolutionary and existential perspectives, we focus our discussion on evolutionary ideas about the origins and functions of religion from Boyer (2001), Norenzayan et al. (2016), and Graham and Haidt (2010), and the origins of morality from Schweder, Much, Mahapatra, and Park (1997), and Haidt and Joseph (2004). Our discussion of existential ideas about the functions of religion and mortality is focused primarily on the thinking of Kierkegaard (1844/1957; 1849/1957), Rank (1930), and Becker (1973), as integrated and systematised by terror management theory (TMT; Greenberg, Pyszczynski, & Solomon, 1986; Solomon, Greenberg, & Pyszczynski, 2015).

Evolutionary perspectives on religion and morality

Evolutionary analyses of religion build on Darwin's (1859) concept of natural selection: characteristics of organisms that increase the likelihood that the genes responsible for these features will be passed on to future generations and become more prevalent in populations due to the advantages these characteristics provide. Over many generations, genes that facilitate survival and reproduction become more prominent and over long periods of time new species emerge. Evolutionary accounts of the origins of religion usually emphasise either the appropriation of adaptive tendencies, such as theory of mind, social monitoring of behaviour by others, and credibility enhancing displays that evolved for other purposes, to serve new functions (e.g., Atran, 2004; Bering, 2006; Boyer, 2004), or the utility of religious belief systems in promoting social cohesion of groups and competition with other groups (Graham & Haidt, 2010).

The human proclivity to impute mental experiences, motives, and intentions to others, referred to as theory of mind or mentalising, is viewed as playing a particularly important role in the origins of religious thought. Attribution of mental experiences to others, presumably as a reflection of one's own inner experiences, facilitated communication and cooperation and thus survival and gene propagation in early humans because it enabled people to recognise social cues from group members and predatory behaviour from other animals and enemies (Baron-Cohen, 1999). Our ancestors were a highly social species so tendencies to monitor each other's behaviour and be sensitive to the fact that one's own behaviour was monitored by others were selected for evolutionarily because they increased the likelihood of surviving and reproducing in the small group contexts in which they lived.

Given their proclivity to perceive intentions in others, early humans applied this tendency to forces of nature, leading them to anthropomorphise physical phenomena as living entities and imagine them as possessing feelings, intentions, and desires, similar to those they experienced in themselves and perceived in other humans. For example, a god might cause thunder when it became angry or help with a hunt when it was pleased. Lacking the knowledge gleaned from millennia of scientific and philosophical progress, using their newly emerged cognitive propensities to imagine that entities in nature had experiences similar to themselves was a reasonable assumption for early homo sapiens.

Based on observations of contemporary hunter-gather societies, anthropologists and religious historians speculate that the earliest spirits were conceived of as capricious beings that cared little about the welfare of humans (e.g., Wright, 2009); given the many inconsistencies in the world in which they lived, and the lack of cultural knowledge of the consistencies and patterns that emerged over time, this imputation of capriciousness fit their observations. Though the deities of many hunter-gatherer societies seem to show little interest in the behaviour of humans, the idea of watchful spirits that monitor and reward or punish human behaviour is common to most larger scale societies (Norenzayan et al., 2016). Thus as our species progressed, the spirits our ancestors imagined became increasingly powerful and focused on human welfare and morality (e.g., Boehm, 2008; Wright, 2009). Presumably this reflects the human tendency to monitor and respond to the behaviour of other humans projected onto spiritual entities. It is also a likely consequence of the gradual accumulation of culturally shared knowledge about the workings of the world and the patterns in nature and human behaviour that were being discovered.

Adaptationist evolutionary theories of religion emphasise the utility of religious beliefs and behaviour for facilitating social cohesion, cooperation within groups, and successful competition with other groups. Espousing watchful gods that meted out rewards and punishments to people based on their behaviour was an effective form of social control that promoted prosocial behaviour within groups and preferential treatment of ingroup over outgroup members. Cultures that embraced these more demanding 'big gods' had an advantage over those that did not because they were more cooperative and cohesive, were more successful in intergroup competition, were able to impose their beliefs by force on less successful groups that lacked such beliefs, and their success led other groups to copy their beliefs.

From an adaptationist perspective, religious rituals, ceremonies, and extravagant sacrifices are viewed as *credibility-enhancing displays.* This is viewed as an extension of the more general tendency for people to affiliate with others who mark their group membership by costly actions that would not be undertaken by those not deeply committed to a group. Thus, costly rituals and ceremonies are seen as evolving because they provided valuable information about commitment to the group (Bering, 2006).

Norenzayan et al. (2016) recently proposed a theory of the emergence of 'big gods' that combines the evolutionary by-product and adaptationist approaches, positing that the initial emergence of spirit concepts to natural phenomena resulted from extending the socially adaptive tendency to impute mental states to other humans to anthropomorphise physical aspects of nature. They further argue that primitive concepts of a spirit world that resulted from such tendencies eventually morphed into complex belief systems that included deities who cared about the behaviour of humans and intervened in their affairs. These beliefs were adopted by cultures because they facilitated social cohesion. From this perspective, cognitive proclivities, such as theory of mind, coupled with increasing beliefs in gods that were concerned with the morality of people and could offer punishment or rewards for behaviours, enabled people to develop ways to cooperate with strangers on larger scales which facilitated living in increasing large groups. The resulting religious societies were more successful than societies without religion or with gods who did not monitor human activities because, as Norenzayan (2013) explains, 'watched people are nice people' (p. xiii). Members of groups with gods who were punishing, omnipotent, and omniscient were more likely to behave in group-enhancing ways, which enabled them to live in increasingly larger groups, villages, and cities.

Evolutionary theories of the origins of morality generally point to instances of behaviour in other species similar to the moral behaviour of humans to suggest that gut-level moral intuitions are primitive early adaptations that preceded the emergence of language and sophisticated intellect characteristic of modern humans. For example, chimpanzees, macaques, and bonobos display pre-moral behaviours such as food sharing and conflict management (Flack & de Waal, 2000); even deer, elephants, and vampire bats display signs of moral inclinations toward their conspecifics (Beckoff & Pierce, 2009). From this perspective, moral intuitions evolved through natural selection to promote and maintain social order for group living. When animals are guided by a set of innate moral rules, their groups become more successful due to increased cooperation and reduced harmdoing. Moral foundations theory (Graham & Haidt, 2010; Haidt & Joseph, 2004) posits that these primitive moral intuitions were the building blocks upon which our more intelligent early human ancestors developed moral beliefs and values. These evolved pre-linguistic moral foundations were the 'first draft' of human morality that was later edited and modified by cultures in ways that fit their unique circumstances. Moral foundations theory follows in the adaptationist tradition of viewing morality as functioning to promote intra-group harmony and successful intergroup competition which ultimately facilitated survival, reproduction, and propagation of genes. These ideas fit well with Norenzayan et al'.s (2016) synthesis of evolutionary perspectives on religion, in that morality became the primary concern of the big gods who watched over human behaviour and meted out rewards and punishment in accordance with people's behaviour to enforce morality — all in the service of social cohesion and gene survival.

Evolutionary theories of religion and morality provide important insights regarding how the earliest forms of religious thought developed from evolutionarily advantageous human cognitive proclivities and how cultures with compelling religious beliefs systems were more successful and became more common over time. But these analyses fall short of providing a comprehensive explanation of the transition from merely projecting human qualities onto physical phenomena to religions as we know them today — what Norenzayan et al. (2016) refer to as 'big god' religions. And though they offer insight into the societal level adaptive utility of allegiance to gods who monitored human activities and meted out rewards and punishments accordingly, they are unable to explain many of the most important features of the most successful religions that have stood the test of time, influenced culture and history, and continue to influence thought and behaviour today. Though ideas of watchful gods were clearly useful once they took hold, what inspired the idea that the gods cared about human behaviour and allotted rewards and punishments in accordance with that behaviour? Importantly, what led to the idea that life continues after physical death, when all signs of existence are gone from the deceased? Acknowledging the adaptive consequences of such beliefs does not explain what led to the emergence and appeal of such beliefs. Perhaps most importantly, such approaches do not provide compelling explanations of what motivates religious belief and behaviour in contemporary humans.

Clearly the emergence of the complex and elaborate systems of belief that constitute religion could not have resulted from random mutations in neural structures, nor is it plausible that they reflect cynical attempts to manipulate the masses to promote social order and the power of the elites. Although this may well have sometimes occurred in later stages in the development of religion and society, when leaders and elites realised they could manipulate the masses with tales of a world beyond the physical one in which people lived, it is extremely unlikely that the early architects of religion promoted ideas in which they themselves did not believe. A comprehensive theory of the origins of religion should explain what led to the *emergence* of a broad class of functionally similar ideas across diverse groups of people, what made them appealing enough to individuals for them to be widely accepted and eventually instituted as shared cultural knowledge, and what motivates people to maintain belief in them, engage in costly displays, and even give their lives because of the credence they put in them.

Existential theories, death, and terror management

TMT posits that human beings are unique among animals in their possession of evolved cognitive capacities that make them aware of death and its inevitability. Awareness of death in an animal with diverse motive systems oriented toward sustaining life creates the potential for overwhelming terror, which is both highly aversive and likely to disrupt goal-directed behaviour. TMT posits that our ancestors used the same sophisticated intellectual abilities that gave rise to this problem to produce a partial solution to it by using the understandings of reality that were gradually emerging and becoming central parts of cultural worldviews as a bulwark against existential terror.

Emerging awareness of death put a 'press' on emerging ideas about the world in which our ancestors lived, such that ideas that helped manage death-related anxiety were more likely to occur to people and attract their interest, leading them to be communicated to others who likely also found them comforting, and gradually spread within groups to become part of emerging *cultural worldviews*. Ideas about an invisible spirit world that influenced human affairs emerged and spread because they met individual psychological needs. These ideas became more complex and specific as cultural knowledge developed as a result of human ingenuity and creativity (broad classes of cognitive abilities that evolved for other reasons) being employed to manage anxiety. Cultural worldviews provide: (1) a theory of reality that imbues life with meaning, structure, significance, and permanence; (2) standards of value that define the behaviour and attributes of good and bad people; and (3) the hope of literally and/or symbolically transcending death.

Literal immortality is provided by the ideas suggesting that life continues in some form after physical death, such as in heaven, reincarnation, or the merger of one's soul with the spirits of one's ancestors. Though the vast majority of cultures, past and present, include literal immortality beliefs in some form, the specifics of these beliefs vary widely across cultures (see Solomon et al., 2015 regarding the diversity of afterlife beliefs). *Symbolic immortality* entails the possibility of being a valuable part of something greater than oneself that is believed to be eternal. Group identifications, such as families, nations, religious and ethnic groups, or even seemingly trivial things such as sports team affiliations and *alma maters*, provide symbolic immortality. Symbolic immortality is enhanced by valued contributions to one's groups, such as children, monuments, inventions, monetary contributions, or deeds and stories that will persist after one has died. Though fortune and fame are obviously useful in ordinary life, TMT suggests they are also important sources of symbolic immortality (for a review of evidence supporting this claim, see Solomon et al., 2015).

Managing existential terror by qualifying for either literal or symbolic immortality requires faith in the absolute validity of one's worldview and believing that one is living up to the standards of value that are derived from it. Religious teachings about literal immortality usually require both faith and good behaviour to qualify for a desirable afterlife. Similarly, common experience and cultural teachings make it clear that not all who die are remembered, and that being a good group member who believes in and exemplifies the values of the group is the best route to symbolic immortality. This sense of being a valued part of a meaningful universe is the essence of self-esteem, which keeps anxiety in check as one goes through life. Self-esteem develops its anxiety-buffering properties as a result of a complex interplay of evolved attachment tendencies and culturally prescribed socialisation experience (for a discussion of this process, see Pyszczynski, Solomon, & Greenberg, 2015, or Solomon et al., 2015).

In order for one's worldview and self-esteem to effectively shield one from anxiety, people must remain confident of the absolute validity of their worldviews and that they are in fact living up to its standards. Because the most important aspects of cultural worldviews are abstract ideas and values that cannot be directly verified by one's senses, and some of these run counter to observable reality, faith in them is maintained through social consensus. Others who share one's beliefs and values and attest to one's value increase one's certainty; those who see things differently challenge this certainty. A single person who believes in a fantasy afterlife is unlikely to feel relief from the finality of death, but millions of believers who share the same views provide a compelling cultural worldview that can stave off existential dread. Protection from death-related anxiety provided by worldviews and self-esteem causes people to react positively to those who validate their views and negatively to those who threaten them. The way others impinge on people's faith in their worldview and personal value, and thus their ability to manage anxiety, is a major determinant of their attitudes and behaviour toward them.

In sum, TMT posits that the potential for anxiety that resulted from awareness of the inevitability of death was made more manageable by beliefs that imbued life with meaning, purpose, and significance, and cultural standards that enabled individuals to construe themselves as valuable contributors to a meaningful and eternal reality. From this perspective, religion is a cultural innovation that functions to manage the potential for existential anxiety that provides hope of transcending death, either literally in a spirit world where life continues after physical death, or symbolically by being part of something greater than oneself and making enduring contributions to these entities.

Hundreds of experiments conducted in diverse cultures the world over support hypotheses derived from TMT (for recent reviews, see Greenberg, Vail, & Pyszczynski, 2014; Pyszczynski et al., 2015). Research has shown that (1) boosting self-esteem reduces self-reported anxiety, physiological arousal in the face of threat, and death-denying cognitive distortions; (2) reminders of death (mortality salience; MS) increase defensive reactions to people and ideas that impinge on one's worldview and self-esteem, striving to enhance self-esteem, discomfort when violating cultural norms, estimates of social consensus for one's attitudes, and preference for well-structured information; (3) threats to worldviews or self-esteem make death-related thoughts come to mind more rapidly (increase death thought accessibility; DTA); (4) increasing self-esteem or affirming one's worldview decreases DTA and reduces or eliminates defensive responses to MS; and (5) evidence of the existence of an afterlife reduces the increased worldview defense and self-esteem striving that MS otherwise produces.

These logically distinct lines of research provide converging evidence for TMT and document these effects across diverse aspects of worldviews and self-esteem, including political attitudes, religious beliefs, charitable donations, romantic love, attitudes toward sex, desire for children, support for war and terrorism, physical aggression, and reaction to those who are different. Although alternative explanations have been proposed for some aspects of some studies, we know of no viable alternative to TMT as a comprehensive explanation for this literature (for discussions of critiques and alternative explanations for TMT research, see Pyszczynski et al., 2015).

Research has shown that MS increases belief in supernatural beings and an afterlife, and some (but not all studies) show this occurs even for spiritual beings not associated with one's own faith (e.g., Batson & Stocks, 2004; Norenzayan, Dar-Nimrod, Hansen, & Proulx, 2009; Osarchuk & Tatz, 1973). Research also shows that challenges to one's religious beliefs increase DTA (e.g., Schimel, Hayes, Williams, & Jahrig, 2007). Other research has shown that MS increases distress among people when using religious objects for mundane purposes (Greenberg, Simon, Porteus, Pyszczynski, & Solomon, 1995). Research also shows that death reminders increased the impact of recently primed moral values, but only if they are framed in religious ways. For example, Rothschild, Abdollahi, and Pyszczynski (2010) found that although MS increased support for military action or terrorist attacks among American and Iranian religious fundamentalists (respectively), this was reversed when they were first primed with verses from the Bible or Koran that promoted compassion. When primed with compassionate religious values, MS decreased support for war and terrorism. Similarly, priming ideas of shared humanity reverse the typical tendency of MS to increase support for war (Motyl et al., 2011). Consistent with the death-denying function of morality posited by TMT, research documents a role for terror management processes in behaviour relevant to reactions to all five of the moral foundations posited by MFT (for a review, see Kesebir & Pyszczynski, 2011; see Vail et al., 2010 for a review of research on the role of death concerns in religious attitudes and behaviour).

The invention of spirits, gods, and religion

We believe these ideas fit well with contemporary evolutionary theories of religion and that combining evolutionary by-product, existential, and cultural adaptationist perspectives provides a more compelling and comprehensive account of the origins and function of religion than any of these perspectives do in conceptual isolation. Our intelligent design integration of these perspectives posits that evolved cognitive and social proclivities both set the stage for the most rudimentary beliefs in an invisible spirit world and gave rise to existential fears that motivated people to use these beliefs as building blocks for more elaborate belief systems that protected them from these fears. People then used other aspects of their personal experience to fill in the details of this dimension. Thus the spirits and gods they imagined were fleshed out to have human attributes similar to what they experienced in the people with whom they interacted.

As human curiosity about the workings of the world increased (likely in the service of choosing adaptive courses of action to deal with the environmental challenges they faced), early humans likely found it useful to impute power over things that mattered to the gods and spirits. Thus they imbued these spirits with power over the weather, availability of food, safety from predators, and harmonious relationships with other members of their groups. As the power imputed to the spirits increased, their similarity to powerful humans likely increased as well. It is probable that gods were created in the image of parents, chiefs, tribal leaders, and others high in the dominance hierarchies in which our ancestors lived. This might explain the obedience, devotion, fealty, and sacrifice that people assumed the gods demanded from them in return for both improving the nature of earthly existence and granting admission to the afterlife. Worship may have emerged as a projection onto the gods of the deference and submission that powerful humans demanded.

This use of powerful humans as models for the gods that our ancestors invented may help explain the egotistic, insecure, and cruel nature of many versions of supreme beings that comedians such as George Carlin and Louis C.K. have pondered as a source of humor. Ironically, the reason many people find such musings offensive is because of their fear that the gods might unleash their wrath and smite anyone who finds humor in such challenges to their desire for fealty. Along these lines, American evangelist Jerry Falwell opined that the 9/11 terrorist attacks were God's punishment for American acceptance of feminists, homosexuals, and promiscuity (Ambinder, 2011). Fear of a vengeful God who does not play by the rules he set for his children persists in many contemporary religious belief systems.

TMT posits that awareness of the inevitability of death was a byproduct of sophisticated human intellectual abilities. Though the emergence of increasingly sophisticated cognitive capacities and the consequent awareness of death probably gradually unfolded and spread over millennia, this was a seismic realisation that changed the nature of the spirit world that our ancestors were inventing and refining. Emerging awareness of death encouraged attributing increased power to the spirits and extending this power beyond people's immediate physical needs to solving to the problem of death and existential dread. Though different cultural groups resolved this problem in different ways, imagining that human beings became part of the unseen spiritual dimension after they died was likely an appealing and compelling idea, reinvented by many people across the expanding environment that our ancestors populated.

Though the earliest iterations of these ideas were probably fairly vague, as civilisation progressed and some individuals took on specialised roles of interfacing with the spirit and ascertaining their nature, these ideas became more complex and fleshed out. The knowledge of this dimension that shamans professed likely increased their power and the influence they had over emerging religious beliefs. Similarly, the power possessed by tribal leaders likely led their preferred beliefs to be widely emulated and often forcefully imposed on the less powerful. Indeed, throughout history, leaders were often viewed as chosen by and having special relationships with the local deities. In many cases, as in Egypt, China, and Japan, leaders were themselves viewed as gods, a practice that continues to this day in some places. In others, such as the Roman Empire and most of Europe, leaders were seen as being chosen by the deity and having a special relationship with him (it was usually, though not always, a him!). This assumption of a relationship between god and country is reflected in the beliefs held by some that divine intervention led to the election of modern American presidents.

The overarching theme of this chapter is that emerging awareness of death had a profound impact on the function and nature of the gods and religions that humankind was creating, which ultimately changed the dynamics of the moral intuitions and social norms that controlled behaviour. Although most cultures teach that morality is derived from the preferences of deities (or in some cultures, especially Asian ones, less personal spiritual forces that lie outside of the realm of human nature), contemporary theories of morality pay surprisingly little attention to the role of gods and spirits in promoting morality. However, for many if not most people, staying in the good graces of God is viewed as the primary impetus for moral behaviour and declining religious faith is feared as portending moral chaos and God's wrath.

Moral foundations theory (Haidt & Joseph, 2004) suggests that moral intuitions evolved in our pre-human ancestors long before the emergence of language and meaning systems because they were useful for maintaining cohesion within groups and minimising conflict. With the emergence of modern humans, these moral intuitions were verbalised and codified into cultural norms and values, and then integrated into more comprehensive cosmologies. Thus, moral values were tied to the emerging cultural worldviews that give meaning and purpose to life and explain why moral behaviour is important. TMT suggests that awareness of death and the emergence of increasingly powerful gods who provided a path to literal immortality to those who stayed in their good graces changed the motivational impetus for moral behaviour from staying in the good graces of others to pleasing the gods and continuing to exist after one's physical death. As one's fate after death became contingent on supernatural judgement, the consequences of moral and immoral behaviour became far greater.

This is not to say that the influence of other humans was eliminated by the invention of gods who controlled the afterlife, but this emergence of a new impetus for moral behaviour became an increasingly powerful force that promoted morality. Indeed, obtaining validation of one's faith and validation of one's virtue from those in one's group is essential for maintaining faith in one's worldview and self-esteem. As moral behaviour became the major criterion for admission to the afterlife by the deities, this further increased the importance that mortal humans put on it for their relationships with other humans. Part of the reason parents and other socialising agents place such great value on the moral behaviour of children is their commitment to the death transcendence of their offspring — which, in turn, increases their own prospects for both literal and symbolic immortality. This may be yet another reason why moral values are generally the most highly valued bases of both self-esteem and social judgment (e.g., Skitka, Bauman, & Sargis, 2005).

From individual equanimity to cultural success and back

As adaptationist theories suggest, societies and cultures that have compelling religious belief systems are indeed likely to be more successful, leading to larger populations and spreading of both their worldviews and genes (e.g., Norenzayan et al., 2016). By motivating individuals within societies to behave toward their neighbours in a more pro-social and less destructive way, religious beliefs have the potential to promote social cohesion and reduce chaos. We argue that allegiance to religious beliefs and conforming to the values they promote is motivated largely by the respite from existential anxiety that the promise of a blissful afterlife provides. Of course this is not the only motivating factor, and social pressure from one's peers or powerful others surely plays a part as well.

Religion transforms death from an unsolvable problem that cannot be controlled to a solvable and controllable one by providing a pathway to literal immortality through virtuous behaviour. Religion has the potential to both quell anxiety and promote a more cohesive society. More cohesive societies promote the welfare of individuals and the propagation of their genes, which leads them to further spread the cherished beliefs that give them equanimity, either by persuasion and example or brute force. Getting more people to share one's beliefs, whether such conversions occur through missionary activity or forceful imposition (or both), provides further consensus for the veracity of those beliefs, and thus increases faith in them and consequently their ability to buffer anxiety.

Unfortunately, using religious belief to quell anxiety is not without costs. Though the increased impetus for moral behaviour, above and beyond staying in the good graces of one's neighbours, is likely to promote social cohesion within groups, it often contributes to disdain hostility, and violence toward both other groups and members of one's own group who do not share one's devotion. From early tribal wars, through the Crusades and Spanish Inquisition, to the wave of religious terrorism currently enveloping much of the world, the threat to one's cherished beliefs posed by those with other beliefs has a long history of promoting bloody conflicts (for a review of research on the role of fear of death and religious beliefs in promoting war and terrorism, see Pyszczynski, Vail, & Motyl, 2010).

The underlying dynamic here is the human tendency to base certainty about beliefs on social consensus, and the wide diversity of religious beliefs that always have been and probably always will be central sources of emotional security for people. Though many religions promote universal love and compassion for all, and research has shown that reminders of these teachings can reverse the effect of existential threat on hostility toward outgroups (Rothschild et al., 2009), the proclivity to live up to these values often run counter to the need for certainty about beliefs that can never be definitively proven. This conflict between the hostility toward those with different beliefs produced by the difficulty of believing in what cannot be seen, and the compassion towards such people that the compassion teachings of religion demand, is a vexing paradox that explains why religious commitment sometimes promotes peace but often encourages violence.

An intelligent design perspective on religion offers a small ray of hope for moving beyond this seemingly insurmountable conflict between the need for certainty about one's beliefs and mandates to live up to the values associated with one's beliefs. If religious belief systems are the product of human ingenuity, it may be possible for people to find ways of resolving these competing proclivities. As moral foundations theory suggests, though moral precepts are built upon ancient evolved intuitions, cultures revise these precepts and this has the potential to be an ongoing process. Indeed, it has been argued that violence and war has been generally decreasing over the course of history (Pinker, 2011). This may reflect a gradual process of moral evolution that promotes putting greater value on compassion, fairness, and a sense of shared humanity over allegiance to one's group, respect for authority, and devotion to purity and sanctity. Compassion for those who are different from oneself has been a part of many religious traditions for at least a few millennia. The challenge for intelligent designers of future moral systems is to find ways of making these values win out over the desire for certainty about one's own worldview.

References

Ambinder, M. (2011, September 14). Falwell suggests gays to blame for attacks. *ABC News*. Retrieved from http://abcnews.go.com

Atran, S. (2004). *In gods we trust: The evolutionary landscape of religion.* Oxford, England: Oxford University Press.

Baron-Cohen, S. (1999). The evolution of a theory of mind. In M. Corballis & S. Lea. (Eds.), *The descent of mind: psychological perspectives on hominid evolution.* Oxford, England: Oxford University Press.

Batson, C.D., & Stocks, E.L. (2004). Religion: Its core psychological functions. In J. Greenberg, S.L. Koole, & T. Pyszczynski (Eds.), *Handbook of experimental existential psychology* (pp. 141–155). New York, NY: Guilford Press.

Becker, E. (1973). *The denial of death.* New York, NY: Free Press.

Bekoff, M., & Pierce, J. (2009). *Wild justice: The moral lives of animals.* Chicago, IL: University of Chicago Press.

Bering, J.M. (2006). The cognitive science of souls: Clarifications and extensions of the evolutionary model. *Behavioral and Brain Sciences, 29*(5), 486–493.

Boehm, C. (2008). Purposive social selection and the evolution of human altruism. *Cross-Cultural Research, 42*(4), 319–352.

Boyer, P. (2001). *Religion explained: The evolutionary origins of religious thought.* New York, NY: Basic Books.

Darwin, C. (1859). On the origin of species by means of natural selection, or, the preservation of favoured races in the struggle for life. London, England: J. Murray.

Flack, J.C., & De Waal, F.B.M. (2000). 'Any animal whatever': Darwinian building blocks of morality in monkeys and apes. *Journal of Consciousness Studies, 7*(1–2), 1–29.

Graham, J., & Haidt, J. (2010). Beyond beliefs: Religions bind individuals into moral communities. *Personality and Social Psychology Review, 14*(1), 140–150.

Greenberg, J., Pyszczynski, T., & Solomon, S. (1986). The causes and consequences of a need for self-esteem: A terror management theory. In R.F. Baumeister (Ed.), *Public self and private self* (pp. 189–212). New York, NY: Springer-Verlag.

Greenberg, J., Porteus, J., Simon, L., Pyszczynski, T., & Solomon, S. (1995). Evidence of a terror management function of cultural icons: The effects of mortality salience on the inappropriate use of cherished cultural symbols. *Personality and Social Psychology Bulletin, 21*(11), 1221–1228.

Greenberg, J., Vail, K., & Pyszczynski, T. (2014). Terror management theory and research: How the desire for death transcendence drives our strivings for meaning and significance. *Advances in Motivation Science, 1,* 85–134.

Haidt, J., & Joseph, C. (2004) Intuitive ethics: How innately prepared intuitions generate culturally variable virtues. *Daedalus, 133*, 55–66.

Kierkegaard, S. (1954). *The sickness unto death* (W. Lowrie, Trans.). New York, NY: Princeton University Press. (Original work published 1849)

Kierkegaard, S. (1957). *The concept of dread* (W. Lowrie, Trans.). Princeton: Princeton University Press. (Original work published 1844)

Kesebir, P., & Pyszczynski, T. (2011). The role of death in life: Existential aspects of human motivation. In R. Ryan (Ed.), *The Oxford Handbook of Motivation*. New York, NY: Oxford University Press.

Motyl, M., Hart, J., Pyszczynski, T., Weise, D., Maxfield, M., & Siedel, A. (2011). Subtle priming of shared human experiences eliminates threat-induced negativity toward Arabs, immigrants, and peace-making. *Journal of Experimental Social Psychology, 47*(6), 1179–1184.

Norenzayan, A. (2013). *Big gods: How religion transformed cooperation and conflict*. Princeton University Press.

Norenzayan, A., Dar Nimrod, I., Hansen, I.G., & Proulx, T. (2009). Mortality salience and religion: Divergent effects on the defense of cultural worldviews for the religious and the non religious. *European Journal of Social Psychology, 39*(1), 101–113.

Norenzayan, A., Shariff, A.F., Gervais, W.M., Willard, A.K., McNamara, R.A., Slingerland, E., & Henrich, J. (2016). The cultural evolution of prosocial religions. *Behavioral and Brain Sciences, 39*. doi:10.1017/S0140525X14001356

Osarchuk M., & Tatz S. (1973). Effect of induced fear of death on belief in afterlife. *Journal of Personality and Social Psychology, 27*(2), 256–260.

Pinker, S. (2011). *The better angels of our nature: The decline of violence in history and its causes*. London, England: Penguin Books.

Pyszczynski, T., Solomon, S., & Greenberg, J. (2015). Thirty years of terror management theory: From genesis to revelation. *Advances in Experimental Social Psychology, 52*, 1–70.

Pyszczynski, T., Vail, K.E., & Motyl, M.S. (2010). The cycle of righteous killing: Psychological forces in the prevention and promotion of peace. In T. Pick, A. Speckhard, & B. Jacuch (Eds.), *Homegrown terrorism: NATO Science for Peace and Security Series — E: Human and Societal Dynamics*. (pp. 227–243). Amsterdam, the Netherlands: IOS Press.

Rank, O. (1931). *Psychology and the soul*. (W. Lowrie, Trans.). New York, NY: Perpetua Books.

Rothschild, Z.K., Abdollahi, A., & Pyszczynski, T. (2009). Does peace have a prayer? The effect of mortality salience, compassionate values, and religious fundamentalism on hostility toward out-groups. *Journal of Experimental Social Psychology, 45*(4), 816–827.

Schimel, J., Hayes, J., Williams, T., & Jahrig, J. (2007). Is death really the worm at the core? Converging evidence that worldview threat increases death-thought accessibility. *Journal of Personality and Social Psychology, 92*(5), 789.

Shweder, R., Much, N., Mahapatra, M., & Park, L. (1997). Divinity and the 'big three' explanations of suffering. *Morality and Health, 119*, 119–169.

Skitka, L.J., Bauman, C.W., & Sargis, E.G. (2005). Moral conviction: Another contributor to attitude strength or something more? *Journal of Personality and Social Psychology, 88*(6), 895.

Solomon, S., Greenberg, J., & Pyszczynski, T. (1991). A terror management theory of social behavior: The psychological functions of self-esteem and cultural worldviews. *Advances in Experimental Social Psychology, 24*, 93–159.

Solomon, S., Greenberg, J., & Pyszczynski, T. (2015). *The worm at the core: On the role of death in life.* New York, NY: Random House.

Statius, C. (2003). *Thebaid.* (D.R.S. Bailey, Trans.). Cambridge, MA: Harvard University Press. (Original work published 92 CE)

Vail, K.E., Rothschild, Z.K., Weise, D.R., Solomon, S., Pyszczynski, T., & Greenberg, J. (2010). A terror management analysis of the psychological functions of religion. *Personality and Social Psychology Review, 14*(1), 84–94.

Wright, R. (2010). *The evolution of God: The origins of our beliefs.* New York, NY: Little, Brown.

Chapter 7

Death anxiety and psychopathology

Lisa Iverach

Transdiagnostic constructs have been implicated in the development, course, and maintenance of psychopathology. A transdiagnostic approach to psychopathology focuses on symptoms and predispositions evident across multiple diagnostic categories of mental disorders. Examples of transdiagnostic constructs that are regarded as risk and maintaining factors for a range of mental disorders include perfectionism (Egan, Wade, & Shafran, 2011), rumination (McLaughlin & Nolen-Hoeksema, 2011), behavioural inhibition and avoidance (Dozois, Seeds, & Collins, 2009), and intolerance of uncertainty (Mahoney & McEvoy, 2012). Although treatments for mental disorders have traditionally focused on disorders as distinct and separate (Dozois et al., 2009), treating transdiagnostic constructs in conjunction with treatment for specific disorders can improve symptoms and outcomes, prevent the development of comorbid disorders, and increase cost-effectiveness (Dozois et al., 2009; Egan et al., 2011; Kutlesa & Arthur, 2008; McLaughlin & Nolen-Hoeksema, 2011; Lundh & Ost, 2001). It also extends the traditional medical model of categorical classification and treatment towards a more contemporary approach based on empirically supported shared dimensions (Brown & Barlow, 2009; Maxfield, John, & Pyszczynski, 2014).

Death anxiety as a transdiagnostic construct

Death can elicit fears of separation, powerlessness, loss of control, and meaninglessness (Noyes, Stuart, Longley, Langbehn, & Happel, 2002). According to terror management theory (TMT), cultural worldviews and self-esteem provide a buffer against existential fear of death (Burke, Martens, & Faucher, 2010; Greenberg, 2012; Greenberg et al., 1992; Hayes, Schimel, Arndt, & Faucher, 2010; Pyszczynski, Greenberg, & Solomon, 1999; Routledge, 2012; Strachan et al., 2007). However, the capacity to apply these buffers against anxiety may be disturbed by such factors as genetic predispositions, insecure attachment, temperament, adverse childhood events, trauma, and other life difficulties (Maxfield et al., 2014). These threats to meaning and self-esteem are likely to result in psychological vulnerability, anxiety, and distress (Maxfield et al., 2014).

As a result, psychopathology is considered to reflect maladaptive efforts to cope with death awareness and existential fear (Maxfield et al., 2014; Strachan, Pyszczynski, Greenberg, & Solomon, 2001; Strachan et al., 2007; Yalom, 1980). However, death anxiety may not always be obvious, with associated psychological difficulties often focused on 'smaller and more manageable threats, such as spiders, germs, or other common phobic objects' (Maxfield et al., 2014, p. 42). Hence, death anxiety is regarded as a basic fear underlying the development, course, and maintenance of a range of mental disorders (Arndt, Routledge, Cox, & Goldenberg, 2005; Furer & Walker, 2008). Numerous studies have evaluated the presence of death anxiety across obsessive–compulsive disorder (OCD), somatic symptoms disorders, depressive disorders, posttraumatic stress disorder (PTSD), schizophrenia, eating disorders, and manic-depression (Arndt et al., 2005; Cheung, Dennis, Easthope, Werrett, & Farmer, 2005; Giles, 1995; Furer & Walker, 2008; Khanna, Khanna, & Sharma, 1988; Strachan et al., 2007; Thorson & Powell, 2000).

For instance, the transdiagnostic nature of death anxiety is particularly evident in compulsive handwashing and checking, where individuals engage in behaviours designed to reduce the likelihood or threat of death (e.g., handwashing to prevent diseases, and checking of stoves and power points to prevent fire and death). Similarly, many of the feared objected reported by individuals with specific phobia are associated with harm or death, such as spiders, blood, and heights.

Death anxiety and psychopathology: The present review

Given that death features prominently across many mental disorders, the purpose of this chapter is to review evidence regarding the role of death anxiety across a range of mental disorders, including OCD, panic disorder, specific phobias, social anxiety disorder, agoraphobia, separation anxiety, somatic symptom disorders (hypochondriasis), PTSD, depressive disorders, and eating disorders (also see Iverach, Mezies, & Menzies, 2014).

Obsessive-compulsive disorder and death anxiety

Several researchers have noted that many obsessive-compulsive tendencies are associated with death-related fears about self or loved ones, such as diseases, danger, and germs (Iverach et al., 2014; Menzies & Dar-Nimrod, 2017; Menzies, Menzies, & Iverach, 2015; Strachan et al., 2007). Most recently, it has been argued that the dread of death may be a central driver of most OCD presentations (Menzies & Dar-Nimrod, 2017; Menzies et al., 2015). The most influential research to date was conducted by Menzies and Dar-Nimrod (2017), who explored the relationship between death anxiety and various markers of psychopathology in 171 OCD patients. Moderate to large correlations were found between death anxiety scores and OCD severity, number of hospitalisations, medications, and diagnoses of comorbid anxiety-related disorders. In an additional experiment, Menzies and Dar-Nimrod randomly allocated 66 OCD washers and 66 OCD nonwashers to either a mortality salience or dental pain priming condition. After this priming, participants completed several distraction tasks involving skin conductance recording, and were then able to wash conductive gel off their hands. The OCD washers washed their hands for longer and used more soap and paper towel than OCD nonwashers. Furthermore, participants in the mortality salience condition demonstrated greater cleaning than participants in the dental pain condition. These findings suggest that fear of death may drive OCD washing behaviour.

Previous experimental research conducted by Strachan and colleagues (2007) has also confirmed that death awareness is capable of exacerbating compulsive behaviours. For instance, when compared to participants who scored low on compulsive handwashing, Strachan and colleagues found that compulsive handwashers spent more time washing their hands, and used more paper towel to dry their hands, following a mortality salience induction. This highlights the potential for death anxiety to be a factor underlying obsessive-compulsive disorder, thereby providing some explanation for the exaggerated attention that people with OCD focus on reducing or eliminating danger and disease (Strachan et al., 2007).

This view has been advocated by Jones and Menzies (1997a), who conducted a laboratory contamination task to evaluate whether expectancy of life-threatening illness drives handwashing behaviour. Obsessive-compulsive washers were found to give high estimates of the 'probability of illness' and 'severity of illness' ratings when asked to place their hands in a mixture of potting soil, food scraps, and animal hair. Severity of illness ratings were also found to be highly correlated with anxiety, urge to wash, and time spent washing. Moreover, when severity of illness ratings on a single item 'death scale' were held constant, no other potential mediators remained significantly related to OCD, including perfectionism, self-efficacy, and perceived responsibility. According to Jones and Menzies (1997a), these findings lend weight to the argument that washing behaviour is driven by the expectancy of life-threatening illness.

Additional support for this perspective was provided by Jones and Menzies (1997b), who found that severe OCD patients could be returned to relatively normal functioning following 6 to 12 sessions of cognitive therapy targeting disease expectancy, known as danger ideation reduction therapy (DIRT). The DIRT program is used as a novel approach to treatment-resistant OCD with contamination fears, and has been shown to be effective across a range of studies (Govender, Drummond, & Menzies, 2006; Hambridge & Loewenthal, 2003; Jones & Menzies, 1997b, 1998, 2002; Krochmalik, Jones, & Menzies, 2001; Krochmalik, Jones, Menzies, & Kirkby, 2004).

Anxiety-related disorders and death anxiety

Death anxiety has been implicated across a range of anxiety disorders (Arndt et al., 2005; Strachan et al., 2001), and has been shown to exacerbate anxious responding in individuals with anxiety-related problems (Strachan et al., 2007). According to Strachan and colleagues (2007), 'If the fear of nonexistence lies at the core of the human capacity for anxiety, then reminding people of this deeply rooted fear should exacerbate anxious responding among people with anxiety-related problems' (p. 1138). This suggests that anxiety disorders may be the result of a maladaptive anxiety-buffering system (Maxfield et al., 2014). A range of studies have explored the relationship between death anxiety and several anxiety-related disorders, including panic disorder, agoraphobia, specific phobias, social phobia, and separation anxiety.

Panic disorder and death anxiety

Several researchers have argued that death anxiety is common in panic disorder (Furer & Walker, 2008; Randall, 2001; Starcevic, 2007; Torres & Crepaldi, 2002). A study by Furer, Walker, Chartier, and Stein (1997) examined the relationship between death anxiety and psychopathology in a sample of 21 panic disorder patients, 23 social phobia patients, and 22 controls. When compared to social phobia patients and controls, panic disorder patients reported substantially higher death anxiety. Nearly half of the panic disorder patients also met criteria for hypochondriasis. Of interest, higher death anxiety was found for patients with comorbid panic disorder and hypochondriasis (Furer & Walker, 2008; Furer et al., 1997). Similar findings have been reported by Radanovic-Grguric and colleagues (2004), with a significantly higher rate of death anxiety found among 14 panic disorder patients when compared to 14 major depressive patients. However, half of the panic disorder patients met criteria for major depressive disorder, and two-thirds of major depressive disorder patients met criteria for panic disorder, showing the high rate of comorbidity across disorders. In addition, research has shown that panic disorder patients may in fact have a higher rate of mortality due to death by unnatural causes, when compared to patients with unipolar depression (Coryell, Noyes, & Clancy, 1982).

Taken together, these findings support the transdiagnostic nature of death anxiety, and indicate that heightened death anxiety may be associated with the presence of comorbid psychological conditions. Randall (2001) has argued that death anxiety may be a presenting issue for many patients with panic disorder, highlighting the importance of addressing death-related thoughts and fears in order to address the associated symptoms of the disorder. This supports the need to target death anxiety as part of standard treatment for panic disorder (Randall, 2001), including the application of such strategies as realistic appraisal of bodily threats, and modification of attitudes to health, illness, death, and the body (Starcevic, 2007).

Although large controlled trials are lacking, single case studies have examined the impact of targeting death anxiety in the treatment of panic disorder. For instance, Randall (2001) reported on a single case study of a panic disorder patient treated with existential therapy to treat death anxiety. Therapy focused on fear of death, isolation, freedom, meaning, and life re-evaluation, and was associated with remission of symptoms after three weeks. In addition, Ishiyama (1986) reported on the case study of a Japanese cognitive behavioural treatment, Morita therapy, to treat fear of death during panic attacks. Treatment focused on the existential meaning of anxiety, and was associated with reduced fear of death during anxiety attacks within a single session. These single case study findings suggest the need for larger controlled trials, and further research to explore the role of death anxiety in comorbid disorders.

Specific phobias and death anxiety

Nearly a century ago, Kingman (1928) argued that fear of death is a universal fear underpinning all phobias. It has also been suggested that the development of phobias, and the obsessional symptoms used to displace death-related fears, is founded upon life-threatening experiences with self or loved ones (Meyer, 1975). According to Strachan and colleagues (2007), phobias may develop when death anxiety is focused onto smaller and more manageable threats, such as spiders. For instance, 'a spider phobic's feeling that a spider is threatening, when it actually poses no harm, would make more sense if the spider phobic experienced the spider as a reminder of death even when the spider is not deadly' (Strachan et al., 2007; p. 1149). In 2001, Strachan and colleagues conducted the first series of experiments to evaluate the relationship between death anxiety and anxious responding, with particular focus on the impact of mortality salience on phobic behaviours. Of note, increased fear reactions to spider-related stimuli were found for 32 spider phobics reminded of their own death, but this effect was not found for 30 nonphobic controls who were also reminded of their own death.

Several researchers have advocated the application of therapeutic interventions to address death anxiety associated with specific phobias, including blood phobia (Perez San Gregorio, Borda Mas, & Blanco Picabia, 1995; Persons, 1986). In a multiple baseline study of a single female patient presenting with death anxiety, Persons (1986) found that treatment of death anxiety using exposure treatment for phobias was associated with improvements in fear of losing control. However, it is clear that more research is required to establish the efficacy of well-established therapeutic interventions in treating death anxiety associated with a range of specific phobias.

Social anxiety and death anxiety

Social anxiety is another disorder associated with death anxiety. Given the potential for mortality salience to increase phobic responding to spiders and compulsive handwashing, Strachan and colleagues (2007) investigated the impact of mortality salience on social anxiety and avoidance in 66 undergraduate students with low versus high social anxiety. Participants were assigned to a mortality salience or aversive control induction condition, and social avoidance was subsequently evaluated by measuring how long participants took to complete a free-writing exercise before joining a staged group discussion. Socially anxious participants exposed to a mortality salience induction left less time to join the group discussion, when compared to socially anxious participants in the control condition and nonsocially anxious participants in the morality salience condition. This supports the view that mortality salience exacerbates social anxiety and avoidance.

Given that attentional bias is a core feature of social anxiety, Finch, Iverach, Menzies, and Jones (2015) recently examined the impact of mortality salience on attentional bias in social anxiety with 36 socially anxious and 37 nonsocially anxious individuals who were randomly allocated to a mortality salience or control induction condition. Following the induction procedure, an eye-tracker was used to evaluate initial bias towards, and late-stage avoidance of, socially threatening facial expressions. Socially anxious participants in the mortality salience condition showed significantly more initial bias towards social threat than nonsocially anxious participants in the mortality salience condition and socially anxious participants in the control condition. However, no effect was found for late-stage avoidance of social threat. These findings indicate that death anxiety may increase initial vigilance towards social threat, confirming and extending the work of Strachan and colleagues (2007). Nevertheless, more research is needed to confirm this relationship, and to determine the value and efficacy of treating death anxiety associated with social anxiety.

Agoraphobia, separation anxiety, and death anxiety

The relationship between death anxiety and agoraphobia is supported by evidence that the onset of agoraphobia is preceded by traumatic events, such as physical threats or the loss of loved ones (Foa et al., 1984; Torres & Crepaldi, 2002). In addition, many symptoms associated with agoraphobia involve death-related themes, such as fear of harm when outside the home, heightened focus on internal sensations, death-related catastrophe fears, and hypochondriacal concerns (Foa et al., 1984). A small number of studies have explored this relationship. For instance, Fleischer-Mann (1995) found that death anxiety and separation anxiety were positively correlated for 25 agoraphobic adults, indicating that death anxiety may increase as a result of heightened fears about separation from loved ones. Similarly, a strong relationship between death anxiety, separation anxiety, and quality of attachment was found in a sample of 140 undergraduate students (Caras, 1995). Of note, higher affective quality of parental relationships and a more secure attachment style was associated with lower death anxiety. In addition, when compared to 20 controls, Walser (1985) found heighted death anxiety and separation anxiety among 20 borderline and 20 schizophrenia patients, and concluded that separation anxiety and death anxiety may be phenomenologically linked, with the potential for separation to mask death anxiety.

In a related manner, Mikulincer, Florian, Birnbaum, and Malishkevich (2002) conducted three studies to investigate the impact of separation reminders on death thought accessibility. In Study 1, participants imagined separation from a relationship partner, death of a relationship partner, or a TV program. In Study 2, participants imagined separation from a relationship partner, separation from an acquaintance, or an academic failure. In Study 3, participants imagined separation from a relationship partner that was short-term, long-term, or final. Across these studies, participants completed measures of death-thought accessibility and attachment style. According to Mikulincer and colleagues, 'Thoughts of separation from a relationship partner led to heightened death-thought accessibility mainly when thoughts were focused on long-term or final separations and among persons scoring high on attachment anxiety' (p. 287). This confirms the death-anxiety buffering function of close relationships, and suggests that death anxiety may play a role in separation anxiety.

Despite this evidence, research investigating the treatment of death anxiety associated with agoraphobia or separation anxiety is lacking. Several decades ago, Foa and colleagues (1984) suggested the application of imaginal exposure techniques to treat separation anxiety and death anxiety in order to treat agoraphobia symptoms. Bea and Sicart (1989) also reported on the treatment of separation anxiety and death anxiety in a single patient. However, evidence is lacking regarding the efficacy of these approaches.

Somatic symptom disorders and death anxiety

In 2013, based on the release of the fifth edition of the *Diagnostic and statistical manual of mental disorders* (5th ed.; DSM-5; American Psychiatric Association, 2013), hypochondriasis was removed as a disorder and replaced by the somatic symptom and related disorders. However, research regarding death anxiety and hypochondriasis is reviewed here for the purposes of the present chapter.

A pathological fear of death has been implicated in the sense of bodily threat that is reported by individuals with somatic symptom disorders such as hypochondriasis and health anxiety (Furer & Walker, 2008; Furer, Walker, & Stein, 2007; Starcevic, 2005). In particular, patients with somatic symptom disorders may experience symptoms related to death and dying, such as fears of bodily failure, pain, separation, and loss of power and control (Noyes et al., 2002; Starcevic, 2005). Hence, some researchers have claimed that death anxiety is a central feature of somatic symptom disorders, rather than an associated feature (Hiebert et al., 2005; Noyes et al., 2002). However, the relationship between death anxiety and somatic symptoms disorders like hypochondriasis has received little research attention (Hiebert et al., 2005; Noyes et al., 2002).

Noyes and colleagues (2002) explored death anxiety in 49 hypochondriasis patients and 113 general medical patients. For the hypochondriasis group, positive correlations were found between death anxiety, fear of separation, and loss of meaning. Kellner, Abbott, Winslow, and Pathak (1987) also found that hypochondriasis patients reported more fears of death and disease, and were more likely to attend closely to bodily sensations and seek medical care, than matched family practice patients, nonpatient employees, and nonhypochondriacal psychiatric patients. Moreover, death anxiety has been found in patients with medically unexplained symptoms (Sumathipala et al., 2008). Together, these studies suggest that death anxiety may feature across the somatic symptom and related disorders.

Therefore, targeting death anxiety in the assessment and treatment of somatic symptom and related disorders may improve outcomes (Furer & Walker, 2008; Hiebert et al., 2005; Noyes et al., 2002; Starcevic, 2005, 2007). This may include application of CBT strategies, such as cognitive reappraisal, targeting reassurance seeking, safety behaviours, and exposure to death-related themes (Furer & Walker, 2008). To this end, Hiebert and colleagues (2005) randomly allocated 39 adults with hypochondriasis to group CBT or a 4-month waitlist control group. When compared to the waitlist control group, the CBT group demonstrated reductions in death anxiety and hypochondriacal symptoms. These findings indicate the need for larger treatment trials to evaluate the efficacy of this approach (Furer & Walker, 2008; Hiebert et al., 2005).

Posttraumatic stress disorder and death anxiety

Several researchers have highlighted the relationship between death anxiety and posttraumatic stress disorder (PTSD; Chatard et al., 2012; Cheung et al., 2005; Kesebir, Luszczynska, Pyszczynski, & Benight, 2011). In particular, the two-factor model of death anxiety (Gilliland & Templer, 1985; Lonetto & Templer, 1986; Templer, 1976) suggests that exposure to life-threatening events increases death anxiety, which subsequently triggers the development of PTSD symptoms (Cheung et al., 2005). Similarly, according to the anxiety buffer disruption theory, PTSD may result from disruption of the anxiety buffering system that typically protects individuals from death anxiety (Abdollahi, Pyszczynski, Maxfield, & Lusyszczynska, 2011; Kesebir et al., 2011; Maxfield et al., 2014).

This hypothesis has been investigated across a range of trauma-related groups (Abdollahi et al., 2011; Chatard et al., 2012; Martz, 2004; Safren, Gershuny, & Hendriksen, 2003). For instance, Chatard and colleagues (2012) found that, following mortality salience induction, individuals with high PTSD symptoms following a civil war demonstrated increased death-thought accessibility, compared to individuals with low PTSD symptoms. Mortality salience was also associated with increased trauma symptoms for individuals with high exposure to war, but not for those with low exposure. These findings indicate that PTSD symptomatology may indeed be influenced by disruption to the normal anxiety buffering mechanisms that protect individuals from death anxiety (Chatard et al., 2012). Similar findings have been reported for earthquake survivors (Abdollahi et al., 2011), HIV patients (Safren et al., 2003), veterans and civilians with spinal cord injuries (Martz, 2004), and domestic violence victims (Kesebir et al., 2011). Moreover, in light of the current wave of terrorism occurring in Israel, Hamama-Raz and colleagues (2016) evaluated the relationship between death anxiety and PTSD symptom severity in 429 Israeli adults. Death anxiety was found to be a significant predictor of PTSD symptom severity, and the personality traits of emotional stability and conscientiousness were found to moderate this relationship. Overall, findings suggest that death anxiety may be an appropriate target for psychological treatment in cases of PTSD (Martz, 2004; Safren et al., 2003). Further research is required to explore the effectiveness of such treatment approaches.

Depressive disorders and death anxiety

Existential fear and meaninglessness also feature in the depressive disorders (Ghaemi, 2007; Havens & Ghaemi, 2005; Simon, Arndt, Greenberg, Solomon,

& Pyszczynski, 1998). In a similar manner to anxiety disorders, when viewing depressive disorders from the perspective of TMT, a maladaptive anxiety-buffering mechanism has been implicated in the development of depressive symptoms, including lack of meaning and impaired connectedness with others (Maxfield et al., 2014; Simon et al., 1998). Hence, the Templer Death Depression Scale–Revised has been developed to assess the depressive components of death anxiety, including anhedonia, anergia, existential vacuum, and death sadness (Templer et al., 2001).

In support of this perspective, research evidence has confirmed the presence of death anxiety across the depressive disorders (Brubeck & Beer, 1992; Ongider & Eyuboglu, 2013; Saggino & Ronco, 1997; Simon, Greenberg, Harmon-Jones, Solomon, Pyszczynski, 1996). For instance, experimental research has confirmed greater worldview defence in response to mortality salience for mildly depressive individuals when compared with nondepressed individuals (Simon et al., 1996). Furthermore, the opportunity for worldview defence in response to mortality salience has been associated with greater self-reported life meaning for mildly depressed individuals, when compared to mildly depressed individuals not given the opportunity for worldview defence (Simon et al., 1998). This suggests that depressed individuals may need more protection against death-related fears (Simon et al., 1998).

Additional research has shown that death anxiety is associated with increased depression among patients with depressive disorders (Ongider & Eyuboglu, 2013), and it has been suggested that this relationship may be influenced by age (Thorson & Powell, 2000). For instance, when compared to younger adults (16–35 years), Thorson and Powell found that older adults (65–92 years) reported lower death anxiety and depression, and higher religiosity. However, when both age groups were combined, higher death anxiety was associated with higher depression, and higher religiosity was associated with lower death anxiety.

Taken as a whole, these research findings support the application of existential and related therapies to treat death anxiety associated with depressive disorders (Ghaemi, 2007; Stalsett, Gude, Ronnestad, & Monsen, 2012). A small number of studies have explored this issue. For instance, Chait (1998) reported on the use of psychoanalytic therapy in the treatment of depression and fear of dying in a 7 year old child. Focus on early and ongoing separations related to the child's fears resulted in improved internal structure and family bonds. Furthermore, Hussian (1983) also reported on the use of operant therapy and cognitive therapy to treat depression and high-frequency verbalisations about death and dying in two elderly institutionalised patients. However, larger controlled trials are needed to evaluate the efficacy of well-established treatment strategies for death anxiety associated with depressive symptoms and/or disorders.

Eating disorders and death anxiety

It has been argued that, 'for many patients who starve, purge, or mutilate themselves, the body is speaking of death' (Farber, Jackson, Tabin, & Bachar, 2007, p. 289). Though less researched than other disorders, a small number of studies have explored the role of death anxiety in eating disorders (Alantar & Maner, 2008; Farber et al., 2007; Goldenberg, Arndt, Hart, & Brown, 2005; Hochdorf, Latzer, Canetti, & Bachar, 2005). Across these studies, there is evidence that death anxiety may underlie the desire to be thin, and may play an integral role in the cognitive behavioural profile of anorexia patients (Giles, 1995; Goldenberg et al., 2005). Most recently, Le Marne and Harris (2017) reviewed research evidence on this topic, and also reported on a study of 164 participants who completed a range of measures relating to eating attitudes, death anxiety, perfectionism, and self-esteem. Death anxiety and self-esteem were found to be independent predictors of disordered eating, and perfectionism was only a predictor of disordered eating when death anxiety and self-esteem were not included the regression model. These findings suggest the death anxiety may be a stronger predictor of disordered eating than well-established variables such as perfectionism.

In addition to these findings, higher death anxiety has also been reported by females with anorexia nervosa when compared to matched controls (Giles, 1995). This is not surprising given that anorexia has the highest mortality rate of any mental disorder, which may lead to a preoccupation with death (Farber et al., 2007). Increased rates of suicide are also noted across the eating disorders (Crow et al., 2009). Experimental evidence has shown that reminders of death are associated with subsequent restricted food intake for females, but not males (Goldenberg et al., 2005). This experiment was repeated in a group setting where social comparison was likely, and women with a high body mass index were subsequently found to restrict eating after mortality salience priming. In a further experiment, women with a high body mass index in the mortality salience condition perceived themselves as more discrepant from their ideal thinness. Taken together, findings from these experiments suggest a relationship between death anxiety and eating-related behaviour for females specifically. Further research is needed to examine the impact of treatment for death anxiety on eating disorder symptoms. Farber and colleagues (2007) have suggested that treatment for eating disorder patients should determine their 'personal construct of death' (p. 289).

Discussion

Death anxiety appears to be a basic fear underlying a range of mental disorders (Becker, 1973; Furer & Walker, 2008; Greenberg, 2012; Starcevic, 1989; Strachan et al., 2007). The evidence reviewed in this chapter confirms the transdiagnostic nature of death anxiety in the development, course, and maintenance of psychopathology. Findings across several studies indicate that mortality salience is a unique psychological threat that has the power to exacerbate anxious responding and behaviour (Hayes et al., 2010). That is, 'maladaptive attempts to cope with insufficiently buffered death anxiety' may lead to the development of psychopathology (Strachan et al., 2007, p. 1149).

Clinical implications and future research

Given the compelling nature of this evidence, several therapeutic approaches have been recommended and evaluated in the treatment of death anxiety. For instance, existential psychotherapy acknowledges that existential fear is a significant source of anxiety that can impact personal, physical, social, and spiritual existence (Yalom, 1980). According to this therapeutic approach, death anxiety may not always be obvious, but the defensive psychological structures surrounding death anxiety are often evident (Yalom, 1980). Existential psychotherapy can be applied across a range of psychological disorders (Goldner-Vukov, Moore, & Cupina, 2007; Randall, 2001; Stalsett et al., 2012), with treatment of death anxiety resulting in improved psychological functioning (Yalom, 1980).

Existential therapies have the potential to inform other therapeutic approaches in the treatment of death anxiety and psychopathology. For instance, Ottens & Hanna (1998) have recommended the integration of existential therapies with cognitive behaviour therapy (CBT), in order to strengthen the anxiety-buffering system, improve self-esteem and meaning, and treat death anxiety across a range of mental disorders. This can include the application of CBT treatment strategies, such as exposure, cognitive reappraisal, and systematic desensitisation, in order to address existential concerns and related psychopathology (Ottens & Hanna, 1998). Recent evidence with hypochondriasis has confirmed that CBT can be successfully applied as a transdiagnostic treatment for death anxiety (Furer & Walker, 2008; Hiebert et al., 2005).

Future research is needed to determine whether these well-established therapeutic approaches are associated with improvements in death anxiety and psychopathology (Furer et al., 2007; Greenberg, 2012; Iverach et al., 2014). Research is also needed to evaluate and refine currently available death anxiety assessments and inventories (Hiebert et al., 2005), for use in both clinical practice and research. This may include the development of new, multi-dimensional measures designed specifically to evaluate death anxiety as a transdiagnostic construct in relation to psychological difficulties and distress (Iverach et al., 2014).

Conclusion

In conclusion, the evidence reviewed in this chapter confirms that death anxiety underpins a range of mental disorders, and is also a key therapeutic issue (Martz, 2004; Solomon, Greenberg, & Pyszczynski, 2004). Death anxiety has the power to significantly impact everyday functioning, even when it is not in conscious awareness (Hayes et al., 2010). Given the transdiagnostic nature of death anxiety, Iverach and colleagues (2014) have argued that the following questions must be addressed in future research and clinical practice:

> … can mental disorders be successfully treated without addressing the underlying fear of death? Is it possible that death anxiety left untreated may contribute to a 'revolving door' for patients seeking treatment for mental disorders? For example, are patients with a complex history of disorders (e.g., separation anxiety disorder in childhood, obsessive–compulsive washing in late adolescence, followed by panic disorder in early adulthood) simply displaying manifestations of an underlying fear of death? If so, will successful treatment of death anxiety significantly impact the outcomes of treatment for mental disorders?'

Understanding these mechanisms will significantly improve theoretical knowledge and clinical approaches to the management of death anxiety as a transdiagnostic construct underlying psychopathology.

References

Abdollahi, A., Pyszczynski, T., Maxfield, M., & Lusyszczynska, A. (2011). Posttraumatic stress reactions as a disruption in anxiety-buffer functioning: Dissociation and responses to mortality salience as predictors of severity of post-traumatic symptoms. *Psychological Trauma: Theory, Research, Practice, and Policy, 3*, 329–341.

Alantar, Z. & Maner, F. (2008). Eating disorders in the context of attachment theory. *Anadolu Psikiyatri Dergisi, 9*, 97–104.

American Psychiatric Association (2013). *Diagnostic and statistical manual of mental disorders*, (5th ed.). Washington, DC: Author.

Arndt, J., Routledge, C., Cox, C.R., & Goldenberg, J.L. (2005). The worm at the core: A terror management perspective on the roots of psychological dysfunction. *Applied and Preventative Psychology, 11*, 191–213.

Bea, J. & Sicart, J. (1989). Separation anxieties and death anxieties. *Revista Catalana de Psicoanalisi, 6*, 11–28.

Becker, E. (1973). *The denial of death*. New York, NY: Free Press.

Brown, T.A., & Barlow, D.H. (2009). Aproposal for a dimensional classification system based on the shared features of the DSM-IV anxiety and mood disorders: Implications for assessment and treatment. *Psychological Assessment, 21*, 256–271.

Brubeck, D. & Beer, J. (1992). Depression, self-esteem, suicide ideation, death anxiety, and GPA in high school students of divorced and nondivorced parents. *Psychological Reports, 71*, 755–763.

Burke, B.L., Martens, A., & Faucher, E.H. (2010). Two decades of terror management theory: A meta-analysis of mortality salience research. *Personality and Social Psychology Review, 14*, 155–195.

Caras, G.W. (1995). The relationships among psychological separation, the quality of attachment, separation anxiety and death anxiety. *Dissertation Abstracts International, Section B: The Sciences and Engineering, 56*, 3436.

Chait, I. (1998). Terror of dying: Separation anxiety and the potential for psychic change in the psychotherapy of a 7-year-old boy. *Psycho-Analytic Psychotherapy in South Africa, 6*, 29–40.

Chatard, A., Pyszczynski, T., Arndt, J., Selimbegovic, L., Konan, P.N., & Van der Linden, M. (2012). Extent of trauma exposure and PTSD symptom severity as predictors of anxiety-buffer functioning. *Psychological Trauma: Theory, Research, Practice, and Policy, 4*, 47–55.

Cheung, M.C., Dennis, I., Easthope, Y., Werrett, J., & Farmer, S. (2005). A multiple-indicator multiple-cause model for posttraumatic stress reactions: Personality, coping, and maladjustment. *Psychosomatic Medicine. 67*, 251–259.

Coryell, W., Noyes, R., & Clancy, J. (1982). Excess mortality in panic disorder a comparison with primary unipolar depression. *JAMA Psychiatry, 39,* 701–703.

Crow, S.J., Peterson, C.B. Swanson, S.A., Raymond, N.C., Specker, S., Eckert, E.D., & Mitchell, J.E. (2009). Increased mortality in bulimia nervosa and other eating disorders. *The American Journal of Psychiatry, 166,* 1342–1346.

Dozois, D.J.A., Seeds, P.M., & Collins, K.A. (2009). Transdiagnostic approaches to the prevention of depression and anxiety. *Journal of Cognitive Psychotherapy, 23,* 44–59.

Egan, S.J., Wade, T.D., & Shafran, R. (2011). Perfectionism as a transdiagnostic process: A clinical review. *Clinical Psychology Review, 31,* 203–212.

Farber, S.K., Jackson, C.C., Tabin, J.K., & Bachar, E. (2007). Death and annihilation anxieties in anorexia nervosa, bulimia, and self-mutilation. *Psychoanalytic Psychology, 24,* 289–305.

Finch, E.C., Iverach, L., Menzies, R.G., & Jones, M. (2016). Terror mismanagement: Evidence that mortality salience exacerbates attentional bias in social anxiety. *Cognition and Emotion, 30,* 1370–1379.

Fleischer-Mann, J. (1995). Exploration of attachment-separation, fear of death and separation anxiety in agoraphobia. *Dissertation Abstracts International, Section B: The Sciences and Engineering, 56,* 2370.

Foa, E.B., Steketee, G., & Young, M.C. (1984). Agoraphobia: Phenomenological aspects, associated characteristics, and theoretical considerations. *Clinical Psychology Review, 4,* 431–457.

Furer, P., & Walker, J.R. (2008). Death anxiety: A cognitive-behavioral approach. *Journal of Cognitive Psychotherapy, 22,* 167–182.

Furer, P., Walker, J.R., Chartier, M.J., & Stein, M.B. (1997). Hypochondriacal concerns and somatization in panic disorder. *Depression and Anxiety, 6,* 78–85.

Furer, P., Walker, J.R., & Stein, M.B. (2007). *Treating health anxiety and fear of death: A practitioner's guide.* New York, NY: Springer.

Ghaemi, S.N. (2007). Feeling and time: The phenomenology of mood Disorders, depressive realism, and existential psychotherapy. *Schizophrenia Bulletin, 33,* 122–130.

Giles, A.H. (1995). Death anxiety toward self and mother in clients with anorexia nervosa. *Dissertation Abstracts International, Section B: The Sciences and Engineering, 56*, 0522.

Gilliland, J.C., & Templer, D.I. (1985). Relationship of death anxiety scale factors to subjective states. *Omega: Journal of Death and Dying, 16*, 155–167.

Goldner-Vukov, M., Moore, L. J., & Cupina, D. (2007). Bipolar disorder: From psychoeducational to existential group therapy. *Australasian Psychiatry, 15*, 30–34.

Goldenberg, J.L., Arndt, J., Hart, J., & Brown, M. (2005). Dying to be thin: The effects of mortality salience and body-mass-index on restricted eating among women. *Personality and Social Psychology Bulletin, 31*, 1400–1412.

Govender, S., Drummond, L.M., & Menzies, R.G. (2006). Danger ideation reduction therapy for the treatment of severe, chronic and resistant obsessive-compulsive disorder. *Behavioural and Cognitive Psychotherapy, 34*, 477–480.

Greenberg, J. (2012). Terror management theory: From genesis to revelations. In P. R. Shaver, & M. Mikulincer (Eds.). *Meaning, mortality, and choice: The social psychology of existential concerns* (pp. 17–35). Washington DC: American Psychological Association.

Greenberg, J., Solomon, S., Pyszczynski, T., Rosenblatt, A., Burling, J., Lyon, D., Simon, L., & Pinel, E. (1992). Assessing the terror management analysis of self-esteem: Converging evidence of an anxiety-buffering function. *Journal of Personality and Social Psychology, 63*, 913–922.

Hamama-Raz, Y., Shamir-Mahat, M., Pitcho-Prelorentzos, S., Zaken, A., David, U.Y., Menachem, B.-E., & Bergman, Y.S. (2016). The link between death anxiety and post-traumatic symptomatology during terror: Direct links and possible moderators. *Psychiatry Research, 245*, 379–386.

Hambridge, J. & Loewenthal, M. (2003). Treating obsessive-compulsive disorder: A new role for infectious diseases physicians? *International Journal of Infectious Diseases, 7*, 152–155.

Havens, L.L., & Ghaemi, S.N. (2005). Existential despair and bipolar disorder: The therapeutic alliance as a mood stabilizer. *American Journal of Psychotherapy, 59*, 137–147.

Hayes, J., Schimel, J., Arndt, J., & Faucher, E.H. (2010). A theoretical and empirical review of the death-thought accessibility concept in terror management research. *Psychological Bulletin, 136*, 699–739.

Hiebert, C., Furer, P., McPhail, C., & Walker, J.R. (2005). Death anxiety: A central feature of hypochondriasis. *Depression and Anxiety, 22*, 215–216.

Hochdorf, Z., Latzer, Y., Canetti, L., & Bachar, E. (2005). Attachment styles and attraction to death: Diversities among eating disorder patients. *American Journal of Family Therapy, 33*, 237–252.

Hussian, R.A. (1983). A combination of operant and cognitive therapy with geriatric patients. *International Journal of Behavioral Geriatrics, 1*, 57–61.

Ishiyama, F.I. (1986). Positive reinterpretation of fear of death: A Japanese (Morita) psychotherapy approach to anxiety treatment. *Psychotherapy: Theory, Research, Practice, Training, 23*, 556–562.

Iverach, L., Menzies, R.G., & Menzies, R.E. (2014). Death anxiety and its role in psychopathology: Reviewing the status of a transdiagnostic construct. *Clinical Psychology Review, 34*, 580–593.

Jones, M.K. & Menzies, R.G. (1997a). The cognitive mediation of obsessive-compulsive handwashing. *Behaviour Research and Therapy, 35*, 843–850.

Jones, M.K. & Menzies, R.G. (1997b). Danger ideation reduction therapy (DIRT): Preliminary findings with a cognitive treatment for obsessive-compulsive washers. *Behaviour Research and Therapy, 35*, 955–960.

Jones, M.K. & Menzies, R.G. (1998). Danger ideation reduction therapy (DIRT) for obsessive-compulsive washers: A controlled trial. *Behaviour Research and Therapy, 36*, 959–970.

Jones, M.K., & Menzies, R.G. (2002). Danger ideation reduction therapy. In G. Zimmar, M. Hersen, & W. Sledge (Eds.), *Encyclopedia of psychotherapy* (pp. 615–619). New York, NY: Academic Press.

Kellner, R., Abbott, P., Winslow, W.W., & Pathak, D. (1987). Fears, beliefs, and attitudes in DSM-III hypochondriasis. *Journal of Nervous and Mental Disease, 175*, 20–25.

Kesebir, P., Luszczynska, A., Pyszczynski, T., & Benight, C. (2011). Posttraumatic stress disorder involves disrupted anxiety-buffer mechanisms. *Journal of Social and Clinical Psychology, 30*, 819–841.

Khanna, N., Khanna, R., & Sharma, R.G. (1988). A study on death anxiety. *Journal of Personality and Clinical Studies, 4*, 47–51.

Kingman, R. (1928). Fears and phobias: Part II. *Welfare Magazine, 19*, 303–308.

Krochmalik, A., Jones M.K., & Menzies, R.G. (2001). Danger ideation reduction therapy (DIRT) for treatment-resistant compulsive washing. *Behaviour Research and Therapy, 39*, 897–912.

Krochmalik, A., Jones, M.K, Menzies, R.G., & Kirkby, K. (2004). The superiority of danger ideation reduction therapy (DIRT) over exposure and response prevention (ERP) in treating compulsive washing. *Behaviour Change, 21*, 251–268.

Kutlesa, N., & Arthur, N. (2008). Overcoming negative aspects of perfectionism through group treatment. *Journal of Rational-Emotive Therapy and Cognitive-Behavior Therapy, 26*, 134–150.

Le Marne, K.M., & Harris, L.M. (2017). Death anxiety, perfectionism and disordered eating. *Behaviour Change, 33*, 193–211.

Lonetto, R., & Templer, D.I. (1986). *Death anxiety.* Washington, DC: Hemisphere.

Lundh, L.G., & Ost, L.G. (2001). Attentional bias, self-consciousness and perfectionism in social phobia before and after cognitive-behaviour therapy. *Scandinavian Journal of Behaviour Therapy, 30*, 4–16.

Mahoney, A.E.J., & McEvoy, P.M. A transdiagnostic examination of intolerance of uncertainty across anxiety and depressive disorders. *Cognitive Behaviour Therapy, 41*, 212–222.

Martz, E. (2004). Death anxiety as a predictor of posttraumatic stress levels among individuals with spinal cord injuries. *Death Studies, 28*, 1–17.

Maxfield, M., John, S., & Pyszczynski, T. (2014). A terror management perspective on the role of death-related anxiety in psychological dysfunction. *The Humanistic Psychologist, 42*, 35–53.

McLaughlin, K.A., & Nolen-Hoeksema, S. (2011). Rumination as a transdiagnostic factor in depression and anxiety. *Behaviour Research and Therapy, 49*, 186–193.

Menzies, R.E., & Dar-Nimrod, I. (2017). Death anxiety and its relationship with obsessive-compulsive disorder. *Journal of Abnormal Psychology, 126*, 367–377.

Menzies, R.G., Menzies, R.E., & Iverach, L. (2015). The role of death fears in Obsessive Compulsive Disorder. *Australian Clinical Psychologist, 1*, 6–11.

Meyer, J.-E. (1975). The theme of death and the origin and course of obsessional neuroses. *Psychotherapie und Medizinische Psychologie, 25*, 124–128.

Mikulincer, M., Florian, V., Birnbaum, G., & Malishkevich, S. (2002). The death-anxiety buffering function of close relationships: Exploring the effects of separation reminders on death-thought accessibility. *Personality and Social Psychology Bulletin, 28*, 287–299.

Noyes, R., Stuart, S., Longley, S.L., Langbehn, D.R., & Happel, R.L. (2002). Hypochondriasis and fear of death. *The Journal of Nervous and Mental Disease, 190*, 503–509.

Ongider, N., & Eyuboglu, S.O. (2013). Investigation of death anxiety among depressive patients. *Journal of Clinical Psychiatry, 16*, 34–46.

Ottens, A.J., & Hanna, F.J. (1998). Cognitive and existential therapies: Toward an integration. *Psychotherapy: Theory, Research, Practice, Training, 35*, 312–324.

Perez San Gregorio, M.A., Borda Mas, M., & Blanco Picabia, A. (1995). Fear of death in blood phobia patients: A proposal and a therapeutic programme. *Analisis Y Modificacion De Conducta, 21*, 249.

Persons, J.B. (1986). Generalization of the effects of exposure treatments for phobias: A single case study. *Psychotherapy, 23*, 161–166.

Pyszczynski, T., Greenberg, J., & Solomon, S. (1999). A dual-process model of defence against conscious and unconscious death-related thoughts: An extension of terror management theory. *Psychological Review, 106*, 835–845.

Randall, E. (2001). Existential therapy of panic disorder: A single system study. *Clinical Social Work Journal, 29*, 259–267.

Routledge, C. (2012). Failure causes fear: The effect of self-esteem threat on death-anxiety. *Journal of Social Psychology, 152*, 665–669.

Safren, S.A., Gershuny, B.S., & Hendriksen, E. (2003). Symptoms of posttraumatic stress and death anxiety in persons with HIV and medication adherence difficulties. *AIDS Patient Care and STDs, 17*, 657–664.

Saggino, A. & Ronco, A. (1997). Depression, state anxiety, trait anxiety and social desirability as predictive variables for death anxiety. *Giornale Italiano di Psicologia, 24*, 629–638.

Simon, L., Arndt, J., Greenberg, J., Solomon, S., & Pyszczynski, T. (1998). Terror management and meaning: Evidence that the opportunity to defend the worldview in response to mortality salience increases the meaningfulness of life in the mildly depressed. *Journal of Personality, 66*, 359–382.

Simon, L., Greenberg, J., Harmon-Jones, E., Solomon, S., & Pyszczynski, T. (1996). Mild depression, mortality salience and defence of the worldview evidence of intensified terror management in the mildly depressed. *Personality and Social Psychology Bulletin, 22*, 81–90.

Solomon, S., Greenberg, J., & Pyszczynski, T. (2004). The cultural animal: Twenty years of terror management theory and research. In J. Greenberg,

S. L. Koole, & T. Pyszczynski (Eds.), *Handbook of experimental existential psychology* (pp. 13–34). New York, NY: Guilford.

Stalsett, G., Gude, T., Ronnestad, M.H.; & Monsen, J.T. (2012). Existential dynamic therapy ('VITA') for treatment-resistant depression with Cluster C disorder: Matched comparison to treatment as usual. *Psychotherapy Research, 22*, 579–591.

Starcevic, V. (1989). Pathological fear of death, panic attacks, and hypochondriasis. *The American Journal of Psychoanalysis, 49*, 347.

Starcevic, V. (2005). Fear of death in hypochondriasis: Bodily threat and its treatment implications. *Journal of Contemporary Psychotherapy, 35*, 227–237.

Starcevic, V. (2007). Body as the source of threat and fear of death is hypochondriasis and panic disorder. *Psihijatrija Danas, 39*, 73–82.

Strachan, E., Pyszczynski, T., Greenberg, J., & Solomon, S. (2001). Coping with the inevitability of death: Terror management and mismanagement. In C.R. Snyer (Ed.), *Coping with stress: Effective people and processes* (pp. 114–136). Oxford, England: Oxford University Press.

Strachan, E., Schimel, J., Arndt, J., Williams, T., Solomon, S., Pyszczynski, T., & Greenberg, J. (2007). Terror mismanagement: Evidence that mortality salience exacerbates phobic and compulsive behaviors. *Personality and Social Psychology Bulletin, 33*, 1137–1151.

Sumathipala, A., Siribaddana, S., Hewege, S., Sumathipala, K., Prince, M., & Mann, A. (2008). Understanding the explanatory model of the patient on their medically unexplained symptoms and its implication on treatment development research: A Sri Lanka study. *BMC Psychiatry, 8*, 54.

Templer, D.I. (1976). Two factor theory of death anxiety: A note. *Essence: Issues in the Study of Ageing, Dying, and Death, 1*, 91–93.

Templer, D.I., Harville, M., Hutton, S., Underwood, R., Tomeo, M., Russell, M., Mitroff, D., & Arikawa, H. (2001). Death Depression Scale-Revised. *Omega: Journal of Death and Dying, 44*, 105–112.

Thorson, J.A. & Powell, F.C. (2000). Death anxiety in younger and older adults. In A. Tomer (Ed.), *Death attitudes and the older adult: Theories, concepts, and applications* (pp. 123–136). New York, NY: Brunner-Routledge.

Torres, A.R. & Crepaldi, A.L. (2002). Panic disorder and hypochondriasis: A review. *Revista Brasileira de Psiquiatria, 24*, 144–151.

Walser, C.B. (1985). Death anxiety and separation anxiety in borderline and schizophrenic patients. *Dissertation Abstracts International, Section B: The Sciences and Engineering, 46,* 667.

Yalom, I.D. (1980). Existential psychotherapy. New York, NY: Basic Books.

Section 2: Treatment Approaches

Chapter 8

Death in existential psychotherapies: A critical review

Joel Vos

Existential psychotherapists seem obsessed with death, at least in the public domain. Google searches show that that there are five times more pages on death in existential therapy than in psychodynamic and cognitive behaviour therapies. This fascination with death seems to have been particularly promoted by two frequently cited publications. First, Yalom's (1980) *Existential psychotherapy* centres around four unavoidable givens that all of us have to cope with in life, which evoke anxiety and which we subsequently try to avoid or deny: death, freedom, isolation and meaninglessness. Second, Becker (1973/2007) describes in *Denial of death* how our fear and subsequent denial of death are primary motivations in life.

Both Yalom and Becker explicitly write that they derived their focus on death from existential philosophers such as Kierkegaard, Heidegger and Tillich. However, it may be argued that they have misinterpreted these philosophers (Craig, 2015). Existential philosophers are less obsessed with death, and describe our confrontation with mortality as '*one of the many ways* to open the gates to [full] existence' (Heidegger, 1927, par. 45). Fromm (1941) wrote that the core message of existential philosophers was about freedom, not death. For example, Kierkegaard (1844/1980) wanted to reveal the lack of existential freedom in his era, which was revealed in angst. This experience of angst is a broad existential phenomenon which reaches much further than only death anxiety, as there are many different types of angst which are about different parts of our existence, such as anxiety for the loss of self. Death anxiety itself is also a multi-layered phenomenon, as it could refer to the fear of not-being, physical suffering, and so on. Thus, one size does not fit all: different individuals have different existential experiences.

The existential philosophers were interested in the totality of our existence. In *Being and time*, Heidegger (1927) discussed death from the perspective of the totality our being, how we are stretched in time and space. Heidegger (1927, par. 37) refers to Dilthey who called this our 'time-play-space': the space and time between birth and death in which we can live fully and authentically, and the time and space between individuals, and the world and history in which they are embedded. Heidegger metaphorically compares this with an open space in a forest: he is interested in the openness of the space, and not only in the boundaries where the space stops and the forest starts (Wrathall, 2011). Death is one of the many components of the totality of our being.

Early existential philosophers would describe the existential-psychotherapeutic obsession with death as reductionist. By reducing death to a discrete phenomenon and defence mechanisms that we must confront, patients are being taught a reductionist mind-set which has been shown in clinical trials to be ineffective and even detrimental for some clients (cf. Vos, Craig, & Cooper, 2015). This chapter will introduce existential philosophers who laid the foundations of existential psychotherapies, followed by reductionist and nonreductionist existential psychotherapists. Finally, an integrative existential-psychotherapeutic perspective on death will be suggested, with an overview of specific competences and empirical evidence.

Seven existential-philosophical perspectives on death

Totality-of-being instead of being-an-object

Early existential philosophers and psychologists such as Heidegger, Dilthey and Jaspers shared their antipathy towards the reductionist psychologism of our inner life, including our experience of death. Heidegger described how psychologists reduced ('objectified') the totality of our subjectively lived experiences into discrete objects (Heidegger, 1913). For example, psychoanalysts in Heidegger's time seemed to reduce death to an underlying fight between psychological-emotional drives, *Thanatos* and *Eros*. Furthermore, cognitive behaviourists wrote how we fear death because of unhelpful or unrealistic ideas or behaviour. Thus death does not have inherent meaning but we give it meaning, in line with the Ancient Greek philosopher Epicurus (trans., 1994). Heidegger (1987) called this reductionism a major threat:

> the view that psychology — which turned long ago in psychoanalysis — is taken ... as a substitute for philosophy (if not for religion) ... [they are] representative of modern science which is based on the fact that the human being posits himself as an authoritative subject to whom everything which can be investigated becomes an object. (Heidegger, 1987, p. 94, 310)

Heidegger suggested that we should not reduce death to a specific physical or emotional phenomenon, but understand death from the totality of our being: the period in-between and beyond our birth and death, connected in time and space (Heidegger, 1927). Reductionist psychological approaches only describe objectified distinct phenomena ('ontic') and do not fundamentally reveal the totality and fundaments of our being ('ontology'), although death is actually about the end of our full being. In his early work, Heidegger described how our human perspective is limited by death and made possible by the totality of our existence that we have been thrown in when we were born. For instance, he uses the terms 'being-towards-death' and 'death as a possible gate to existence' to describe how our being here-and-now always refers to death. In his later work, he does not start from the perspective of humans, but from the perspective of the totality of Being; in this wider context, he shows how our personal death is part of a much larger totality (Vos, 2015). For example, he uses the metaphor of wide surroundings — heaven and earth, gods and mortals — within which individuals build houses. The walls of the house — our human limitations such as death and our uniqueness — define what is inside and outside, but seen from the perspective of the wide surroundings, the house is only temporary and the surroundings are already inside the house (Vos, 2015). Thus, Heidegger criticises psychologists who focus on death as a specific experience which we can objectify in psychological laboratories or psychotherapies.

Being instead of objectivity

Dilthey (1887/2010) wanted to understand life from the perspective of life itself, and not explain it from the distant perspective of a researcher or therapist: what do my experiences here-and-now tell about my total life and the world in which I am embedded? Death is not like other phenomena: it is not an object that we as subjects relate to, it is the end of being-a-subject, and as such death is always there in our experiences as we live-until-death (Heidegger, 1927). Death differs from other biological or psychological phenomena, as death is 'the highest court' where we can be judged (Heidegger, 1927, p. 230) and 'one possible authentic existential interpretation' giving entrance to the subjective totality of our being (Heidegger, 1927, par. 45). Thus, we cannot speak about death in mere objective or subjective terms, but should transcend this subject-object distinction.

Phenomenology instead of psychotherapeutic models

How can we transcend the subject-object distinction and understand death from the perspective of the totality of Being? The early existential philosophers developed a phenomenological method, which tries to let the phenomena reveal themselves instead of us objectively explaining what they are. Husserl and Heidegger developed three phenomenological steps (Spinelli, 2005). First, we need to temporarily set aside our usual approach to our being ('bracketing'), such as stopping to objectify death. Second, phenomenologists try to describe and not explain their experiences (Dilthey, 1887/2010). They try to perceive the situation neutrally with all senses, and not only in theoretical-intellectual ways. What do you feel? What do you see? What is actually there? Third, phenomenologists avoid placing any *initial* hierarchies of significance or importance upon the items of description. That is, they initially treat all experiences as having equal value or significance. For example, before psychotherapists meet clients, they should not assume that death must be an important topic for this individual. Therefore, phenomenological-existential psychotherapists such as Binswanger and Boss, tried to avoid building psychological models and instead focused on phenomenological analyses of their client's lived experiences.

Realism instead of naïve heroism

In our daily life, we often do not have an authentic perspective on the totality of life and death. We are 'first and foremost fallen' to an inauthentic and incomplete approach of our self and death (Heidegger, 1927). This means for instance that we run away, deny and avoid the experience of our being, rationalise, objectify, or follow fashionable opinions. For Heidegger, inauthenticity is a given part of life, as authentically facing our totality requires a courageous decision, and not everyone is always able to 'stare at the sun' (Yalom, 2008). Similarly, existential psychotherapists such as Van Deurzen acknowledge the struggles of life: we cannot always approach life and death as an archetypical hero (Vos, 2015).

In contrast, later existential-philosophers such as Sartre (1958) denounced denial of death as 'bad faith'. Similarly, existential-humanistic psychotherapists such as Yalom are negative about individuals denying the totality of being, and demand a more heroic approach. Their psychotherapy focuses on addressing our resistances, and embracing what we fear. They put a pressure on 'turning tragedy into triumph', that is finding meaning despite adversity (Frankl,1946/1986). They describe the confrontation and denial of death as an inherently positive — albeit challenging — experience, which can even be the source of culture and civilisation (Becker, 1973). Life means being responsible in finding the right answer to its problems and fulfil the tasks which it constantly sets for each individual (Frankl, 1946/1986). For example, Frankl's work has been used extensively in short psychotherapeutic interventions in individuals with chronic or life-threatening physical diseases, as quick pragmatic answers to their confrontation with their vulnerability and mortality (Vos, 2016b). By the end of the 20th century, this positive existential-psychotherapeutic attitude towards death contributed to the emergence of the positive psychology movement, which has been criticised for the 'tyranny' of positivity, and the lack of balance between positive and negative life-experiences (Held, 2004; Kashdan & Biswas-Diener, 2014; Wong, 2015). Clinical trials confirm that existential-psychotherapies which put a one-sided focus on heroically and/or positively confronting death — regardless of the strength and readiness of the person- are ineffective or even lead to worse mental health such as psychosis (Vos et al., 2015).

Many ways lead to the gate of full existence

Individuals can suddenly experience a call of their existential conscience, calling them back to the totality of their being and appeal to become authentic (Heidegger, 1927, par. 45). Many ways can lead to the 'gate of full existence', of which death may be the most poignant. For example, the existential-psychiatrist Jaspers (1922/2013) wrote that there is an unlimited number of 'boundary situations' — such as suffering, fate, guilt — in which we can become 'enlightened in our existence'. Frankl described the 'tragic triad' of guilt, suffering and death (Lukas, 1990). Tillich (1952) mentioned three types of existential anxiety, relating to fate and death, guilt and condemnation, meaninglessness and emptiness. Yalom mixed these authors when he developed his fourfold of death-freedom-isolation-meaninglessness. Finally, Bugental and Sterling (1995) addressed the sextet of finiteness, potential-to-act, choice, embodiment, awareness and separateness. However, the identification and categorisation of such discrete life-enlightening situations seem inconsistent with the Sartrian adage that 'existence precedes essence', that is: the totality of our subjective lived experience can never be perfectly categorised. Furthermore, ontic and ontological dimensions seem inaccurately mixed in some of these descriptions (Craig, 2015).

From a phenomenological perspective, each individual can become aware of the totality of their being in their own unique life situations (cf. Spinelli, 2005). Furthermore, Heidegger (1927) described that existence is revealed differently in different eras: every era has a different existential mood ('*Grundstimmung*'). Death anxiety was the mood of the interbellum in the 30s, while the post-WWII period may have been dominated by boredom. Our era may be determined by a different mood, which can only be revealed by personal phenomenological analyses and which may not be universally predefined.

Existential Copernican revolution
Reductionist psychologists seem to focus on what individuals say and do about death, but existential-philosophers focus on what death tells about us: death opens the gate to existence (Heidegger, 1913). For example facing the death of a loved one or our mortality could make us aware that we are physical beings, thrown into existence, unique and part of larger personal, social, physical and spiritual worlds (Van Deurzen-Smith, 1998; Heidegger, 1927).

Death can also make us aware of the paradoxes of life. Jaspers (1922/2013, p. 229, my trans.) wrote that in boundary situations, our worldview and intentions fail, and we feel like a failing existence: 'there is nothing stable, no undoubtable absolute, no stop, which can hold every thinking. Everything flows, is in movement of continuous questioning, everything is relative, finite, split in paradoxes, and never the totality, the absolute and essential'. We learn from such specific moments that life is fundamentally characterised by failing and being-limited: 'with everything we want, there is a not-wanting, an anti-wanting; our self and the world are antinomically split and against each other'.

Death reminds us that our being inherently harbours a nothing-ness: our decisions are limited, our options, our situation, and our social relationships (Heidegger, 1927; Sartre, 1943). Despite these limitations, we have to make decisions and live our daily life. How do we cope with such paradoxes between our life drive and death drive (Rank, 1959/2004)? How do we cope with losing our desire for autonomy and independence when we are sick and dying (May, 1981)? Existential-psychotherapists help clients with such paradoxes, to live a meaningful life in spite of everything (Vos, 2015).

Freedom

The confrontation with death is 'two-edged, demanding and creating': at the moment when we feel that our stability falls away and we become aware of our limitations, we can also become aware of our Kierkegaardian freedom (Jaspers, 1922/2013, p. 231). We can become aware of the spaciousness and temporality of our time-play-space (Dilthey, 1887/2010), understanding that being-there is being-in-possibilities (Heidegger, 1927). That is, we learn that life situations can change, we can change, and we are able of using our opportunities responsibly and authentically. We may be unable to change the situation — for example, at our deathbed — but we can still change our inner attitude towards the situation. Meaning-centred psychotherapists have developed many ways to help clients experience the freedom to live a meaningful life despite their struggles, albeit that this freedom is always limited and our decisions are imperfect as life inherently harbours a nothingness (Vos, 2018).

Reductionist existential-psychotherapies

Foundations

The terror of WWII seemed to have led to different approaches in Europe and America. While postwar Europe was characterised by relatively complex and dark existential-philosophies, America showed a more positive approach. Influenced by the human potential movement, death was seen as a possibility to realise our potential (Maslow, 1968). Humans are not only living-towards-death or a Freudian *Thanatos* (Jones, 1953), but living-towards-self-congruence (Rogers, 1959). For example, many retreats were organised in the 1970s, in which clients were asked to visualise and act-as-if they were dying, with the intention to help them embrace their finitude and live life to the largest potential. Thus, the complexity of death in our life became reduced to a potential-to-prosper.

These American existential-psychotherapies were strongly influenced by humanistic theologians and psychologists, such as Tillich, Fromm, Becker, Rogers and May. Tillich followed the existential philosophy of Heidegger, and elaborated existential anxiety particularly in the spiritual domain (Chi, 2013). He wrote how our mortality confronts us with our ontic self-affirmation, feelings of condemnation and guilt, emptiness and meaninglessness. We need to have the heroic courage to no longer rely on others telling what will become of us when we die, but seek answers inside ourselves: 'the courage to be is the courage to accept oneself as accepted in spite of being unaccepted' (Tillich, 1952, p. 164). Becker (1973) describes how managing the terror of death could even be a source of creativity and culture. Like Jaspers (1919) already wrote, worldviews and culture can emerge as a way to cope with our anxiety and sense of failure in boundary situations. That is, the confrontation with death can evoke a terrifying fear of annihilation as we desire for self-preservation, and also a fear of the inevitability of death as we become cognitively aware of our mortality (Becker, 1967). We cannot always focus on death as we would be mortified, and therefore we cope via rationalisation (e.g., telling oneself 'death is far away'), repression (denial and avoidance) and identification (submerge in something meaningful such as family, culture, country or religion). Thus we build worldviews in defence of existential anxiety. This Terror Management Theory has been extensively empirically validated (Greenberg, Koole, & Pyzscinksi, 2004).

This existential-humanist approach contrasts Heidegger (1977) who criticised the focus on worldviews, as this focus shifts the attention from the totality, dynamics and temporality of our being (ontology) to fixed objectified views (ontic): they reveal our being only as a mere function of coping-with-death (Goldberg, 2012). Jaspers wrote in 1919, that therapists should not focus on explaining how clients develop fixated and partial worldviews (ontic; '*Weltbild*'), but help them to phenomenologically and dynamically perceive their total being (ontology; '*Weltanschauung*').

Existential-Humanistic-Psychotherapy 1.0
EHP helps clients to become more present and more fully and subjectively alive (Schneider & Krug, 2010). Our attempt to self-realisation is often blocked or resisted by our anxiety, which is usually unconscious (Cooper, 2017). Yalom

(1980) and other EHP therapists combined the Terror Management Theory with the psychodynamic theory of defence mechanisms: we defend ourselves existentially against the terror evoked by life's inevitable givens. These defence mechanisms can stop us from fully functioning. Clients are stimulated to overcome their resistances to life, particularly death anxiety. This 'unpeeling' of resistances (Bugental, 1987) may lead to feelings of guilt, pain, shame, dread or futility. Instead of fleeing from such feelings — like we are inclined to -, EHP suggests clients to stay with these feelings, and learn to tolerate. This is particularly achieved by focusing on what clients experience in the here-and-now and invoking what is 'palpably relevant or charged' (Schneider & Krug, 2010, p. 114). Therapeutic techniques consist of questions about the experiential processes in the here-and-now, staying with feelings, self-expression and free association, identifying and visualising emotions and fostering trust in the ability to bear negative feelings (Cooper, 2017). Similar to stimulating clients to be authentically present, EHP therapists aim to be authentically present for their clients.

Existential-humanistic psychotherapists stimulate clients to confront their ultimate concerns, particularly their mortality which they identify as one of the most prominent causes of resistance to life. The rationale is that these confrontations may help clients overcome their resistances, take their responsibility to live life to the full in the here-and-now, and become more fully present and alive. However, 'death concerns are not conscious to most individuals but must be inferred by disguised manifestations' (Yalom, 2008, p. 78). The fear of death (ontologic anxiety) may be traced in many specific situations and experiences (ontic anxiety), for instance underlying more specific phobias; for example, a client fearing to cross bridges may actually be afraid of crossing death (Wolfe, 2008). Yalom (1980) also describes how our beliefs in our specialness or ultimate rescuer could be denial of death, and May (1969) mentions how others may deny death by focusing on their youth, vitality, or productivity at work or sex and offspring. Thus, existential-humanistic psychotherapists interpret their client's resistance, and try to identify underlying existential anxieties. Clients develop insight in their defence mechanisms and try to face their anxiety. Yalom (1980) describes several exercises to identify death anxiety, such as writing your own obituary or epitaph, visualising your own death, or drawing a line representing your life from birth to death and putting a cross where you are now. This approach has been described as relatively directive and pragmatic, and risking imposing interpretations on clients (Craig, 2015).

Meaning-Centred Psychotherapy & Positive Psychology 1.0

In 1946, Frankl published *Saying yes to life in spite of everything*, which became later known as *Man's search for meaning* (1946/1986). This described his experiences in concentration camps, where individuals were confronted with the tragic triad but were still able to experience meaning. Those who were able to experience meaning-in-spite-of-everything were able to survive, whilst others who lost hope and faith demised. In line with Jaspers (1922/2013), Frankl called this ability 'transcendence': reaching beyond the limitations and finitude of their life situation to 'what can be' and 'what ought to be', and thus transcending our limitations in space and time, accepting our freedom to decide, and developing a larger, more authentic and meaningful perspective on life (Vos, 2016a). The inmate's psychological reactions were not solely the result of their life situation, but also of their freedom to modulate their inner attitude, for example by deciding not to despair but to focus on something more meaningful that transcends the situation, such as connecting with fellow-inmates or having faith.

Frankl's work was based on three central pillars: the assumption that all individuals have an inner striving towards meaning ('will to meaning'), that everyone is always free to take a stance towards any conditions in life ('freedom of will'), and that every situation has the potential of being meaningful (Vos, 2015). The aim of logo-therapy and existential-analysis was to 'turn tragedy into triumph', to help individuals live a meaningful life — via the three main ways — despite life's limitations and finitude. Frankl believed that individuals can always discover meaning by exploring their experiences, being productive-creative and having meaningful-attitudes. Frankl's practices focused on modulation of attitudes (having more beneficial attitudes towards life's challenges), de-reflection (focusing on experiencing instead of intellectualising) and paradoxical intention (breaking the cycle of anxiety by exaggerating and engaging in the feared situation).

Logo-therapists and existential-analysts have been accused of reductionism, authoritarian overtones, pre-set assumptions about meaning, and imposing their worldview on clients (May, 1978; Yalom, 1980). For example, they seem to assume that life is good and that despite the terror of death, meaning can always be found (Cooper, 2017). From the perspective of Sartre (1958) and Camus (1955) it may be argued that logo-therapy stimulates bad faith, as its focus on meaning may avoid or soften the existential terror caused by the absurdity and meaninglessness of life. Van Deurzen (2001) questioned whether such directive therapy can be called existentialist at all.

Nonreductionist existential psychotherapies

Philosophy

Nonreductionist existential psychotherapists often orientate explicitly at Heidegger's approach of death, as described above, and particularly at the phenomenological method. These therapies aim at uncovering how clients relate to the totality and dynamics of being, and help them live a meaningful and authentic life while embracing the finitude, paradoxes and uncertainties of life.

Daseinsanalysis

Binswanger and Boss applied Heidegger's methodology to clients (Cohn, 2002). Daseinsanalysts aim to help clients open up to the totality of their being, and live a more authentic life. The basic attitude is one of let-it-be-ness ('*Gelassenheit*'), which means trying not to impose our ideas and expectations on our experiences, but being open for what phenomenologically reveals itself in our experiences (Vos, 2018): perceiving, not explaining (Condrau, 1988). Boss's classical Daseinsanalysis follows a phenomenological approach and thus focuses on the totality of the client's lived experiences. Finitude may come up as a relevant theme for some clients, but this is only described as part of how they relate to the totality, dynamics and possibilities of Being. In contrast, other Daseinanalysts, such as Holzhey-Kunz (2014), more strongly emphasise our psychological suffering and mortality.

Daseinsanalysts borrow techniques from psychoanalysis, such as free association and dream analyses, which help therapists and clients to stay open to the totality of their clients' being-in-the-world: 'to enable the client to unfold all his world-disclosing possibilities of relating toward the particular beings which he encounters' (Boss, 1963, p. 253). They assume that psychological problems and psychopathology show how individuals are closed to parts of their world, by privation, blocking or constriction of their potentiality (Boss, 1988). Daseinsanalysts try to bracket their assumptions and not objectify therapeutic relationships, but be authentic and nondirective, and focus at creating a supportive space in which clients feel free to explore and accept all experiences. Daseinsanalysts do not replace the responsibility of their clients (Heidegger called this 'leaping in') but anticipate and give insight to their client's potential ('leaping ahead'). However, the practices of Daseinsanalysts have been criticised for too conservatively following Heidegger and being reductionist in their interpretations.

Phenomenological-existential approaches

By the end of the 20th century, a diverse group of psychotherapists in the United Kingdom, such as Van Deurzen-Smith (1988) and Spinelli (1997), developed an existential psychotherapeutic approach centring around a descriptive nondiagnostic exploration of clients' lives and experiences, with an emphasis on the therapeutic relationship (Cooper, 2017). This approach was strongly influenced by Heidegger (Spinelli, 1996) and in line with constructivist and narrative-psychotherapeutic approaches (Neimeyer, Burke, Mackay, & van Dyke Stringer, 2010).

For Spinelli, the psychotherapeutic attitude of un-knowing ('phenomenological bracketing') is particularly important, to be able to tap into the stream of experiencing and 'worlding' of clients. In line with Heidegger (1927), he describes how our being is related to others and the world around us. Our world is inherently characterised by change, uncertainty and anxiety. We often create reflective reductionist 'worldviews' to structure these experiences. Spinelli (2005) does not follow the reductionist existential-psychotherapeutic obsession with death: he has no specific demands of clients to face a pre-given range of ultimate givens or unravel their existential defence mechanisms. The aim of therapy is to 'clarify descriptively that which the client experiences as disruptive to the continuity of the worldview so that its sedimentations and dissociations can be explored inter-relationally' (2005, p. 87). Thus unlike Jaspers, Spinelli does not break open the clients' ontic worldviews to help them understand the totality of being, but he focuses on the worldview as it is currently being-lived. Via an in-depth relational approach, Spinelli helps clients to understand their worldview and their lived experiences, and how this worldview may have led to dilemmas and difficulties.

Similarly, Van Deurzen does not specifically focus on ultimate concerns such as death, but is interested in the general difficulties, limitations, ambiguities and uncertainties that individuals may experience in everyday life. We do not need confrontations with the death of our loved ones or our own mortality to understand existence: our daily life gives many examples of the fundamental Jaspersian paradoxical nature of life. Van Deurzen phenomenologically stays with the client's descriptions of daily life, and if the theme of death arises she explores this, but she would not assume or impose the theme of death on clients. Similar to her mentor Henry (1973), Van Deurzen seems to assume that life perpetually oscillates between suffering and joy. She writes that 'life is an endless struggle where moments of ease and blissful happiness are the exception rather than rule', and reaching heaven-on-earth is unlikely (Van Deurzen, 2015, p. 181). She agrees with Jaspers that the positive intentions of individuals are inevitably confronted with injustices, paradoxes and failures in endless numbers of boundary situations. Individuals often find it difficult to accept the reality that life is an endless struggle, for instance by fantasising about a perfect and problem-free life. Such unrealistic expectations lead to frustration and more suffering, as these expectations will inevitably fail in daily life (Van Deurzen & Adams, 2011/2016). In the role of an empathic and nondirective mentor and fellow-human-being, Van Deurzen helps clients to embrace the totality of being and wake up from self-deception, and in this process realise that they may be stronger than they may think. This helps clients to move beyond a fear of life, discover life's potentiality and experience life as worth living.

Van Deurzen asks descriptive-phenomenological questions such as 'could you tell me more about your experience' and 'what does this mean for you'? These questions aim at clarifying how clients understand the totality of being. Based on the work of Heidegger and Binswanger, she suggests four interlinked dimensions of existence which can be systematically explored with clients (Van Deurzen & Arnold-Baker, 2005). She identifies a physical world of things ('*Umwelt*'), social world ('*Mitwelt*'), Personal world ('*Eigenwelt*') and Spiritual world ('*Uberwelt*'). For example, the experience of death and mortality can be examined from the perspective of each of these worlds. These four dimensions largely overlap with the fundamental motivations of meaning-centered therapist Längle (2007). Vos (2016b) empirically confirmed this categorisation in his systematic literature review of 109 studies in more than 45,000 individuals worldwide about what they experience as meaningful, valuable or important in life: materialist-hedonic, self-oriented, social, larger and existential-philosophical meanings. The meanings that individuals experience in each world are inevitably confronted by tensions and paradoxes. While facing paradoxes — such as living-towards-death — in each different world of meanings, Van Deurzen helps clients to identify what is really important and meaningful.

Existential-Humanistic Psychotherapy 2.0

Within the American humanistic-existential school, psychotherapists such as Bugental, Schneider, and Hoffman developed a nonreductionist approach (Schneider & Krug, 2010). Instead of explaining existential defence mechanisms and stimulating clients to face life's ultimate givens, they stimulate clients to use their human potential to rediscover *awe* in their lives: humility and wonder, thrill and anxiety, towards the totality and mystery of being (Schneider & Krug, 2010). They aim at 'setting people free', not by focusing on their limitations but by embracing their full range of experiences (Schneider, 2008). This approach is less psychodynamic than Yalom, integrates techniques from other psychotherapeutic approaches, is more client-centred (Rogers, 1959) and uses focusing techniques that help clients to embrace their experiences in the here-and-now ('felt-sense'; Gendlin, 1996).

Meaning-centred and positive psychotherapy 2.0

Many modern logo-therapists and existential-analysts, such as Wong, Ivtzan, and Vos, have developed less reductionist versions of meaning-centred and positive psychotherapies (Vos, 2018; Ivtzan, Lomas, Hefferon, & Worth, 2015; Wong, 2015). Meaning is not imposed or assumed, but revealed by phenomenologically and systematically analysing the client's experiences, for instance via Socratic dialogues, similarly to Van Deurzen's worlds (Vos, 2018). Meaning is also regarded as only one aspect of the broad range of existential experiences about life (Wong, 2015). Wong pleas for an integration of positive and existential psychotherapies into an 'existential positive psychology', to bring out the best in individuals in spite of and because of the dark side of human existence (Wong, 2015).

Thus experiences of death and existential anxiety are explored and embraced, while experiences of meaningfulness are not regarded as a definitive answer or solution to this. Meaning-centred therapists focus on how to live with life's paradoxes and embrace life in its totality, including its triumphs and tragedies (Vos, 2016a). Paradoxes are inherent to life: 'there is no joy of life without despair' (Camus, 1968, p. 56) and 'the ultimate paradox is that negation becomes affirmation' (May, 1981, p. 164). Awareness of death is essential to meaningful living, and personal awareness of death can contribute to personal transformation (e.g., Bretherton & Ørner, 2004; Schneider & Krug, 2010; Vos, 2018). Furthermore, the focus is not only on the stimulation of individual meaning and happiness, but on the position of the individual towards human kind (Wong, 2015).

Based on the works of Heidegger and Frankl, and mimicking Van Deurzen's assumption that life is an endless struggle, Vos (2018) summarises the meaning-centred psychotherapeutic aims as living a meaningful and satisfying life despite life's struggles, including our mortality. This means that the reality and irreducibility of death is acknowledged, and that meaning is not regarded as an answer to death but as an independent answer parallel to embracing the dread of death (Vos, 2018). 'This treatment will not change [or get rid of] your [psychological problems, physical limitations, your finitude], or totally reduce the pain you feel. This treatment will also not expect you to fight like a hero, because I do not want you to be like a Don Quixote, fighting against the unfightable. However, what this treatment can help you with, is to live a meaningful and satisfying life despite your [problems]. Some patients say that this helps them to deal better with their [suffering], and they feel better able to distance themselves from their pain and other limitations. Many clients find this message relieving as I recognise the reality that their fight to the unchangeable is not helpful. They often tell that friends, family and doctors expect them to fight like an archetypic hero' (Vos, 2018, chapter 11). With such a dual attitude, clients will not arrive at reductionist inauthentic 'meanings' (the Anglo Saxon term 'meaning' is etymologically derived from the reductionist term '*Meinung*') but at authentic perceiving (in non-English languages the term '*Sinn*' is used instead of 'meaning', which is derived from the Latin '*sentire*', and which means 'perceiving with all senses' and is linked to a phenomenological understanding of the totality of being; Vos, 2018, Chapter 1).

Thus, death anxiety and death acceptance co-exist according to these meaning-centred psychotherapists (cf. Wong's Dual-Systems-Model, 2012; Death Attitude Profile in Wong, Reker, & Gesser, 1994). Vos (2018) calls this a 'dual attitude', an attitude which simultaneously accepts existential paradoxes, such as meaning in life for sceptics, and experiencing meaning in the face of life's limits. Instead of reducing one side of the duality to the other side (e.g., be totally sceptical about the ability to live a meaningful life in the face of death, or focusing rigidly on meaning and denying death), both life's positive and negative sides are simultaneously accepted. This assumes the tolerance for discomfort that may arise from existential paradoxes. Different explanations have been given for how individuals can have a dual attitude, such as switching or quickly oscillating between two sides, or seeing one side as background and the other as foreground in the attention (Vos, 2018). Clients can learn to embrace the dark side by becoming wiser through synthesis of opposites, becoming more flexible and balanced, appreciating contrast-effects, becoming stronger and more spiritual through self-transcendence, and having a mindset focusing on meaning as independent from success or failure (Wong, 2015). Ivtzan, Lomas, Hefferon & Worth (2015) have identified different ways of restoring and maintaining the duality, such as appraisal and the principles of co-valence and complementarity. This dual attitude may help them to live a meaningful and satisfying life in the face of adversity such as death (Vos, 2016a).

Integration, competences and empirical evidence

Thus, existential philosophy seems to have emerged as a response to reductionist approaches in philosophy and psychology. As part of this existential-philosophical movement, some philosophers thematised death, as they regarded this as a prominent gate to understanding the totality of Being. Similarly, some psychotherapists also primarily focused on death, and they stimulated clients to face death, death anxiety and denial. This death-anxiety-defence-model may indeed be relevant for some — although not necessarily all — clients, as empirical studies confirm (Greenberg et al., 2004). However, it is reductionist to assume that all clients in all life situations can and should heroically embrace being in its totality and death in more particular, and that psychological problems can always be interpreted as death denial. To examine whether death and/or other (existential) topics are relevant for individuals, psychotherapists may use phenomenological and client-centred methods.

This chapter described how the field of existential-psychotherapy showed some reductionist tendencies in the past, but seems to be turning towards more nonreductionist and integrative approaches. What would an integrative-existential approach to death look like? This would most likely consist of phenomenological client-centred methods, combined with a large therapeutic toolkit. Vos (2016a, 2018) has suggested how psychotherapeutic integration could happen at different levels. At a macro-level, the client and therapist explore what the general needs and skills of the client are. These explorations happen relationally at an equal level, like mentor-mentee, with a strong focus on psycho-education, and transparency about the different psychotherapeutic possibilities. When an informed shared decision has been made, the therapist could select a specific approach or treatment manual. For example, if the client needs and desires a confrontational approach, an existentialist-humanistic approach may be applied. If clients do not know how to live a meaningful life in the face of life's finitude, meaning-centred support may be offered. Regardless of which approach is selected, the existential-psychotherapists will be phenomenologically sensitive to the subjectively lived micro-experiences of clients in daily life, and not impose their views or meanings.

Integrative-existential psychotherapists could systematically explore how death creates tensions and paradoxes in each of the different Van Deurzian worlds, Langlian fundamental motivations, or Vossian types of meaning. For example, psychotherapists could explore how death challenges material-hedonic, self-oriented, social, higher or existential-philosophical meanings (Vos, 2016a, 2106b). For example, when I become aware of my finitude, I start to realise that I will not able to enjoy health in the same way anymore as I do now. I acknowledge that my drive towards self-development will be limited by my physical vulnerability. I may feel isolated from my loved ones as I need to undergo this existential process of dying on my own, although this may also stimulate me to have more authentic relationships and leave a positive social legacy. My death could also create an existential urgency, motivating me to commit myself to larger purposes in my life, contribute to a more just world, or turn towards religion. I may also become aware of the existential nature of my life, such as my uniqueness and freedom. In each world, I will need to cope with the tensions between the existential reality of my mortality and my desires, expectations or fundamental assumptions about living in an understandable, controllable and benevolent world (Janoff-Bulman, 1992).

Practically, this integrative-existential approach assumes that psychotherapists have a broad toolkit of many psychotherapeutic competenceis. Vos (2016a, 2018) describes a pluralistic approach to meaning-centred psychotherapy, which integrates 39 psychotherapeutic skills that he grouped as assessment, meaning-specific, relational, existential, phenomenological, mindfulness and experiential psychotherapeutic competences. These skills have been identified as the common denominator of all evidence-based meaning-centred therapies. Furthermore, the effectiveness of each of these skills are supported by systematic empirical evidence (Vos, 2016a, 2018). Over the years, meaning-centred psychotherapists have developed a wide range of practical psychotherapeutic exercises, helping clients to live a meaningful life despite their confrontation with life's struggles and finitude (see an overview; Vos, 2018).

This integrative-existential approach seems to be supported by clinical trials. A systematic review and meta-analyses of all existential therapies show that nonreductionist meaning-centred therapies have large significant effect sizes on psychological well-being and quality-of-life, while reductionist existentialist-humanistic approaches have small or nonsignificant effect sizes (Vos et al., 2015). There are no trials on Daseinsanalysis, and there is one promising trial on phenomenological-existential psychotherapy. Unpublished moderator-analyses showed that existential psychotherapies were more effective when these did not merely address existential givens such as death but simultaneously addressed how individuals experience meaning-despite-life's-challenges. This means that, in line with Becker's (1973) hypotheses, death should be addressed simultaneously with its defence mechanisms of creating a meaningful worldview. Clients should be taught how to experience meaning-in-spite-of-everything (Frankl, 1946/1986). Confronting death without allowing (defensive) meaning-making could lead to nonsignificant or even negative effects.

A follow-up meta-analysis on all 60 clinical trials on meaning-centred therapies confirmed that meaning-centred psychotherapies have large effects on psychological well-being and quality-of-life, even larger than control-groups and the dodo-bird-effect which claims that all therapies have modest effects thanks to common therapy factors (Vos & Vitali, 2018). Moderator-analyses showed that the less reductionist meaning-centred psychotherapies were, the more effective they became. That is, meaning-centred practices had larger effects when these did not include religious-spiritual formulations, were structured, explicitly stimulated clients to set and experiment with achievable goals in daily life, used mindfulness exercises, explicitly discussed one type-of-meaning/world per session, addressed self-worth, discussed existential limitations such as death, mentioned the coherence of time, focused on creating a positive therapeutic relationship, and systematically addressed the large possible number of meanings in different Van Deurzian/Langlian/Vossian worlds.

These empirical studies seem to confirm the psychological importance of not reducing the totality of our being to only-death or only-meaning. The core question is how clients can live a meaningful and satisfying life within their limited lifetime, without denying these limitations. Each individual may be confronted at different times with different limitations in their existence, which may not be restricted to death anxiety, but also boredom or other fundamental moods. Existential-psychotherapists can phenomenologically unpeel the lived experiences of each individual, and identify the possible relevance of death and other existential givens for their clients.

References

Becker, E. (1973/2007). *The denial of death*. New York, NY: Simon and Schuster.

Boss, M. (1963). *Psychoanalysis and daseinsanalysis*. New York, NY: Basic Books.

Boss, M. (1988). Martin Heidegger's Zollikon Seminars. *Review of Existential Psychology and Psychiatry, 16,* 7–20.

Bretherton, R. & Ørner, R.J. (2004). Positive Psychology and Psychotherapy: An Existential Approach. In P.A. Linley & S. Joseph, *Positive psychology in practice*. New York, NY: Wiley.

Bugental, J.F.T (1987). *The art of the psychotherapist*. New York, NY: Norton.

Bugental, J.F., & Sterling, M.M. (1995). *Existential-humanistic psychotherapy: New perspectives*. London, England: Guilford.

Camus, A. (1955). *The myth of Sisyphus, and other essays*. Paris, France: Vintage.

Camus, A. (1968). *Lyrical and critical essays*. Paris, France: Vintage.

Chi, S.W. (2013). *The Heideggerian legacy in Paul Tillich's ontology and theological anthropology* (Doctoral dissertation), Boston University.

Cohn, H.W. (2002). *Heidegger and the roots of existential therapy*. London, England: SPC.

Condrau, G. (1988). A seminar on daseinsanalytic psychotherapy. *The Humanistic Psychologist, 16*(1), 101.

Cooper, M. (2017). *Existential therapies* (2nd ed.). London, England: SAGE.

Craig, E. (2015). The lost language of being: Ontology's perilous destiny in existential psychotherapy. *Philosophy, Psychiatry, & Psychology, 22*(2), 79–92.

Dilthey, W. (2010). *Understanding the human world* (Vol. 2). Princeton, NJ: University Press. (Original work published 1887)

Epicurus. (1994). *The Epicurus reader: Selected writings and testimonia*. Cambridge, MA: Hackett.

Frankl, V. E. (1946/1986). *Man's search for meaning*. New York, NY: Washington Square Press.

Fromm, E. (1941). *Escape from freedom*. New York, NY: Avon.

Gendlin, E. (1996). *Focusing-orientated psychotherapy*. London, England: Guildford.

Goldberg, S. (2012). Epistemic extendedness, testimony, and the epistemology of instrument-based belief. *Philosophical Explorations, 15*, 181–198.

Greenberg, J., Koole, S.L., & Pyszczynski, T.A. (Eds.). (2004). *Handbook of experimental existential psychology.* London, England: Guilford Press.

Heidegger, M. (1913). *The doctrine of judgment in psychologism,* GA1. Frankfurt, Germany: Klostermann.

Heidegger, M. (1927). *Sein und zeit.* Frankfurt, Germany: Klostermann.

Heidegger, M. (1977). *Holzwege,* Vol. 5. Frankfurt, Germany: Klostermann.

Heidegger, M. (1987). *Zollikon seminars: Protocols, conversations, letters.* Evanston, IL: Northwestern University Press.

Held, B.S. (2004). The negative side of positive psychology. *Journal of Humanistic Psychology, 44*(1), 9–46.

Henry, M. (1973). *The essence of manifestation.* The Hague: Martinus Nijhoff.

Holzhey-Kunz, A. (2014). *Daseinsanalyse: der existenzphilosophische Blick auf seelisches Leiden und seine Therapie.* Vienna: Facultas-WUV.

Ivtzan, I., Lomas, T., Hefferon, K., & Worth, P. (2015). *Second wave positive psychology: Embracing the dark side of life.* New York, NY: Routledge.

Jaspers, K. (1919). *Psychologie der Weltanschauungen,* GA17. Frankfurt, Germany: Klostermann.

Jaspers, K. (2013). *Allgemeine psychopathologie.* Berlin, Germany: Springer-Verlag. (Original work published 1922)

Kashdan, T., & Biswas-Diener, R. (2014). *The upside of your dark side: Why being your whole self — not just your 'good' self — drives success and fulfillment.* New York, NY: Penguin.

Kierkegaard, S. (1980). *The concept of anxiety* (Trans.). Princeton, NJ: Princeton University Press. (Original work published 1844)

Längle, A. (2007). The search for meaning in life and the existential fundamental motivations. *International Journal of Existential Psychology and Psychotherapy, 1*(1), 2–14.

Lukas, E. (1990). Overcoming the 'tragic triad'. *International Forum for Logotherapy, 13*(2), 89–96.

May, R. (1969). *Love and will.* New York, NY: W.W. Norton

May, R. (1978). Response to Bulka's article. *Journal of Humanistic Psychology, 18*(4), 55–55.

May, R. (1981). *Freedom and destiny.* London, England: Norton.

Maslow, A.H. (1968). *Toward a psychology of being.* New York, NY: Van Nostrand.

Neimeyer, R.A., Burke, L.A., Mackay, M.M., & van Dyke Stringer, J.G. (2010). Grief therapy and the reconstruction of meaning: From principles to practice. *Journal of Contemporary Psychotherapy, 40*(2), 73–83.

Rank, O. (2004). *The myth of the birth of the hero, and other writings.* London, England: Random House. (Original work published 1959)

Rogers, C. (1959) *A theory of therapy, personality, and interpersonal relationships: As developed in the client-centered framework.* New York, NY: McGraw-Hill.

Sartre, J.P. (1958). *Being and nothingness: A phenomenological essay on ontology.* New York, NY: Philosophical Library.

Schneider, K.J. (2008). Theory of the existential-integrative (EI) approach. In *Existential-integrative psychotherapy: Guideposts to the core of practice* (pp. 35–48). New York: NY, Routledge.

Schneider, K.J., & Krug, O.T. (2010). *Existential-humanistic therapy.* Washington DC: American Psychological Association.

Spinelli, E. (1996). Martin Heidegger's influence upon British psychology and psychotherapy'. *Journal of the Society for Existential Analysis, 8*(1), 28–38.

Spinelli, E. (1997). *Tales of un-knowing: Therapeutic encounters from an existential perspective.* New York, NY: New York University Press.

Spinelli, E. (2005). *The interpreted world: An introduction to phenomenological psychology* (2nd ed.). London, England: SAGE.

Tillich, P. (1952). *The courage to be.* New Haven, CT: Yale University Press.

Van Bruggen, V., Vos, J., Westerhof, G., Bohlmeijer, E., & Glas, G. (2015). Systematic review of existential anxiety instruments. *Journal of Humanistic Psychology, 55*(2), 173–201.

Van Deurzen, E. (2015). *Paradox and passion in psychotherapy: An existential approach.* London, England: Wiley.

Van Deurzen, E., & Adams, M. (2011/2016). *Skills in existential counselling & psychotherapy.* London, England: SAGE.

Van Deurzen, E., & Arnold-Baker, C. (Eds.). (2005). *Existential perspectives on human issues: a handbook for therapeutic practice.* London, England: Palgrave Macmillan.

Van Deurzen-Smith, E. (1988). *Existential counselling in practice.* London, England: SAGE.

Vos, J. (2015). Meaning and existential givens in the lives of cancer patients: A philosophical perspective on psycho-oncology. *Palliative & Supportive Care, 13*(4), 885–900.

Vos, J. (2016a). Working with meaning in life in chronic or life-threatening disease: A review of its relevance and the effectiveness of meaning-centred therapies. In P. Russo-Netzer, S. Schulenberg, & A. Batthyany (Eds.), *Clinical Perspectives on Meaning* (pp. 171–200). New York, NY: Springer.

Vos, J. (2016b). Working with meaning in life in mental health care: A systematic literature review of the practices and effectiveness of meaning-centred Therapies. In P. Russo-Netzer, S. Schulenberg, & A. Batthyany (Eds.), *Clinical Perspectives on Meaning* (pp. 59–87). New York, NY: Springer.

Vos, J. (2018). *Meaning in life: an evidence-based handbook for practitioners.* London, England: Palgrave McMillan.

Vos, J., Craig, M., & Cooper, M. (2015). Existential therapies: a meta-analysis of their effects on psychological outcomes. *Journal of consulting and clinical psychology, 83*(1), 115.

Vos, J. & Vitali, D. (2018). Meaning-centered therapies: a systematic literature review and meta-analysis. *Journal of Supportive and Palliative Care* (in press).

Wolfe, B.E. (2008). Existential issues in anxiety disorders and their treatment. In K.J. Schneider (Ed.), *Existential-integrative psychotherapy: Guideposts to the core of practice* (pp. 204–216). New York: NY, Routledge.

Wong, P.T.P. (2015). *What is second wave positive psychology and why is it necessary?* Retrieved from http://www.drpaulwong.com/what-is-second-wave-positive-psychology-and-why-is-it-necessary.

Wong, P.T., Reker, G.T., & Gesser, G. (1994). Death Attitude Profile – Revised: A multidimensional measure of attitudes toward death. In R.A. Neimeyer (Ed.), *Death anxiety handbook: Research, instrumentation, and application*, p. 121–148. Washington, DC: Taylor and Francis.

Wrathall, M. (2011). *Heidegger and unconcealment: Truth, language, and history.* New York, NY: Cambridge University Press.

Yalom, I.D. (1980). *Existential psychotherapy.* New York, NY: Basic Books.

Yalom, I.D. (2008). *Staring at the sun: Overcoming the dread of death.* New York, NY: Scribe.

Chapter 9

Cognitive and behavioural procedures for the treatment of death anxiety

Rachel E. Menzies

All of us will encounter a variety of death-related events in our lives, some of which are likely to cause moderate or significant distress. While some individuals may develop adaptive mechanisms for coping with fears of death, thoughts of death may engender paralysing terror in others, and result in unhelpful coping mechanisms (e.g., Kastenbaum, 2000). Further, researchers have proposed that death anxiety underpins many mental health disorders (see Chapter 7 for a thorough exploration of the role of death fears in psychopathology). For example, fears of death may manifest in hypervigilance towards the body (i.e., monitoring of changes in heart rate) in panic disorder (Schmidt, Lerew, & Trakowski, 1997), compulsive handwashing and contamination concerns in obsessive-compulsive disorder (OCD; Menzies & Dar-Nimrod, 2017), and in the feared subjects of common specific phobias, such as heights, spiders, or flying, almost all of which can directly result in fatality (Marks, 1987).

Despite recent arguments that clients with a variety of disorders may benefit from a transdiagnostic intervention targeting death anxiety (e.g.,

Furer, Walker & Stein, 2007; Iverach, Menzies & Menzies, 2014), standard psychological treatments do not typically address fears of death. This may be due to the death anxiety of the clinicians and researchers themselves which may lead to a reluctance to work directly with concerns about mortality (Yalom, 2008), or which may result in not only avoidance, but hostility, when the subject is raised (Burton, 1962). As such, the understanding of the use of cognitive and behavioural procedures for targeting death anxiety is somewhat limited, and only a handful of studies have rigorously evaluated the efficacy of these methods.

This chapter will first review the types of cognitive and behavioural procedures that have been proposed as effective methods with which to address the dread of death, including exposure therapy, behavioural experiments and cognitive reappraisal. Second, the evidence for these techniques, including studies which have trialled cognitive behaviour therapy (CBT) methods in either clinical or nonclinical populations, will be reviewed. Lastly, the implications of these findings will be discussed.

Cognitive approaches in the treatment of death anxiety

All of us hold a variety of beliefs about death. Whilst many of these beliefs may be adaptive, such as the belief that death is a natural part of life, the development of maladaptive beliefs about mortality may produce excessive fear, and may interfere with the individual's life (Yalom, 2008). As such, for clients who hold unhelpful or unrealistic beliefs about death, treatment should focus some attention on assisting them in developing a more balanced perspective on mortality. A thorough assessment prior to commencing treatment is therefore necessary in order to ascertain the client's particular concerns and beliefs about death, and to develop an accurate case formulation (Furer & Walker, 2008). While some of these beliefs may be realistic and adaptive (e.g., 'death is an inevitable part of being human'), others (e.g., 'death is unfair, and shouldn't happen to me') may be contributing to the resulting anxiety around death, and avoidance of death-related thoughts or situations. Furer et al. (2007) propose the use of cognitive reappraisal in order to provide corrective information to clients who often hold unrealistic or maladaptive beliefs about death. For example, a client's belief that 'if I die before my children are grown, it will ruin their lives forever' may be substituted with the more realistic belief that 'leaving my children behind will be difficult but there are other people who care about them who will help them' (p. 156). Similarly, beliefs about not being able to emotionally cope with a diagnosis of a terminal illness may be substituted with the belief that many people are understandably anxious after a terminal diagnosis, but most manage to cope with dignity at the end of life (Furer et al., 2007). Even for those who have been diagnosed with a terminal illness, it has been argued that it is crucial to assess and challenge problematic assumptions and maladaptive cognitions about the illness and death (Onyechi et al., 2016), such as 'it would be awful if I died this way' (p. 17).

Cognitive approaches may also involve drawing on recent research in other areas, such as palliative care, in order to provide the client with realistic information about death. For instance, clients with a dread of death may hold particular beliefs about dying involving unbearable pain or suffering (Furer & Walker, 2008). Such clients may benefit from being provided with information about the effectiveness of pain relief for the dying (Furer et al., 2007), as well as research outlining the physical stages of the dying process, such as the painlessness of the 'death rattle', and the gradual loss of desires such as hunger and thirst. In contrast, beliefs that suffering is an inevitable part of death may be challenged with a more philosophical approach. For example, Yalom (2008) suggests the use of Epicurus' 'symmetry argument' in dealing with the dread of death, noting: 'after death, I will be in the same state of nonbeing as before birth' (p. 296). Similarly, for people who hold beliefs concerning death being an unjust or catastrophic inevitability, one approach may be to ask them to calculate the probability of their parent's initial meeting, (Menzies, 2012). By encouraging a focus on the immense improbability of their own unique DNA sequence coming into being at all, this may help to challenge beliefs centered on the assumption that death is an inherently negative event.

Behavioural procedures to reduce fears of death

Behavioural experiments

Behavioural experiments offer clients the opportunity to 'test out' the beliefs underlying their anxiety or distress (Bennett-Levy et al., 2004). Given the prevalence of death-related concerns across a range of disorders, behavioural experiments have been suggested to challenge maladaptive or unrealistic beliefs about death and dying (e.g., Kirk & Rouf, 2004; Silver, Sanders, Morrison & Cowey, 2004). For example, patients with health anxiety frequently report thoughts demonstrating a higher than average cost attributed to dying, such as 'My partner's life would be destroyed if I die', 'I would not be able to emotionally cope with a terminal diagnosis' or 'Nobody will miss me if I die'. Many of these beliefs can be tested directly or indirectly. For example, to challenge a patient's belief that their own death would result in their children ending up in social services' care due to their partner's inability to cope, Silver et al. (2004) have proposed asking the patient to develop a survey and give this to their partner, siblings and parents. A questionnaire can be used in this manner to assess the family's coping strategies and ability to manage care of their children in the event of their death. This experiment may also allow the patient to talk about their concerns about death with their loved ones, serving both as an exposure task and opportunity to challenge any unrealistic or catastrophic beliefs around death and dying.

While it is important for behavioural interventions to reduce the cost of dying, the probability of this in certain situations should also be examined. Kirk and Rouf (2004) have proposed the use of behavioural experiments to challenge beliefs around the likelihood of death and dying in specific phobias such as heights (e.g., 'If I stand near the edge, I'll fall and die'), water (e.g., 'Nobody will save me if I drown'), transport (e.g., 'We'll crash, I'll be trapped and burn to death') and being alone (e.g., 'An intruder will break in and murder me'). For example, for phobic patients who believe they may actually die of anxiety if confronted with the object of their fear, Kirk and Rouf suggest that a behavioural experiment may allow them to learn that their heart will not simply 'give way' from fear. Similarly, treatment for a height phobia may involve targeting the use of safety behaviours and the belief that 'Unless I hold on to the railing I'll fall and die'. A behavioural experiment requiring the patient to cross a bridge without tightly gripping the railing may prove valuable in demonstrating the unnecessary nature of the safety behaviour, as well as challenging the high probability of dying in this context. Kirk and Rouf (2004) also propose challenging the perceived role of safety behaviours in reducing the probability of death within driving phobias. For instance, a patient can be asked to sit in the passenger seat of a moving car, and keep their eyes closed for increasing amounts of time, in order to challenge the belief that 'Both the driver and I will be killed unless I am a hypervigilant passenger'.

A number of authors have therefore encouraged the use of behavioural experiments to reduce patients' beliefs about the cost and probability of death, either to the self or others, across a range of disorders, including panic disorder (Hackman, 2004), posttraumatic stress disorder (PTSD; Mueller, Hackmann & Croft, 2004), and OCD (Morrison & Westbrook, 2004). However, while behavioural experiments may reduce patients' beliefs about the probability of death in particular situations, the certainty of one's own death at one time or another remains unchangeable. Given this, it has been suggested that treatments which focus on disputing threat appraisal of the patient's current death theme (e.g., disputing the likelihood of falling to one's death), may actually not be addressing the underlying worries that death is inescapable (Menzies, 2012). In fact, it has been argued that treatment targeting these proximal threats of death may not only fail to address the root of the patient's problem, they may contribute to the 'revolving door' often seen in mental health (Iverach et al., 2014). For example, while a patient may seek treatment for various mental illnesses across their lifespan (e.g., a specific phobia in childhood, panic disorder in adolescence, followed by illness anxiety disorder in adulthood), if these disorders are manifestations of an underlying dread of death, leaving this untreated may not result in long-term successful treatment outcomes. As such, additional treatment components may be necessary to cultivate acceptance of the inevitability of death, rather than disputing its probability in one form or another (e.g., by challenging the likelihood of having a heart attack in panic disorder, or of dying from a spider bite in specific phobias). Exposure therapy may therefore play a central role in reducing avoidance and denial, and to expose clients to the inevitable nature of their own death.

Exposure therapy

Avoidance is one of the most common methods of dealing with the dread of death (e.g., McKenzie, Brown, Mak & Chamberlain, 2017). Today, more than any other time in history, death in the Western world is sequestered from society, and our contact with death is often sanitised, if not completely hidden (Willmott, 2001). While developments in science and modern medicine have significantly extended the average lifespan, a death is no longer the visible and communal event it once was, and the care of the deceased, once left for the hands of close family members, is now reserved for hospital staff and the funeral industry. Many people avoid thinking about mortality completely, and may choose to live their lives as though death does not exist (Firestone, 1994). Given this often pervasive avoidance, exposure tasks may play a crucial role in the treatment of death anxiety by encouraging clients to gradually confront their fears. While a variety of possible exposure exercises exist to target death anxiety in general, these tasks should be tailored wherever possible to the client's particular fears surrounding mortality. For example, exposure to situations (e.g., funerals), themes (e.g., cancer or terminal illness) or stimuli (e.g., images of skulls or skeletons) which a client has deliberately and systematically avoided should warrant priority (Furer et al., 2007).

Several authors have suggested the use of imaginal exposure tasks to allow clients to confront their death fears and prepare for the inevitable (e.g., Bohart & Bergland, 1979; Carrera & Elenewski, 1980). Furer et al. (2007) suggest that clients write detailed stories imagining their own imminent death, with a deliberate attempt to incorporate the client's specific fears about death. For example, a client may write a story describing their visualisation of sitting in a doctor's office and hearing for the first time that they have been diagnosed with a terminal illness. Similarly, as part of a group therapy intervention, researchers have led participants through an imaginative 'death fantasy trip' (Bohart & Bergland, 1979, p. 384), in order to expose them to the idea and inevitability of their own death, as well as the death of others. Further, clients with a particular fear of the death of loved ones may also be encouraged to write vivid stories depicting these; starting with a diagnosis, for example, before describing the event of the death itself, and ending with the funeral and grieving process. As an additional exposure task, Furer et al. (2007) suggest clients read obituaries online or in a newspaper, and specifically look for those who died at around their own current age.

Of course, cognitive and behavioural procedures are not owned by CBT clinicians, and have been effectively incorporated into and expanded within other therapy traditions. In a similar vein to the exposure techniques described earlier, acceptance and commitment therapy (ACT) practitioners have developed innovative means of reflecting on one's own eventual demise, and using this as motivation to improve one's life. One powerful exercise emerging from ACT asks clients to write different versions of their own eulogy, as well as their own tombstone inscription (Hayes & Smith, 2005). Numerous similar procedures appear within existential psychotherapy. For instance, Yalom (2008) also outlines tasks that could easily be considered forms of exposure therapy. In addition to encouraging clients to visualise their own death, Yalom suggests they draw a line, with one end symbolising their birth and the other symbolising their death, and draw a cross representing where they are on that line at present, and to meditate on this image. These sorts of experiential tasks may not only serve as powerful exposure exercises, they may also trigger an important process of self-reflection.

Visiting places associated with death, such as hospitals, funeral homes, or cemeteries may also be a useful exposure exercise (e.g., Bohart & Bergland,

1979), particularly if it is a place that others would not typically avoid due to anxiety (e.g., the grave of a loved one). Preparing or updating a will may likewise serve as not only a valuable exposure task, but an important practical task for clients who may have avoided doing this throughout their life (e.g., Henderson, 1990). Considering funeral arrangements for oneself, consulting with a local funeral home to assist with the planning process, or discussing one's end of life preferences with a partner or close family member may prove similarly useful. Whilst these exercises may all act as effective exposure tasks, it may also serve an important dual purpose: By encouraging a client to specify their end of life wishes, they may gain both a sense of control over their own death, as well as the assurance of a dignified passing. This increased perceived control may in turn lessen his or her fears about their eventual death (Henderson, 1990). Further, by starting to prepare for one's own death while still alive, this behavioural change may inadvertently help challenge beliefs such as: 'My family will not be able to cope when I die'. Taking pragmatic action such as making funeral arrangements, may in fact make the aftermath of their death and the grieving process smoother for those around them — particularly if the process of preparing for death involved discussions with loved ones.

Exposure may also involve clients confronting first-person accounts of people dealing with death. This may involve interacting with someone who is nearing the end of life (e.g., Bohart & Bergland, 1979), or confronting death-related material. Films related to death and dying (e.g., *Beaches, The Green Mile*) have also been implemented as exposure tasks (Bohart & Bergland, 1979; Dadfar, Farid, Lester, Vahid, & Birashk, 2016), and television programs (e.g., *Six Feet Under,* and episodes of *Black Mirror* which touch on mortality, such as 'Be Right Back') may prove equally useful as may songs (e.g., *Don't Fear the Reaper* by Blue Öyster Cult, *All Things Must Pass* by George Harrison, *Let Me Die in My Footsteps* by Bob Dylan, or the album *See You in the Morning Light* by Deep Pools — a poignant example of the grieving process at its most creative, written and recorded after a musician lost his father to stomach cancer), or novels (e.g., Tolstoy's *The Death of Ivan Ilyich*). With the 'death positivity' movement finding a burgeoning popularity, numerous nonfiction books have also been published on the subject in recent years (e.g., Atul Gawande's *Being Mortal*, Paul Kalanithi's *When Breath Becomes Air,* or Caitlin Doughty's two books on the topic: *Smoke Gets in Your Eyes: And Other Lessons From the Crematorium,* and *From Here to Eternity*). While some material may provide a lighthearted and humorous perspective on this typically dark subject (such as the film *Death at a Funeral*), others may offer clients a sense of meaning and continuity in the face of death (such as Mitch Albom's memoir *Tuesdays with Morrie*, or the children's animated film *Coco*). In either case, prolonged exposure to a variety of death-relevant materials is likely to reduce anxiety for clients who typically avoid any material featuring the fearful subject of mortality.

Empirical findings of cognitive behaviour therapy treatment studies

Despite a large body of research investigating CBT treatments of disorders closely linked with death fears (i.e., illness anxiety disorder, panic disorder), such studies typically do not report measures of death anxiety. Further, empirical studies of CBT treatments of such disorders generally do not include a component specifically focused on death anxiety. Despite this, clients will encounter a variety of death-related events in their lives, and by failing to target concerns around death, it has been argued that standard treatments may result in symptoms returning in the future (Iverach et al., 2014; Furer et al., 2007). Given this, more research is warranted investigating the effect of cognitive and behavioural treatments of death anxiety in clinical populations.

Despite the general absence of strategies designed to target death fears among standard treatment procedures, some empirical studies have shed light on this area. In 1969, Cautela proposed that excessive fears of death among the elderly can be reduced using desensitisation techniques, in a manner similar to the reduction of other fears. However, the first experimental study to explore the use of desensitisation in reducing death anxiety was conducted by Peal, Handal, and Gilner in 1981. In order to establish an effective exposure hierarchy of death-related scenes, Peal et al. developed the Death Hierarchy Scene Questionnaire. This questionnaire enables participants to rate how anxious they would feel in response to experiencing over fifty death-related images (e.g., 'You're lying in bed and notice that your heart is skipping beats' and 'You see someone's pet run over and killed by a car'). Peal et al. (1981) then used the anxiety ratings of highly death anxious undergraduate students to create an exposure hierarchy made up of the 21 scenes that were agreed to cause 'some', 'moderate', and 'great' anxiety. Participants randomly allocated to the desensitisation condition then began to work through this hierarchy in groups, across an average of eight sessions. On two separate measures of death anxiety, the desensitisation group resulted in significant reductions in fears of death post-treatment, and no significant reductions were found for a no-treatment control group, or a group assigned to receive regular training in deep muscle relaxation. However, the use of an undergraduate psychology student sample limits the generalisability of these findings to treatment-seeking individuals, while the absence of any follow-up results suggests that the efficacy of the intervention in the long-term is unknown.

In a follow-up study, White, Gilner, Handal, and Napoli (1983) expanded on the previous findings, using systematic desensitisation which was similarly based on a common hierarchy of death scenes assembled from the participants' responses to the Death Hierarchy Scene Questionnaire (Peal et al., 1981). The results demonstrated that among highly death anxious nursing students, ten or less sessions of a group systematic desensitisation procedure led to significant improvements on two separate measures of death anxiety at immediate post-test. No significant reductions were found within the control group. At five month follow-up, however, although one measure of death anxiety showed maintained gains, the second measure indicated a deterioration of any improvements made, suggesting mixed findings regarding long-term treatment efficacy. In addition, despite the high levels of death anxiety in the sample, the diagnostic status of the participants was not known. That is, it is unknown whether any participants had a diagnosed anxiety disorder, and it was not a treatment-seeking sample.

Contrary to these findings, Testa (1981) found that five sessions of a group systematic desensitisation program did not lead to significant reductions in death anxiety among a sample of nurses. The failure to find any improvements in this study, in comparison with those found by White et al. (1983), may possibly reflect the need for more frequent sessions in order to reap benefits across treatment. Alternatively, it is possible that the improvements found by White and colleagues reflect the larger potential treatment gains made possible by participants who are already high in death anxiety.

Only one study has investigated the efficacy of a CBT intervention for death anxiety within a clinical sample. Hiebert, Furer, McPhail and Walker (2005) conducted a randomised controlled trial of group CBT for adults with a DSM-IV diagnosis of hypochondriasis. The treatment program consisted of 14 weekly group therapy sessions, with a focus on both illness-specific fears, as well as broader death-related concerns. For example, as per standard treatment for illness anxiety, imaginal and in vivo exposure to illness was conducted, as was cognitive reappraisal and the reduction of checking behaviours and reassurance seeking. In addition, death anxiety was specifically addressed using techniques such as exposure to death-related concerns and situations, enhancing acceptance of the inevitability of dying, increasing satisfaction with life, and cognitive challenging of maladaptive beliefs about death. The CBT group resulted in significant improvements in symptoms of hypochondriasis and one measure of death anxiety, while no differences were found for the waitlist control condition. Unfortunately, given that the CBT treatment addressed both broad illness anxiety as well as specific death fears, it is difficult to know whether the novel death-related components enhanced treatment outcomes above and beyond the effects of standard CBT. However, it is also possible that the techniques used to target illness anxiety inadvertently reduce death fears, and some may view these as an indirect form of exposure to death. For instance, asking clients to reduce their checking behaviours and reassurance seeking may be seen as reducing their attempts to control death, rather than purely targeting illness anxiety alone.

Empirical findings of 'death education' programs

More recently, various 'death education' programs have been developed and implemented in the hope of increasing awareness of the dying process, and reducing fears of death. Death education programs are often categorised as fitting either a 'didactic' or 'experiential' framework. While the didactic format often includes lectures and audio-visual presentations about the dying process and stages of grief, experiential programs typically focus on utilising open group discussion and role plays in order to allow participants to share their thoughts and concerns about death. Despite not being an explicit CBT treatment approach, death education programs could be considered one form of exposure therapy. For instance, talking about death with others in an open space may not only allow participants to work through their own individual fears about death, it may also help to reduce the avoidance of death commonly encouraged by broader society, and to provide a starting ground for these fears to reduce over the course of the workshop. Further, death education might serve as a component of cognitive therapy, in a similar vein to psychoeducation. Just as the danger ideation reduction therapy (DIRT; Krochmalik, Jones, & Menzies, 2001) program for OCD includes the provision of 'corrective information' about the human body (i.e., the strength and efficacy of the immune system), one might expect that a didactic death education program may serve to challenge maladaptive or unrealistic cognitions about death (i.e., 'dying will always be painful') by offering corrective information about the dying process.

A body of research has attempted to evaluate the effects of death education on fears of death, producing mixed results (see Maglio & Robinson, 1994, for a review). In part, this may be due to the fact that studies in the area are often riddled with methodological limitations, frequently lacking a control group or random allocation of participants. Convenience samples of medical and nursing students are often used when implementing death education programs, as are quasi-experimental designs, such as those involving voluntary enrolment of students into a course on death and dying, with the control group consisting of students who chose not to enroll in such a course. Such methodological limitations raise concerns about the generalisability of effects found resulting from some death education programs, and issues of missing data and inadequate measurement of death anxiety in death education studies have been raised (Wass, 2004).

Despite these common limitations, some randomised controlled studies have been conducted investigating the efficacy of death education programs. In an early study of the effects of death education on death anxiety, Vargo and Batsel (1984) randomly allocated participants to a didactic death education program (i.e., a presentation of Ernest Becker and Elizabeth Kubler-Ross's views on dying, followed by discussion of death-related topics), an experiential program (i.e., a group imaginal exercise focused on having just three days left to live after a nuclear reactor malfunction, followed by discussion), a 'nonconscious' treatment condition (i.e., listening to a neutral tape involving focused attention) or a no-treatment control. The results indicated that the experiential treatment resulted in significant reductions in fear of death on two subscales, while the didactic treatment, nonconscious treatment, and control did not produce any change in death anxiety. The authors argued that the efficacy of the experiential treatment was due to participants sharing an intense and highly personal experience with a focus on their immediate fears of their own death, rather than the more detached and theoretical approach adopted by the didactic treatment. It is also likely that the act of imagining one's own impending death for approximately 90 minutes served as a highly vivid and powerful exposure task, in a similar vein to Furer et al.'s (2007) suggestion that death anxious clients write a detailed story depicting their own diagnosis with a terminal illness, as described earlier.

Despite this significant reduction in death fears, other findings are by no means consistent with those of Vargo and Batsel (1984). Following 36 hours of death education workshops, Dadfar and colleagues (2016) failed to find any significant reduction on five separate measures of death anxiety. There is also some evidence that exposure to a death education program may increase death anxiety, with the results of one eight-week program leading the researcher to conclude: 'Initial discussion increased anxiety for some participants, but continued discussion did not lower anxiety for any participants' (Combs, 1981, p. 79).

Further, additional variables, such as age, appear to moderate the effect of death education on not only death anxiety, but also broader attitudes towards death. Abengózar, Bueno, and Vega (1999) investigated the effects of death education programs on various age groups, recruited through a local newspaper. Three groups of young adults (18–34 years), middle-aged adults (35–39 years), and elderly adults (60–75 years) were randomly allocated to a didactic intervention, experiential intervention, or control condition. Similar to the findings of Vargo and Batsel (1984), at immediate post-test, elderly participants who underwent the experiential workshop showed a significant reduction in death anxiety. For young and middle-aged adults, no changes in death anxiety were found as a result of either education format. However, changes in other outcomes related to death attitudes were found: A didactic intervention significantly reduced 'death loneliness' (i.e., fear of dying alone) for young adults, while the experiential intervention significantly improved both 'attitude toward death' (i.e., more positive and accepting attitudes towards death) and 'death finality' (i.e., distress at the shortness of life). In sum, while immediate post-test revealed various changes in attitudes depending on age and program type, only elderly adults in the experiential condition demonstrated a reduction in death anxiety specifically.

Despite this, at four month follow-up, all three age groups who had received the experiential workshop showed a significant reduction in death anxiety. In contrast, young adults who experienced the didactic intervention showed a significant increase in 'death sadness' (i.e., feeling sad at the thought of death), and 'death depression' (i.e., feeling depressed at the thought of death), possibly due to a burgeoning reflection on their own mortality. No significant changes in death-related variables were found for the control group at follow-up. These joint findings appear to add support to the body of research suggesting the efficacy of experiential death education programs over didactic programs (e.g.,

Maglio & Robinson, 1994). However, additional changes in death attitudes found at follow-up paint a far more complex picture. For instance, young adults in both intervention conditions reported a significant increase in 'death despair' (i.e., despair at the meaningless of life). Similarly, despite the aforementioned reduction in death anxiety, middle-aged adults who experienced the experiential workshop showed a significant increase in 'death despair' and 'death loneliness' at four month follow-up.

The finding that an improvement in death anxiety was accompanied in various cases by a worsening of death despair, sadness, or depression, is a slightly surprising one. It is possible that although exposure to death-related material reduced participants' anxieties around death, it increased other negative emotions towards death, as participants were forced to confront and reflect on their own mortality. This reflection may have been associated with not only an increased realisation of the certitude of death, but an accompanying sense of sadness as this realisation sets in. Notably, this study is one of the few to use a more multidimensional measure of attitudes towards death, rather than measuring death anxiety specifically as the sole outcome variable. It is therefore possible that these increases in sadness or despair may also have occurred as a result of other interventions, such as those described above, although only changes in death anxiety were measured and reported. Further research adopting a more multidimensional measurement approach is needed to clarify if this is the case. Although these changes in various death attitudes are slightly perplexing, this study by Abengózar et al. (1999) suggests that the effect of death education on death attitudes broadly may depend not only on the type of intervention used, but also on participant characteristics, such as age. Whilst the findings are notable in their exploration of the complexity of feelings towards death, the nature of the sample (i.e., the use of a nonclinical sample with no known mental health diagnoses) unfortunately limits how easily one can generalise these findings to treatment-seeking individuals with clinical diagnoses.

As methodological limitations in the research designs increase, so too do the contradictory nature of findings. Among studies lacking randomisation of participants, with samples frequently comprised of medical or nursing students, death education programs have not been found to have any significant effect on death anxiety relative to a control condition (Coleman, 1993; Fischer, Gozansky, Kutner, Chomiak, & Kramer, 2003; Hayslip, Galt & Pinder, 1993). However, among studies lacking a control group, there appears to be both evidence for (Hutchison & Scherman, 1992) and against (Claxton-Oldfield, Crain, & Claxton-Oldfield, 2007; Hegedus, Zana, & Szabo, 2008) the efficacy of death education in reducing death anxiety. Notably, research has demonstrated that treatment intervention studies which lack a control condition have been shown to significantly inflate effect sizes. In a study investigating research designs across 45 meta-analyses, Lipsey and Wilson (1993) found a mean effect size of 0.76 for single group intervention studies using a pre–post design, compared to 0.47 for studies which used a control or comparison group, emphasising the difficulty of estimating true effects from uncontrolled designs. Further research, employing more rigorous methodological designs, appears to be needed to clarify the utility of death education programs as a potential treatment component for interventions targeting death anxiety.

Conclusion

Various cognitive and behavioural procedures have been proposed as effective treatments for the dread of death. These procedures include cognitive reappraisal of maladaptive or unrealistic beliefs about death, behavioural experiments targeting the cost of death and dying, and exposure therapy and systematic desensitisation to images, situations, or events associated with death. Despite a theoretical rationale for targeting fears of death specifically using such methods, only a handful of empirical studies have examined the efficacy of these procedures. Two studies have found that eight or more sessions of systematic desensitisation significantly reduced death anxiety among a nonclinical sample, relative to a control condition (Peal et al., 1981; White et al., 1983). Only one randomised controlled trial of CBT has been conducted on a clinical sample, which found that group therapy involving cognitive challenging of beliefs about death and exposure to death-related concerns led to significant reductions in death anxiety, as well as significant improvements in symptoms among adults with hypochondriasis (Hiebert et al., 2005). However, given that the intervention in this study combined the standard CBT treatment with the novel death-related components, the efficacy of the treatments targeting death fears cannot be established. Despite the lack of research exploring CBT treatments of death anxiety, a larger body of research has examined the impact of death education programs on fears of death. Although death education programs typically involve participants sharing their concerns about death and being provided with information about the dying process, rather than direct cognitive challenging, they could be considered one form of exposure therapy. However, the results of death education programs indicate mixed findings, with studies finding no difference in death anxiety, a significant reduction in fears of death, and even a significant increase in death anxiety.

In sum, although there is a strong theoretical rationale behind the use of cognitive and behavioural procedures in treating death anxiety, only a handful of empirical studies have been conducted, indicating early potential of such treatments. More research is clearly needed to determine the efficacy of CBT interventions, particularly among clinical populations, and to explore whether they offer more consistent improvements relative to death education programs, which demonstrate highly variable results.

References

Abengózar, M.C., Bueno, B., & Vega, J.L. (1999). Intervention on attitudes toward death along the lifespan. *Educational Gerontology, 25,* 435–447.

Bennett-Levy, J., Westbrook, D., Fennell, M., Cooper, M., Rouf, K., & Hackmann, A. (2004). Behavioural experiments: Historical and conceptual underpinnings. In J. Bennett-Levy, G. Butler, M. Fennell, A. Hackman, M. Mueller, & Westbrook, D. (Eds.), *Oxford guide to behavioural experiments in cognitive therapy* (1–20). Oxford University Press.

Bohart, J.B., & Bergland, B.W. (1979). The impact of death and dying counseling groups on death anxiety in college students. *Death Education, 2,* 381–391.

Burton, A. (1962). Death as countertransference. *Psychoanalytic Review, 49,* 3–20.

Carrera, R.N., & Elenewski, J.J. (1980). Implosive therapy as a treatment for insomnia. *Journal of Clinical Psychology, 36,* 729–734.

Cautela, J.R. (1969). A classical conditioning approach to the development and modification of behavior in the aged. *The Gerontologist, 9,* 109–113

Claxton-Oldfield, S., Crain, M., & Claxton-Oldfield, J. (2007). Death anxiety and death competency: The impact of a palliative care volunteer training program. *American Journal of Hospital & Palliative Medicine, 23,* 464–468.

Coleman, T. (1993). The effect of an instructional module on death and dying on the death anxiety of emergency medical technician trainees. *Omega: Journal of Death and Dying, 27,* 123–129.

Combs, D.C. (1981). The effects of selected death education curriculum models on death anxiety and death acceptance. *Death Education, 5,* 75–81.

Dadfar, M.M., Farid, A.A.A., Lester, D., Vahid, M.K.A., & Birashk, B. (2016). Effectiveness of death education program by methods of didactic, experiential, and 8A model on the reduction of death distress among nurses. *International Journal of Medical Research & Health Sciences, 5,* 60–71.

Firestone, R.W. (1994). Psychological defenses against death anxiety. In R.A. Neimeyer (Ed.), *Death anxiety handbook: Research, instrumentation, and application* (pp. 217–241). Washington, DC: Taylor & Francis.

Fischer, S.M., Gozansky, W.S., Kutner, J.S., Chomiak, A., & Kramer, A., (2003). Palliative care education: An intervention to improve medical residents' knowledge and attitudes. *Journal of Palliative Medicine, 6,* 391–399.

Furer, P., & Walker, J.R. (2008). Death anxiety: A cognitive-behavioral approach. *Journal of Cognitive Psychotherapy, 22,* 167–182.

Furer, P. Walker, J.R., & Stein, M.B. (2007). *Treating health anxiety and fear of death: A practitioner's guide.* Springer Science & Business Media.

Hackman, A. (2004). Panic disorder and agoraphobia. In J. Bennett-Levy, G. Butler, M. Fennell, A. Hackman, M. Mueller, & Westbrook, D. (Eds.), *Oxford guide to behavioural experiments in cognitive therapy* (pp. 59-78). Oxford University Press.

Hayes, S.C., & Smith, S. (2005). *Get out of your mind and into your life: The new Acceptance and Commitment Therapy.* Oakland, CA: New Harbinger.

Hayslip, B., Galt, C.P., & Pinder, M.M. (1993). Effects of death education on conscious and unconscious death anxiety. *Omega: Journal of Death and Dying, 28,* 101–111.

Hegedus, K., Zana, A., & Szabo, G. (2008). Effect of end of life education on medical students' and health care workers' death attitude. *Palliative Medicine, 22,* 264–269.

Henderson, M. (1990). Beyond the living will. *The Gerontologist, 30,* 480–485.

Hiebert, C., Furer, P., McPhail, C., & Walker, J. (2005). Death anxiety: A central feature of hypochondriasis. *Depression and Anxiety, 22,* 215–216.

Hutchison, T.D., & Scherman, A. (1992). Didactic and experiential death and dying training: Impact upon death anxiety. *Death Studies, 16,* 317–330.

Iverach, L., Menzies, R.G., & Menzies, R.E. (2015). Death anxiety and its role in psychopathology: Reviewing the status of a transdiagnostic construct. *Clinical Psychology Review, 34,* 580–593.

Kastenbaum, R. (2000). *The psychology of death* (3rd Ed.). Springer: New York.

Kirk, J., & Rouf, K. (2004). Specific phobias. In J. Bennett-Levy, G. Butler, M. Fennell, A. Hackman, M. Mueller, & Westbrook, D. (Eds.), *Oxford Guide to Behavioural Experiments in Cognitive Therapy* (pp. 161–171). Oxford University Press.

Krochmalik, A., Jones M.K., & Menzies, R.G. (2001). Danger Ideation Reduction Therapy (DIRT) for treatment-resistant compulsive washing. *Behaviour Research and Therapy, 39,* 897–912.

Lipsey, M.S., & Wilson, D.B. (1993). The efficacy of psychological, educational, and behavioral treatment. *American Psychologist, 48,* 1181–1209.

Maglio, C.J., & Robinson, S.E. (1994). The effects of death education on death anxiety: A meta-analysis. *Omega: Journal of Death and Dying, 29,* 319–335,

Marks, I. (1987). *Fears, phobias, and rituals: Panic, anxiety, and their disorders.* New York, NY: Oxford University Press.

McKenzie, E.L., Brown, P. M., Mak, A.S., & Chamberlain, P. (2017). 'Old and ill': Death anxiety and coping strategies influencing health professionals' well-being and dementia care. *Aging & Mental Health, 21,* 634–641.

Menzies, R.G. (2012). *The dread of death and its role in psychopathology.* Keynote address presented at the 35th National Conference of the Australian Association for Cognitive and Behaviour Therapy, Queensland, October 2012.

Menzies, R.E., Dar-Nimrod, I. (2017). Death anxiety and its relationship with obsessive-compulsive disorder. *Journal of Abnormal Psychology, 126,* 367–377.

Morrison, N., & Westbrook, D. (2004). Obsessive-compulsive disorder. In J. Bennett-Levy, G. Butler, M. Fennell, A. Hackman, M. Mueller, & Westbrook, D. (Eds.), *Oxford guide to behavioural experiments in cognitive therapy* (101–118). Oxford University Press.

Mueller, M., Hackmann, A., & Croft, A. (2004). Post-traumatic stress disorder. In J. Bennett-Levy, G. Butler, M. Fennell, A. Hackman, M. Mueller, & D. Westbrook (Eds.), *Oxford guide to behavioural experiments in cognitive therapy* (183-201). Oxford University Press.

Onyechi, K.C.N., Onuigbo, L.N., Eseadi, C., Ikechukwu-Ilomuanya, A.B., Nwaubani, O.O., Umoke, O.C., … & Utoh-Ofong, A.N. (2016). Effects of rational-emotive hospice care therapy on problematic assumptions, death anxiety, and psychological distress in a sample of cancer patients and their family caregivers in Nigeria. *International Journal of Environmental Research and Public Health, 13,* 929–43.

Peal, R.L., Handal, P.J., & Gilner, F.H. (1981). A group desensitisation procedure for the reduction of death anxiety. *Omega: Journal of Death and Dying, 12,* 61–70.

Schmidt, N.B., Lerew, D.R., & Trakowski, J.H. (1997). Body vigilance in panic disorder: Evaluating attention to bodily perturbations. *Journal of Consulting and Clinical Psychology, 65,* 214–220.

Silver, A., Sanders, D., Morrison, N., & Cowey, C. (2004). Health anxiety. In J. Bennett-Levy, G. Butler, M. Fennell, A. Hackman, M. Mueller, & Westbrook, D. (Eds.), *Oxford guide to behavioural experiments in cognitive therapy* (pp. 81–98). Oxford University Press.

Testa, J.A. (1981). Group systematic desensitization and implosive therapy for death anxiety. *Psychological Reports, 48,* 376–378.

Vargo, M.E., & Batsel, W.M. (1984). The reduction of death anxiety: A comparison of didactic and experiential and nonconscious treatments. *British Journal of Medical Psychology, 57,* 333–337.

Wass, H. (2004). A perspective on the current state of death education. *Death Studies, 28,* 289–308.

White, P.D., Gilner, F.H., Handal, P.J., & Napoli, J.G. (1983). A behavioral intervention for death anxiety in nurses. *Omega: Journal of Death and Dying, 14,* 33–42.

Willmott, H. (2001). Death. So what? Sociology, sequestration and emancipation. *The Sociological Review, 48,* 649–665.

Yalom, I.D. (2008). *Staring at the sun: Overcoming the terror of death.* San Francisco: Jossey-Bass.

Chapter 10

Death acceptance and the meaning-centred approach to end-of-life care

Paul T.P. Wong, David F. Carreno, and Beatriz Gongora Oliver

The final examination that faces all of us is how to die well. Death anxiety, just like test anxiety, in and by itself will not enable us to pass this final test. How can we best prepare ourselves to defeat this common enemy? Is there any way to cure this dread?

There is a trend in favour of hospice and palliative care over aggressive attempts to prolong lives (Teno et al., 2013). The increasing acceptance of physician-assisted suicide further indicates the need for more physicians capable of ending another person's life with dignity, empathy, and comfort.

Death anxiety is responsible for all kinds of psychological disorders (Iverach, Menzies, & Menzies, 2014), when death is perceived as an undefeatable monster capable of destroying all our cherished dreams and everything that makes happy. Religion, philosophy, and psychology all have wrestled with this perennial challenge, as attested by other chapters in this edited volume.

Down through history, human beings have developed elaborate defense mechanisms against the terror of death, both at the individual and cultural levels, leading to a psychological state of denial (Pyszczynski, Greenberg, & Solomon, 2002; Solomon, Greenberg, & Pyszczynski, 2004). At the cultural level, its ubiquitous presence is felt, from the social functions of funeral and memorial services, religion, and entertainment, to medical care (Kearl, 1989). At the personal level, we resort to all kinds of coping responses towards this existential given. Our own death attitudes are often colored by our personal and collective experiences with the loss of loved ones and our efforts to make the terror of death more bearable.

Death attitudes and the medical professions

The medical profession has made it its mission to prolong life; their negative attitude towards death also makes it difficult for physicians to communicate the 'bad news' to patients and provide proper help during end-of-life care. Mortality is considered a medical failure (Gawande, 2014). In countries that have legalised physician-assisted suicides, such as Canada, family doctors often do not have the training and skills to end a patient's life with dignity and efficiency (Hune-Brown, 2017). Therefore, it has become more relevant today for physicians to be informed on the relevance of death attitudes and end-of-life care.

Health professionals' death attitudes and caring for the dying

Research has shown a connection between health professionals' death attitudes and the quality of end-of-life care. For example, nurses low in death acceptance tend to have negative attitudes towards end-of-life care, whereas nurses with high scores in death acceptance tend to cultivate better relationships with terminal patients (Braun, Gordon, & Uziely, 2010; Malliarou et al., 2011).

Similarly, Black (2007) studied the relationships between personal death attitudes of health professionals and communication regarding advance directives. The approach acceptance of death is positively correlated with initiating the discussion of advance directives, while negative death attitudes correlated negatively.

In a recent review article, Nia, Lehto, Ebadi, and Peyrovi (2016) reported that death anxiety is commonly experienced among healthcare providers and is associated with more negative attitudes about caring for dying patients and their families.

Physicians' personal values are also a factor in end-of-life care. Doukas, Gorenflo, and Supanich (1998) found that primary care physicians who most objected to physician-assisted death (PAD) were less likely to have executed an advance directive; furthermore, their findings suggested that personal physician values were relevant in the withdrawal of treatment in terminal care.

The above findings could be attributed to inadequate training in end-of-life issues in medical schools. Sullivan, Lakoma, and Block (2003) reported that medical students and residents in the United States felt unprepared to provide good care for the dying. They also reported that current educational practices and institutional culture in US medical schools do not support adequate end-of-life care.

Education about death attitudes in medical schools can help improve physician-patient communication and make physicians more aware of how their own death attitudes can affect terminal patients' well being and perceived meaning (Dickinson, 2007; Hamama-Raz, Solomon, & Ohry, 2000; Malliarou et al., 2011; Pollak et al. 2011; Servaty, Krejci, & Hayslip, 1996). For example, Schmi et al. (2016) found that medical residents who reported more classroom training during residency on end-of-life communication skills were more comfortable in end-of-life conversations with terminal patients.

In this chapter, we propose that death acceptance and meaning-making are capable of providing an effective antidote to death dread. We explain why this existential positive psychology approach is needed and how we can apply this meaning-centred approach in end-of-life care.

The positive psychology of death anxiety

From the perspective of second wave positive psychology (PP 2.0; Wong, 2011), all emotions, including negative ones, have adaptive value because they help enhance our resilience, meaning, and flourishing. Paradoxically, death holds the key to living a vital, authentic and meaningful life. Yalom (2008) once said that the idea of death has saved many lives. That is, we cannot life fully without becoming aware of the fragility and finiteness of life. The challenge of existential positive psychology is to discover pathways of death acceptance and living a life of significance, meaning, and lasting value. Such positive attitude towards death can enhance our well being (Neimeyer, 2005; Tomer, 2000; Tomer, Eliason, & Wong, 2008).

The positive psychology of death anxiety can be best understood in terms of the dual-system model (Wong, 2012a). According to this model, optimal adaptation depends on our ability to confront and transform the dark side of life in service of achieving positive goals. It also posits that the best defense is offense; the most effective way to protect ourselves against the terror of death is to aggressively pursue the task of living a meaningful life despite the shadow of death.

Both avoidance and approach systems are needed to be free from the prison of death fear and to motivate us to engage actively in what matters to us. From this dual-systems perspective, death fear and death acceptance can co-exist and work together for our well-being.

From death anxiety to death acceptance

Elisabeth Kubler-Ross' (1969, 2009) stage-model of coping with death (denial, anger, bargaining, depression, and acceptance) was a milestone in death studies. She has identified some defence mechanisms (denial and bargaining) and negative emotional reactions (anger and depression) involved in coming to terms with the reality of death — accepting death as the inevitable end. However, in the last fifty years, the psychology of death has been dominated by research on death anxiety (Kastenbaum, 2000; Neimeyer, 1994a, 1994b; Iverach et al., 2014). There was very little research on death acceptance. About 30 years ago, my associates and I conducted a comprehensive study of death acceptance, which led to the development of the Death Attitude Profile (DAP; Gesser, Wong, & Reker, 1988). In addition to death fear and death avoidance, we identified three distinct types of death acceptance: (1) neutral death acceptance — accepting death rationally as part of life; (2) approach acceptance — accepting death as a gateway to a better afterlife; and (3) escape acceptance — choosing death as a better alternative to a painful existence. The DAP was later revised as the DAP-R (Wong, Reker, & Gesser, 1994). Both scales have been widely used worldwide.

Three types of death acceptance

Approach acceptance is rooted in religious/spiritual beliefs in a desirable afterlife. To those who embrace such beliefs, afterlife is more than symbolic immortality, because it is typically associated with theistic religious faith or belief in a transcendental reality. Approach acceptance is based on the social construction of life beyond the grave, thus offering hope and comfort to the dying as well as the bereaved. More specifically, Harding, Flannelly, Weaver, and Costa (2005) reported that scales that measure belief in God's existence and belief in the afterlife were both negatively correlated with death anxiety but positively correlated with death acceptance.

Escape acceptance is primarily based on the perception that death offers a welcome relief from the pain and miseries of being alive. Suicide and physician-assisted suicide are expressions of escape acceptance. For example, Cicirelli (2006) observed that when individuals experience intractable pain or loss of function, they chose to end their lives.

The construct of neutral acceptance means to accept the reality of death in a rational manner and make the best use of the limited time on earth. Cicirelli (2001) has identified four different personal meanings of death: extinction, afterlife, motivator, and legacy. Belief in the afterlife is similar to approach acceptance; extinction, motivator, and legacy can all come under the umbrella of neutral acceptance.

Once one has found something worth dying for, one is no longer afraid of death. When people are doing something significant and fulfilling, and they are totally engaged in doing what they love, they will have no time to worry about death. Thus, whether we focus on avoidance or approach to the reality of death depends on the meaning we attach to it.

Approach acceptance can incorporate neutral acceptance with regard to making the best use of our finite life on earth, but it has the additional benefit of providing hope for continued existence of one's consciousness beyond the grave. We may never know why a majority of people believe in heaven or an afterlife (Bethune, 2013), but such beliefs, regardless of whether they are based on religious or secular convictions, can be a source of comfort and hope in the face of death.

Death acceptance and meaning-making

Our capacities for meaning-seeking and meaning-making play a key role in curing the dread of death and facilitating death acceptance. We can discover something so meaningful and beautiful even in times of death, as we have already alluded to. In fact, Wong has described the meaning management theory (MMT; Wong, 2008) as a conceptual framework to understand death acceptance. MMT posits that meaning is the best protection against the fear of death and dying because meaning management enables us to transform our fears, embrace life, and do what matters most to us.

Meaning-making can help us rise above what is beyond our control and transform our fears into courage and faith. At the same time, meaning-making motivates us to strive towards something that is bigger and longer lasting than ourselves, whether it is a cultural worldview or a personal God.

From terror management theory to meaning management theory

According to terror management theory (TMT), avoidance of death anxiety is the primary motive, because it is triggered by the terror of death. TMT contends that when people feel threatened by death salience, they resort to cultural beliefs and their self-esteem as a refuge. Wong and Tomer (2011) argue that the main thrust of TMT is unconscious and defensive. Such a defensive posture against the fear of death may create a barrier against death awareness and hinder the intention of living fully despite the terror of death.

MMT is based on existential positive psychology (Wong, 2005, 2009) — the recognition that mature positive psychology needs to be situated in the context of the dark side of human existence. MMT proposes it is more productive and fulfilling to courageously and honestly confront our death anxiety and at the same time passionately pursue a meaningful goal (Tomer et al., 2008; Wong & Tomer, 2011)

MMT provides a comprehensive framework to manage our inner life in terms of its meaning-seeking, meaning-making, and meaning-reconstruction processes in the service of survival and thriving. MMT recognises the legitimacy of unconscious defensive mechanisms proposed by TMT, but complements it by emphasising the adaptive benefits of death acceptance and meaning management (Wong & Tomer, 2011).

Wong's (2012a) dual system model provides a conceptual framework to integrate both positive and negative attitudes towards death and provide a more realistic picture of how we cope with personal death. While an avoidance life orientation condemns us to the prison of fear, a positive life orientation enables us to accept the inevitable negatives and move forward to pursue a meaningful and fulfilling life. Yalom (2008) recognises that 'everyone is destined to experience both the exhilaration of life and the fear of mortality' (p. 273). The trick is how to keep our mind on life rather than on death. Kahlil Gibran (1994) also says: 'It is life in quest of life in bodies that fear the grave' (p. 104).

Meaning management is more than cognitive reframing or rationalisation. It actually requires a fundamental shift from pleasure-seeking to the meaning mindset (Wong, 2012b), from self-centredness to self-transcendence (Wong, 2016). Meaning therapy (Wong, 2010, 2012c) equips people to squeeze out meaning and hope from even the darkest moments of life.

Cancer patients and end-of-life care

One of the most extensively studied end-of-life populations is terminally ill patients with cancer. According to the World Health Organization (2015), cancer was the second leading cause of death globally and accounted for 8.8 million deaths in 2015. Given these high numbers, it is likely that throughout life the reader has witnessed someone's death from cancer. Thus, we consider it essential to introduce in this chapter an analysis of the meaning-related psychological problems encountered by terminally ill patients with cancer as well as the most relevant meaning-centred therapies for this population.

Loss of meaning and dignity in cancer patients

Terminally ill cancer patients are very vulnerable to suffer from loss of meaning in life and dignity, resulting in the desire for hastened death. About 17% of cancer patients reported a high desire to terminate their lives primarily because of depression, hopelessness, and loss of meaning rather than pain (Breibart et al., 2000). Similarly, Chochinov et al. (2002) observed that 47% of patients in their last months of life reported certain loss of sense of dignity. Moadel et al. (1999) interviewed 248 cancer patients regarding their spiritual and existential needs. Patients reported the need to receive help with: overcoming their fears (51%), finding hope (42%), finding meaning in life (40%), and finding spiritual resources (39%). Meaning-centred therapies for advanced cancer, some of which are presented below, aim to overcome this lack of meaning and worth in life. For instance, dignity therapy is designed to decrease suffering, enhance quality of life and bolster a sense of dignity; it provides a safe, therapeutic environment for patients to review the most meaningful aspects of their lives in a way that helps restore their core values, such as 'Family', 'Pleasure', 'Caring', 'A Sense of Accomplishment', 'True Friendship', and 'Rich Experience' (Hack et al., 2010).

Meaning, spirituality, and values

One of the core meaning-related areas in terminally ill cancer patients is spirituality, defined as 'the way in which people understand their lives in view of their ultimate meaning and value' (Muldoon & King, 1995, p. 336). The positive relationship between spirituality and well being in cancer has been widely supported (e.g., Visser, Garssen, & Vingerhoets, 2010). For example, Nelson, Rosenfeld, Breitbart, and Galietta (2002) found a strong negative association between spiritual well being and depression in terminally ill patients with cancer and AIDS. In another study with a sample of 160 cancer patients with a life expectancy of less than 3 months, McClain, Rosenfeld, and Breitbart (2003) showed that spiritual well being has an effect on end-of-life despair, including desire for hastened death, hopelessness, and suicidal ideation.

Personal values are also fundamentally related to meaning matters. One of the classic definitions understands a personal value as 'an enduring belief that a specific mode of conduct or end-state of existence is personally or socially preferable to an opposite or converse mode of conduct or end-state of existence' (Rokeach, 1973, p. 5). Fegg, Wasner, Neudert, and Borasio (2005) define values as 'cognitive representations of goals or motivations that are important to people. They can be described as emotionally and cognitively relevant principles guiding people's lives' (p. 154). Other authors understand values as 'verbally construed global desired life consequences' (Hayes, Strosahl, & Wilson, 1999, p. 206). All in all, these definitions seem to refer to values as what really matters in life.

Although values are considered to remain very stable over time, they can change for different reasons, such as socialisation, self-confrontation, cultural upheaval, therapy, or emotionally significant events (Rokeach, 1973). The experience of cancer is undoubtedly such an event. Grezsta and Sieminska (2011) reported that after the diagnosis of cancer, patients significantly gave more importance to religious morality (salvation, forgiving, being helpful, clean), personal orientation (self-respect, true friendship, happiness), self-constriction (self-control, obedience, honesty), family security, and delayed gratification. In the same time, values such as immediate gratification, self-expansion (being capable, ambitious, broadminded), and competence (a sense of accomplishment, being imaginative, intellectual) decreased in importance. Another study by Fegg et al. (2005) showed that the most important values for terminally ill patients with cancer or amyotrophic lateral sclerosis were benevolence, self-direction, and universalism, whereas power, achievement, and stimulation received the lowest importance. In comparison with healthy adults, these patients scored higher in benevolence and self-enhancement values. The data of this study suggested that security, conformity, and tradition (conservative values) can protect the patients' quality of life in the palliative care situation.

A new line of research recently commenced by Carreno et al. (2017) seems to reveal more information about the relationship of personal values and quality of life in cancer patients. Preliminary results suggest that cancer patients, either after a recent nonterminal diagnosis or terminally ill, seem to perceive shifts in the importance and dedication they give to areas such as family, intimate relationships, friendship, leisure, work, health, spirituality, and self. The highest increases of value and personal involvement are produced in the most priority areas of patients' lives, which indicates that they do a prioritisation and reaffirmation on who they are and what is worthy in life. In addition, patients not only indicate changes in what they consider important, but this is related to a greater involvement in their worthy areas, which in turn has a high impact on quality of life. Those who do not show this shift or clarification in the system of personal values indicate statistically lower spiritual well being and quality of life. Thus, these results also reflect that the clarification of the worldview, self, and personal values are relevant for a clinical perspective since they are related to quality of life and spiritual well being.

Meaning-centred end-of-life cancer care

Patients with cancer are normal people; they can present the same psychopathologies as the rest of the population. Thus, in accordance with the problems presented by each patient, the psychological intervention must be oriented either to the psychopathologic treatment or to reestablish the quality of life that has been altered by the illness, helping patients in the process of coping and adapting to cancer with psychological support and strategies from psycho-oncology.

In general, the majority of psychological interventions in oncology have the goal of improving quality of life and the adjustment to the illness of patients and their families. With regard to the specific case of patients with advanced cancer, they show a greater complexity in the management of physical and psychological symptoms. The emotional response of patients in that phase can be very wide, from passivity, anger, self-reproach, and even to the negation of their situation. In this point, the therapy may aim to guide patients in the revision of their personal values and meaning of life.

Meaning-centred therapies for patients with advanced cancer have demonstrated enhancement in areas such as spiritual well being, quality of life, sense of dignity and meaning, depression, anxiety, and desire for death (e.g., Breitbart et al., 2010; Breitbart et al., 2012; Chochinov et al., 2011). Before presenting two of the most validated meaning-centred therapies for advanced cancer, we see it necessary to highlight the core role of personal values in the functioning of these therapies. Wong (2012d) stresses that 'meaning therapy serves the dual function of healing what is broken and bringing out what is good and right about individuals' (p. xii). Wong's 'PURE' model accounts for four ingredients involved in the definition of meaning: purpose, understanding, responsible action, and enjoyment or evaluation. According to this model, having a meaningful life and a meaningful death not only implies making sense or giving coherence to life and death, but that they are worth living as well. It is in this point that personal values play a fundamental role in meaning-centred therapies. In order for life, death, or any event to be worth living, it is necessary to clarify personal values and to live or feel that one has lived according to them.

One of the meaning-centred therapies that makes explicit personal values as the key components is dignity therapy (Hack et al., 2010). This therapy has the goal of increasing the sense of dignity of end-of-life patients. Dignity, defined as the 'quality or state of being worthy, honored, or esteemed (*Webster's new international dictionary*, 1946) is determined as patients approach death by three broad issues: (1) illness-related concerns, (2) dignity conserving repertoire, and (3) Social Dignity Inventory. The protocol of the 1 to 3 sessions of dignity therapy mainly consists of the presentation of nine questions about what is and has been meaningful in the life of the patients. It includes the final words and legacy that the patient wants to transmit to family and loved ones. These questions can be openly responded to in writings or audio-recordings which are transcribed later. Once edited, the patient identifies individuals with whom the transcription must be shared following their death.

Another scientifically validated meaning-centred therapy for advanced cancer is meaning-centred psychotherapy (Breitbart & Applebaum, 2011). This therapy was designed to treat despair, demoralisation, hopelessness, and desire for hastened death in patients with advanced cancer who do not suffer from clinical depression. Its aim is to sustain and enhance a sense of meaning in the face of existential crisis in which patients experiment a loss of meaning, value and purpose in life. In the terms of Breitbart and Applebaum (2011):

> Meaning, or having a sense that one's life has meaning, involves the conviction that one is fulfilling a unique role and purpose in a life that is a gift. This comes with a responsibility to live to one's full potential as a human being; in so doing, one gains a sense of peace, contentment, or even transcendence, through connectedness with something greater than one's self. (p. 138)

The protocol of meaning-centred psychotherapy, both in its group or individual application (Breitbart & Poppito, 2014a, 2014b) is composed of 7 to 8 sessions in which patients reflect on the concept of meaning and the impact that cancer has produced on their identity. Within the rest of the following sessions, the therapy focuses on helping patients connect with various sources of meaning in their lives. In other words, through different exercises and conversations the therapist encourages patients to clarify their personal values and to live in the service of those values. Based on Viktor Frankl's perspective, Breitbart et al. propose four main sources of meaning: (1) creativity (work, deeds, dedication to causes); (2) experience (art, nature, humour, love, relationships, roles); (3) attitude (the stance one takes towards suffering, death, and other existential problems); and (4) legacy (meaning in a historical and familiar context — past, present, and future). Throughout these sources of meaning, meaning-centred psychotherapy intends to (a) encourage patients to seek meaning in their lives, despite the uncertainty and constrains of the illness; (b) find new ways of re-engagement to life, for example, through transcendence; (c) learn to distinguish between constrains that can be changed, and accept what cannot be changed; (d) integrate the diagnosis of cancer in the history of life of the patient; (e) express emotions and feelings; and (f) enhance psychological adjustment through the meaning of life.

Conclusion

In conclusion, the construct of meaning has an important therapeutic value in patients with advanced cancer. Sustaining and encouraging the meaning of life leads to benefits in the enhancement of spiritual and emotional well being, as well as in quality of life. Further development and validation of these meaning-centred therapies in other end-of life populations are needed.

Our review of the literature has shown that in meaning-centred end-of-life care, the personal attributes of medical professionals are as important as the intervention skills. To provide high quality end-of-life care, medical professionals need to have resolved their own fear of death and come to terms with personal mortality. In addition, they need to have resolved their personal existential struggles, regarding the meaning and core beliefs of their own lives. When healthcare professionals are aware of their own calling, personal values, beliefs, and attitudes, especially with respect to their mortality and spirituality, they create deeper and more significant connections with their patients (Puchalski & Guenther, 2012).

The quality of the presence that professionals provide in the relationship with their patients depends on their maturity and spiritual connection. From this point of view, the commitment to the self-care of professionals should be an ethical imperative. Beyond knowing the different models of therapy, whether clinicians feel called to take care of patients in an integrative way and to cultivate spirituality, they must become aware of the need to connect first with their source of well being, peace, and personal harmony, with its own spiritual dimension.

Good end-of-life care requires teamwork, which may include physicians, nurses, psychologists, and pastoral care chaplains. When the team use their collective resources and adopt a holistic approach that recognises the importance of the spiritual-existential dimension in patients and their families, it will benefit both the healthcare professionals and their patients.

Finally, we argue that better end-of-life care education is needed in medical schools, residence training, and continued education for practicing physicians. This is important not only because of increased demand for hospice and palliative care, but also because of increased demands for physician-assisted death in many countries.

References

Bethune, B. (2013, May 7). Why so many people — including scientists — suddenly believe in an afterlife: Heaven is hot again, and hell is colder than ever. *Maclean's*. Retrieved from http://www.macleans.ca/society/life/the-heaven-boom/

Black, K. (2007). Health care professionals' death attitudes, experiences, and advance directive communication behavior. *Death Studies, 31*(6), 563–572. doi:10.1080/07481180701356993

Braun, M., Gordon, D., & Uziely, B. (2010). Associations between oncology nurses' attitudes toward death and caring for dying patients. *Oncology Nursing Forum, 37*(1), 43-49. doi:10.1188/10.ONF.E43-E49

Breitbart, W., & Applebaum, A. (2011). Meaning-centered group psychotherapy. In M. Watson & D. Kissane (Eds.), *Handbook of psychotherapy in cancer care.* (pp. 137–148). Chichester, England: Wiley.

Breitbart, W., & Poppito, S. (2014a). *Individual meaning-centered psychotherapy for patients with advanced cancer: A treatment manual.* New York, NY: Oxford University Press.

Breitbart, W., & Poppito, S. (2014b). *Meaning-centered group psychotherapy for patients with advanced cancer: A treatment manual.* New York, NY: Oxford University Press.

Breitbart, W., Poppito, S., Rosenfeld, B., Vickers, A.J., Li, Y., Abbey, J., ... Cassileth, B.R. (2012). Pilot randomized controlled trial of individual meaning-centered psychotherapy for patients with advanced cancer. *Journal of Clinical Oncology, 30*(12), 1304–1309.

Breitbart, W., Rosenfeld, B., Gibson, C., Pessin, H., Poppito, S., Nelson, C., ... Olden, M. (2010). Meaning-centered group psychotherapy for patients with advanced cancer: A pilot randomized controlled trial. *Psycho-Oncology, 19*(1), 21–28.

Breitbart, W., Rosenfeld, B., Pessin, H., Kaim, M., Funesti-Esch, J., Nelson, C.J., & Brescia, R. (2000). Depression, hopelessness, and desire for hastened death in terminally ill patients with cancer. *The Journal of the American Medical Association, 13*(284), 2907–2911.

Carreno, D.F., Cangas, A.J., Eysenbeck, N., Gongora, B., Uclés-Juárez, R., & Fernández-Miranda, S. (2017). *The impact of cancer on personal values and its implications for spiritual well-being and quality of life.* Manuscript in preparation.

Chochinov, H.M., Hack, T., Hassard, T., Kristjanson, L.J., McClement, S., & Harlos, M. (2002). Dignity in the terminally ill: A cross-sectional, cohort study. *The Lancet, 360*(9350), 2026–2030.

Chochinov, H.M., Kristjanson, L.J., Breitbart, W., McClement, S., Hack, T., Hassard, T., & Harlos, M. (2011). Effect of dignity therapy on distress and end-of-life experience in terminally ill: A randomised controlled trial. *The Lancet, 12*, 753–762.

Cicirelli, V.G. (2001). Personal meanings of death in older adults and young adults in relation to their fears of death. *Death Studies, 25*(8), 663–683.

Cicirelli, V.G. (2006). *Older adults' views on death.* New York, NY: Springer.

Dickinson, G. (2007). End-of-life and palliative care issues in medical and nursing schools in the United States. *Death Studies, 31(8)*, 713–726. doi:10.1080/07481180701490602

Dignity [Def. 1]. (1946). *Webster's new international dictionary* (2nd ed.). Springfield, MA: Merriam-Webster.

Doukas, D., Gorenflo, D., & Supanich, B. (1998). Primary care physician attitudes and values toward end-of-life care and physician-assisted death. *Ethics & Behavior, 9*(3), 219–230.

Fegg, M.J., Wasner, M., Neudert, C., & Borasio, G.D. (2005). Personal values and individual quality of life in palliative care patients. *Journal of Pain and Symptom Management, 30*(2), 154–159.

Gawande, A. (2014). *Being mortal: Medicine and what matters in the end.* Toronto, ON: Doubleday.

Gesser, G., Wong, P.T.P., & Reker, G.T. (1988). Death attitudes across the life span. The development and validation of the Death Attitude Profile (DAP). *Omega, 2*, 113–128.

Gibran, K. (1994). *The prophet.* London, England: Senate Press. (Original work published 1923)Grezsta, E., & Sieminska, M.J. (2011). Patient-perceived changes in the system of values after cancer diagnosis. *Journal of Clinical Psychology in Medical Settings, 18*, 55–64.

Hack, T., McClement, S., Chochinov, H.M., Cann, B. J., Hassard, T., Kristjanson, L.J., & Harlos, M. (2010). Learning from dying patients during their final days: Life reflections gleaned from dignity therapy. *Palliative Medicine, 24*(7), 715–723.

Hamama-Raz, Y., Solomon, Z., & Ohry, A. (2000). Fear of personal death among physicians. *Omega, 41*(2), 139–149.

Harding, S.R., Flannelly, K.J., Weaver, A.J., & Costa, K.G. (2005). The influence of religion on death anxiety and death acceptance. *Mental Health, Religion & Culture, 8*(4), 253–261.

Hayes, S.C., Strosahl, K.D., & Wilson, K. G. (1999). *Acceptance and commitment therapy.* New York, NY: Guilford Press.

Hune-Brown, N. (2017, May 23). How to end a life. *Toronto Life*. Retrieved from http://torontolife.com/city/life/doctors-assist-suicide-like-end-life/

Iverach, L., Menzies, R.G., & Menzies, R.E. (2014). Death anxiety and its role in psychopathology: Reviewing the status of a transdiagnostic construct. *Clinical Psychology Review, 34*(7), 580–593.

Kastenbaum, R. (2000). *The psychology of death* (3rd ed.). New York, NY: Springer.

Kearl, M.C. (1989). *Endings: A sociology of death and dying*. New York, NY: Oxford University Press.

Kubler-Ross, E. (1969). *On death and dying*. New York, NY: Macmillan.

Kubler-Ross, E. (2009). *On death and dying* (40th anniversary ed.). Abingdon, England: Routledge.

Malliarou, M., Pavlos, S., Kiriaki, S., Tatiana, S., Kostantinia, K., Eleni, M., & Eleni, T. (2011). Greek nurses' attitudes towards death. *Global Journal of Health Science, 3*(1), 224–230.

McClain, C., Rosenfeld, B., & Breitbart, W. (2003). Effect of spiritual well-being on end-of-life despair in terminally-ill cancer patients. *The Lancet, 361*, 1603–1607.

Moadel, A., Morgan, C., Fatone, A., Grennan, J., Carter, J., Laruffa, G., ... Dutcher, J. (1999). Seeking meaning and hope: Self-reported spiritual and existential needs among an ethnically diverse cancer patient population. *Psycho-Oncology, 8*, 1428–1431.

Muldoon, M., & King, N. (1995). Spirituality, health care, and bioethics. *Journal of Religion and Health, 34*(4), 329–349.

Neimeyer, R.A. (Ed.). (1994a). *Death anxiety handbook: Research, instrumentation, and application*. New York, NY: Taylor & Francis.

Neimeyer, R. A. (1994b). The threat index and related methods. In R.A. Neimeyer (Ed.), *Death anxiety handbook* (pp. 61–101). New York, NY: Taylor & Francis.

Neimeyer, R. A. (2005). From death anxiety to meaning making at the end of life: Recommendations for psychological assessment. *Clinical Psychology: Science and Practice, 12*(3), 354–357.

Nelson, C.J., Rosenfeld, B., Breitbart, W., & Galietta, M. (2002). Spirituality, religion, and depression in the terminally ill. *Psychosomatics, 43*(3), 213–220.

Nia, H.S., Lehto, R. H., Ebadi, A., & Peyrovi, H. (2016). Death anxiety among nurses and health care professionals: A review article. *International Journal of Community Based Nursing and Midwifery, 4*(1), 2–10.

Pollak, K., Alexander, S., Tulsky, J., Lyna, P., Coffman, C., Dolor, R. ..., Ostbye, T. (2011). Physician empathy and listening: associations with patient satisfaction and autonomy. *Journal of the American Board of Family Medicine, 24*(6), 665–672. doi:10.3122/jabfm.2011.06

Puchalski, C., & Guenther, M. (2012). Restoration and re-creation: Spirituality in the lives of healthcare professionals. *Current Opinion in Supportive Palliative Care, 6*, 254–258.

Pyszczynski, T., Greenberg, J., & Solomon, S. (2002). *In the wake of 9/11: The psychology of terror.* Washington, DC: American Psychological Association.

Rokeach, M. (1973). *The nature of human values.* New York, NY: Collier Maclillian.

Servaty, H., Krejci, M., & Hayslip, J.R. (1996). Relationships among death anxiety, communication apprehension with the dying, and empathy in those seeking occupations as nurses and physicians. *Death Studies, 20*(2), 149–161.

Schmi, J.M., Meyer, L.E., Duff, J.M., Dai, Y., Zou, F., & Close, J.L. (2016). Perspectives on death and dying: A study of resident comfort with end-of-life care. *BMC Medical Education, 16,* 297. doi:10.1186/s12909-016-0819-6

Solomon, S., Greenberg, J., & Pyszczynski, T. (2004). The cultural animal: Twenty years of terror management theory research. In J. Greenberg, S. Koole, & T. Pyszczynski. (Eds.), *Handbook of experimental existential psychology.* New York, NY: Guilford.

Sullivan, A., Lakoma, M., & Block, S. (2003). The status of medical education in end-of-life care: A national report. *Journal of General Internal Medicine, 18*(9), 685–695.

Teno, J.M., Gozalo, P.L., Bynum, J.P., Leland, N.E., Miller, S.C., Morden, N.E., ... Mor, V. (2013). Change in end-of-life care for Medicare beneficiaries: site of death, place of care, and health care transitions in 2000, 2005, and 2009. *JAMA, 309*(5), 470–477.

Tomer, A. (Ed.) (2000). *Death attitudes and the older adult: Theories, concepts, and applications.* Philadelphia, PA: Brunner-Routledge

Tomer, A., Eliason, G.T., & Wong, P.T.P. (2008). *Existential and spiritual issues in death attitudes.* New York, NY: Erlbaum.

Visser, A., Garssen, B., & Vingerhoets, A. (2010). Spirituality and well-being in cancer patients: A review. *Psycho-Oncology, 19,* 565–572.

Wong, P.T.P. (2005). The challenges of experimental existential psychology: Terror management or meaning management? Review of the book Handbook of experimental existential psychology. *PsycCRITIQUES, 50*(52). doi:10.1037/04131412

Wong, P.T.P. (2008). Meaning management theory and death acceptance. In A. Tomer, E. Grafton, & P.T.P. Wong (Eds.), *Death attitudes: Existential & spiritual issues.* Mahwah, NJ: Erlbaum.

Wong, P.T.P. (2009). Existential positive psychology. In S.J. Lopez (Ed.), *Encyclopedia of positive psychology* (Vol. 1, pp. 361–368). Oxford, England: Wiley Blackwell.

Wong, P.T.P. (2010). Meaning therapy: An integrative and positive existential psychotherapy. *Journal of Contemporary Psychotherapy, 40*(2), 85–99.

Wong, P.T.P. (2011). Positive psychology 2.0: Towards a balanced interactive model of the good life. *Canadian Psychology, 52*(2), 69–81.

Wong, P.T.P. (2012a). Toward a dual-systems model of what makes life worth living. In P.T.P. Wong (Ed.), *The human quest for meaning: Theories, research, and applications* (2nd ed., pp. 3–22). New York, NY: Routledge.

Wong, P.T.P. (2012b). What is the meaning mindset? *International Journal of Existential Psychology and Psychotherapy, 4*(1), 1–3.

Wong, P.T.P. (2012c). From logotherapy to meaning-centered counseling and therapy. In P.T.P. Wong (Ed.), *The human quest for meaning: Theories, research, and applications* (2nd ed., pp. 619–647). New York, NY: Routledge.

Wong, P.T.P. (Ed.). (2012d). *The human quest for meaning: Theories, research, and applications* (2nd ed.). New York, NY: Routledge.

Wong, P.T.P. (2016). Self-transcendence: A paradoxical way to become your best. *International Journal of Existential Psychology and Psychotherapy, 6*(1). Retrieved from http://www.drpaulwong.com/wp-content/uploads/2016/03/Self-Transcendence_A-Paradoxical-Way-to-Become-Your-Best-2016-Aug-15.pdf

Wong, P.T.P., Reker, G.T., & Gesser, G. (1994). Death Attitude Profile – Revised: A multidimensional measure of attitudes toward death. In R.A. Neimeyer (Ed.), *Death anxiety handbook: Research instrumentation and application* (pp. 121–148). Washington, DC: Taylor & Francis.

Wong, P.T.P., & Tomer, A. (2011). Beyond terror and denial: The positive psychology of death acceptance. *Death Studies, 35*(2), 99-106.

World Health Organization. (2015). *Cancer*. Retrieved from http://www.who.int/cancer/en/

Yalom, I.D. (2008). *Staring at the sun: Overcoming the terror of death*. San Francisco, CA: Jossey-Bass.

Chapter 11

Continuing bonds between the living and the dead in contemporary western societies: Implications for our understandings of death and the experience of death anxiety

Edith Maria Steffen and Elaine Kasket

This chapter takes the starting point that the fear of death is in part determined by how we relate to our dead and how we conceptualise death, suggesting that cultural factors play an important role in the creation and maintenance of death anxiety. Relevant cultural considerations include ontological questions about the way we define constructs such as reality, life and death and sociocultural questions about whether, for example, we see the dead and the living from an individualistic perspective as separate entities or from a collectivist perspective as connected, and what implications this may have for how we relate to our dead. Since the early 20th century, modern western societies could be said to have had the tendency to sever links with their deceased ancestors. A more collectivist view is represented by the continuing bonds perspective, an interdisciplinary sociocultural perspective that has become an influential new paradigm within bereavement scholarship over the past two decades. In this chapter, we aim to show how the continuing bonds perspective can add a broadening dimension to western understandings of death and thus help reconceptualise what death can mean, which may to some extent mitigate against a fear of a death that is seen as a complete disconnection and as devoid of any sense of continuation. As an example of a new way of extending life beyond death, a special focus of this chapter is on digital forms of survival and the crafting of continuing bonds through social media.

The construction of death, relationships with the dead and death anxiety

What do we mean when we speak of the fear of death? What are we referring to when we talk about death? The meanings we attach to death can be thought of as not only subject to individual variation, but also as situated and defined within particular cultural contexts, which include, for example, languages, places, practices and technologies, and the worldviews that are created through them. Conceptualisations of death — and of life — are as much culturally bounded constructions as our understandings of constructs that seem more readily to refer to 'man'-made categories such as intelligence or beauty. For example, there are significant cross-cultural differences even in how death is defined so that a person who is viewed as dead in one society may be classed as alive in another and vice versa (Rosenblatt, 1997). The distinction between life and death is not even clear-cut from a bio-medical perspective (Davey, 2011), and the difficulty of precisely differentiating between life and death becomes yet more complicated when we ask questions about who or what dies: our bodies, our personalities, our identities? Can we have dead and living parts to us? Can we be dead by degrees?

Beyond an essentialist perspective on death

Such complexity merits deeper philosophical consideration. Yet, the philosophical movement that has given most attention to death, existentialism, has often taken a surprisingly simple perspective on death, tending towards the view that death is the ultimate reality or the only certainty in life, 'an inexorable given of the human condition' (Cooper & Adams, 2005, p. 78), a single thing that cannot be argued with. While existentialism, according to Rollo May (1958), developed to oppose the essentialism of western science and thinking, when it comes to death, an absolutist/essentialist stance is often adopted: 'Death is ... the one fact of my life which is not relative but absolute' (May, 1958, p. 49). Any questioning of this immutable fact becomes quickly framed as a form of denial, a defence mechanism (e.g., Yalom, 1980). It is interesting that existentialism critiques and transcends other dualities, for example the mind-body divide, yet it maintains the idea of the facticity of a sharp life-death distinction above all else. It is suggested here that an absolutist view of death could be seen as fundamentally a modernist western position, grounded in a rationalist, materialist and reductionist way of understanding the world, prone to isolating, separating and atomising phenomena. Existentialism could be accused of the unquestioning adoption of a modernist position here, omitting to view its own thinking about death as situated within a specific sociohistorical context.

Beyond a self-focused perspective on death

Furthermore, existentialist thinking about death and the existentialist concern with death anxiety can also be seen to derive from a somewhat self-focused position which seems to take one's own death as the starting point for thinking about what death means, as in the solitary concept of 'being-towards-death' (Heidegger, 1962), a nonrelational process that places the awareness of one's own mortality at the centre. However, our first-hand empirical knowledge of death comes from seeing others die. We experience death in the first place when our loved ones die, which makes death into a relational and intersubjective event. What death as such means to us is influenced by our experiences as grievers, and our grief is influenced by our conceptualisations of what has happened to loved ones who have died and whether or how we can still be connected with them. When our loved ones die, we are not only faced with their physical absence but also with their changed status as 'dead loved ones': Who are they and where are they now? The bereavement literature has sometimes spoken about the griever needing to 'relocate' the deceased loved one (Prigerson & Parkes, 2010), and while there seems to be less difficulty with re-locating the physical remains, mourners across different belief systems are faced with the problem of conceptualising the ongoing existence of the *person* that has died and to whom they still feel attached. Different belief systems may provide different afterlife conceptualisations that more or less satisfactorily enable the bereaved to conceive of the ongoing existence of this person and the context in which such an existence may take place, but the problem of what it means to be dead may remain unresolved, whether one holds a faith in an afterlife or not.

Beyond an individualistic perspective of death

Conceptions of an afterlife as a place or alternative world are for most people hypothetical, perhaps with the exception of those whose near-death experiences have given them a sense of an empirically validated existence beyond terrestrial life. By contrast, conceptions of the continued existence of the deceased loved one themselves may be more readily available to grievers, as many report to feel comforted by a continued sense of connection, something that can be seen as a central aspect of grieving across many different cultures (Chan et al., 2005; Grimby, 1998; Lindstrom, 1995; Rees, 1971; Yamamoto, Okonogi, Iwasaki, & Yoshimura, 1969). It makes sense that people in more collectivist cultures may have an easier time maintaining a sense of the ongoing existence of the deceased than people in cultures that value separation between individuals. The materialism and individualism of the dominant modernist worldview in the west implies, for example, that the person as a unit is independent and clearly separate from its context. A logical implication of this worldview is that the living and the dead are separate and that no connection exists between them and that someone who is physically 'dead' is also 'gone'. By contrast, an understanding of people as intrinsically connected may mean that a part of the other person stays part of me and vice versa. The view of people as separate has significant implications for how we understand the life and death of people we love and care about as well as for how we understand our own life and death.

The assumption that I can be in a relationship with a person for many years but be instantly thrown into a state of disconnectedness when they die, is likely to engender significant anxiety. By extension, it also means that I can be cut off in an instant from everything and everyone I care about, and being the 'social animals' that we are, fear of being disconnected may contribute substantially to any anxiety about 'mere' physical death.

The continuing bonds perspective and how it is relevant for contemporary western societies

This way of understanding ourselves and the world is so ingrained in our western thinking that it is difficult to imagine it could be otherwise. Yet, the existence of more collectivist cultures shows us that this is not the only way of seeing reality.

Continuing bonds in Japan

As an example, in Japanese culture, one's identity is defined by one's community as it is 'embedded in the sense of social harmony' (Goss & Klass, 2005, p. 22). The Japanese emphasis on interdependence, reciprocity, loyalty and sensitivity to others and the prioritisation of one's role as a member of a group rather than an individual is reflected in communal rites to take care of the dead and maintain connections with the ancestors (Valentine, 2018). Significantly, the deceased ancestors remain members of the family in a mutually dependent relationship and are so much part of the lives of the living, it would be artificial to draw a clear boundary between both worlds. The presence of the *butsudan* (Buddhist altar) in the home, for example, enables family members to continue sharing personal and intimate aspects of their lives with their deceased loved ones, continuing the bonds they had before the death (Klass, 2006). Yet, vitally, the shared ritual which includes communication with the deceased is not separate from the rest of the lives of the living, but instead, cultural and personal narratives become interwoven (Klass, 2006). The significance of how cultural narratives or conceptual frameworks can facilitate or hinder the development and maintenance of continuing bonds between the living and the dead cannot be overestimated. Valentine (2018) conducted a comparative qualitative analysis of continuing bonds in British and Japanese mourners, whereby descriptions of continuing bonds by the British characterised them as 'diverse, idiosyncratic and improvised', whereas the Japanese mourners' continuing bonds were found to be 'grounded in a shared tradition of mutual obligation and harmonious interdependency across the life-death boundary' (Valentine, 2018).

The 'discovery' of continuing bonds in the west

Given such significant cultural differences, one conclusion might be to simply accept that westerners have a harder time relating to their dead and integrating such relationships into their lives and leave it at that. However, one reason the 'discovery' of continuing bonds in cultures such as Japan has been so important for the west is that it addressed a need that was not being met by the contemporary bereavement culture. Approaches to grief and bereavement in the 20th century were characterised by the demand on the bereaved to 'let go' and 'move on'. In Freud's *Mourning and melancholia* (1917), an ongoing attachment to the deceased was viewed as a form of denial or 'hallucinatory wishful psychosis'. This was a marked change from prolonged and extensive mourning traditions in the 19th century, for example in Victorian Britain, and this cultural change, as so sharply analysed by sociologist Tony Walter (1999), could be seen as part of modernist and materialist 20th century western society's need for well-functioning productive individuals who can contribute to that society's consumerist and technological objectives. Hand in hand with this ideology went a medicalisation of people's grief experiences and thus a pathologisation of experiences that didn't fit the dominant materialist worldview. Widows sensing the presence of their deceased husbands were told they were having hallucinations and suffering from pathological grief, and this diagnosis remained the received wisdom for much of the 20th century. However, a study by Yamamoto et al. (1969) changed this picture, as it was shown that 90% of the participating Japanese widows had such experiences and there were no concerns about their mental health, which raised questions about pathologising such experiences in western widows. A large survey by Rees (1971) in Wales, UK, then constituted the first western study to demonstrate the extent of experiencing ongoing contact with the deceased and the comforting impact this had on the bereaved. While this was the beginning of many further surveys and phenomenological studies around such experiences, it was not until the publication of *Continuing Bonds: New Understandings of Grief* by Klass, Silverman and Nickman (1996) that the tables truly turned. This publication, which is often seen as marking a paradigm shift in bereavement scholarship, brought the idea to a wider audience that ongoing relationships with the deceased are normal and can be beneficial, and just over twenty years on, it can be observed that there is now widespread acceptance of this changed understanding (see Klass & Steffen, 2018).

Continuing bonds in contemporary western societies

Since Klass et al. (1996) demonstrated that continuing bonds with the deceased are relevant and significant aspects of grief in western contexts too, a great many studies have explored how people maintain their relationships with their deceased loved ones. Aready mentioned are sense of presence experiences. Approximately 60% of the bereaved report having had such experiences, and these may entail any of the five senses or just a nondistinct 'feeling of presence' (Rees, 1971). The vast majority of these experiences are felt to be beneficial, but a small number are experienced as negative, often made sense of as unfinished business in the relationship. Other forms of continuing bonds can simply be talking to the deceased, for example at the graveside, but also in other places and situations, dreaming of the deceased, talking to others about the deceased, looking at photographs or mementos and using a whole range of different forms of memorialisation. Legacy projects are another way of continuing the bond, from fundraising to starting an enterprise in the deceased person's name. Smaller ways of honouring the deceased can simply entail doing something the way the deceased would have done, cherishing objects, foods, and so forth that the deceased would have enjoyed, adopting certain mannerisms or ways of speaking of the deceased, or taking up new interests and hobbies that strengthen the connection with the deceased. A significant aspect of continuing bonds is that they bestow a continued social existence on the deceased (Klass et al., 1996). Sometimes this can be done through sharing stories about the deceased, as when jointly constructing a biography of the deceased, as Walter (1999) put it, but also through sharing metaphors or rituals that evoke a sense of the deceased's presence. For example, one couple reported that every time a digital clock shows a time with all the same numbers, it signifies their deceased child's presence to them and a confirmation of their continued connection which brings them joy (Gudmundsdottir & Chesla, 2005). Such examples demonstrates not only the comforting impact of continuing bonds but also how this impact is partly socially constituted, creating a sense of social membership for the deceased through the shared understanding of the practice's or the metaphor's meaning. In some instances, these meanings carry with them wider-ranging implications that can stretch far into the future. In a study by one of the authors (Steffen & Coyle, 2011), one man reported after-death communication with his deceased mother and receiving messages including a 'commission' to take care of other still living family members. This example shows how the continuing bond can also be a medium or channel for the transmission of identity-related meaningful tasks or legacy projects, thus constituting a reciprocal relationship of care and responsibility between the living and the deceased.

The persistence of the digital self, and its relationship to death anxiety

It is clear that we traverse a wide spectrum in our varying conceptualisations of death, and of the place of our dead in society. At one end sits the received wisdom of essentialist, self-focused, individualistic cultures, which mark out clear boundaries between the quick and the dead: culturally-sanctioned remembrances may be limited to certain times, such as Memorial Day or All Souls' Day; people who seek out or believe in a closer connection or communication with the deceased, such as spiritualists, may be dismissed as mad or marginal; and those who do not obey Freud's dictum to break attachments with the dead after a seemly period of time are pathologised. At the other end, we find the interdependent, collectivist beliefs of many other cultures: ancestors continue to occupy a place in society; the dead are accepted and integrated into everyday life; and experiences of responding to others' deaths, and anticipating one's own, are inevitably coloured by this perspective. Cutting across countries and cultures, however, is the levelling influence of modern digital technologies, which in unanticipated ways are changing what death means, where the dead 'live', and how the dead continue to possess presence and influence long after breath has left their corporeal bodies. The fact that our digital lives can extend for generations beyond our physical ones may have considerable implications for our experience of death anxiety.

The construction and maintenance of the digital self

Before 2008, the average adult spent just 18 minutes a day on their phones; this has now stretched into many hours (Alter, 2017), although it may be that very little of that time is spent actually speaking to others voice to voice. As we use our devices to photograph, type, upload, post, share, comment, search, hyperlink and retweet, the minutiae of our lives are tracked and logged, sometimes deliberately and sometimes inadvertently. The online sphere comes to house a huge externalised memory bank; a collection of reflections and projections of our bodily-bound selves; and a forum for those digital selves to 'meet' and interact with one another. The traditional duality of which Descartes spoke, the being of body ('res extensa') and being of mind ('res cogitans') have been joined by a third, 'res digitalis' (Kim, 2001), a type of being that sits somewhere between extensa and cogitans and shares features of both. Today's 'digital natives' (Prensky, 2001), virtually born with smartphones in their hands and entirely accustomed to both having a digital self and to communing with other digital selves in the online agora, may find it hard to fathom that a lack of physical proximity was ever a barrier to knowledge, communication, or even intimacy.

Facilitated by the massive increase in data capturing and sharing over the last few years, due to advances in mobile technologies, social networking platforms, and the ease of interface between them, our digital representations may be rich indeed. The vast majority of our verbal and visual data are generated, conveyed and stored in digital rather than analog form, with each creation and transmission adding to our digital footprints. The more detailed one's online presence and the heavier one's social media use, the more tangible that person can continue to seem, even when the physical person behind the digital representation has died. Little wonder, therefore, that bereaved people may describe a well-developed social networking profile as the 'last bit of [the dead person] that's still really real' (Kasket, 2012). Far from being a psychologically concerning development, mourners' ongoing interaction with persistent digital selves or reflections seems to have positive effects. Memorialisation on social networking sites has all the benefits of traditional mourning rituals, with the added positives of accessibility and continuity; it seems to have a facilitative impact on our ability to grieve and cope (e.g., Irwin, 2017; Kasket, 2012), through participation in a community of mourning in which the dead person also continues to be a tangible part. Persistence of digital selves has huge implications for ongoing continuing bonds, and interacting with deceased individuals' continuing online presence — particularly social networking profiles — appears to be a 'new normal' in the bereavement landscape. Beyond this, however, posthumously persistent digital reflections call into question when complete 'death' — inclusive of 'social death' — really occurs.

The digital desegregation of the living and the dead

The industrial revolution in the west helped cement the conceptualisation of life and death as separate in a variety of ways, as already described, but including *topographically*. Take 19th century England as an illustration of this. Prior to the 1830s in England, people were usually buried in the localities in which they had lived, in churchyards or family plots amongst their relatives and communities. As the century progressed and the industrial revolution gathered pace, there was mass migration into rapidly growing cities: the population of London more than doubled. Churchyards were insufficient to handle all of the deceased members of such a mobile and expanding populace, and in the capitol city the newly forged London Cemetery Company responded by establishing seven elegant Victorian cemeteries between 1832 and 1842. These were large, stand-alone cemeteries, unlike the 'graveyards' or 'churchyards' situated within local communities. With these developments, the spaces for the living became more distinct and delineated from the spaces for the dead. People became less likely to walk past graves of grandparents, parents or siblings as they went about their daily business, instead having to make special arrangements and efforts to visit their dead. Valuing productive, effective functioning (Walter, 1999), western industrial societies increasingly managed their dying in hospitals, and allocated their dead to beautiful but clearly separate spaces.

One of the canonical narratives about life in the information age is that digital platforms and technologies are fragmenting society, isolating and disconnecting us from one another and from a sense of true community. While this may be true in some ways, the digital revolution has done wonders for the social lives of the dead, who are more able to stay involved and influential in the lives of the living than ever before. Kittler (1999) points out that the 'realm of the dead is as extensive as the storage and transmission capabilities of a given culture' (p. 13), and the technological culture in which we exist seems to have limitless potential for both. The social networking profiles of the dead remain frequently visited and continuously expanded and embellished with the conversations and memories of the community of grievers, who speak directly to the dead as well as to one another. Dead people's recommendations on Amazon, Goodreads and TripAdvisor still influence others' reading and travelling choices. Their Spotify listening preferences still affect their families' algorithmically generated playlists.

The way the online environment is currently organised, the Facebook profiles, Twitter accounts, book reviews and blog posts of deceased users do not exist in a separate space to that of live users; we encounter the dead everywhere we go online, like navigating tombstones proliferating on a bustling city street. Paradoxically, the more technologically advanced we become, the more we return to something like the pre-industrial era, in which the dead and the living existed cheek by jowl. Perhaps this means that, as in the pre-industrial era, we the living are more conscious of our own mortality, being so much more frequently exposed to the traces of those no longer physically with us. At the same time, though, we may feel more assured of our ongoing significance to our loved ones and communities, seeing how the voices and images of the everyday dead (not just the famous, great and good) are still vivid and accessible online. Ironically, our wondrous modern technologies could drive a global return to a culture of ancestor veneration, even in those industrialised and secularised societies that turned away from it long ago. When we hold our smartphones, we can also hold a *butsudan* in the palms of our hands. While I may know nothing about my great grandmother apart from a name and a faded photograph or two, my daughter may be vivid, influential and inspirational in the lives of her great grandchildren.

This compelling fantasy of immortality, however, has a downside, for the spectre of technological obsolence haunts both our software and hardware. The digital beings on whom we may come to rely for a sense of continuing bonds with our dead can 'either endure forever, without any change, or disappear instantly without leaving a trace. [They] have two contradictory possibilities simultaneously: eternal endurance and instant vanishment' (Kim, 2001, p. 101). Our anxiety about death can, therefore, be both assuaged and triggered by the fact that so much of our legacy — particularly our visual and verbal legacies, which underpin our direct ongoing influence and voice in the world — are likely to be stored in digital form.

Entering the uncanny valley
While our persistent online representations may be helpful in continuing bonds and assuaging our anxieties about our own and others' deaths, there is an additional caveat. Our ever-advancing technologies create some novel possibilities for those who indulge fantasies of cheating death, but the actualisation of those possibilities represent a tipping point, for many, into a territory that feels distinctly uneasy. For example, people report being highly distressed by experiences such as receiving status updates or birthday reminders from dead users' nonmemorialised Facebook accounts. In a case in the United States some years ago, a grieving mother whose young son's death from a rare disease had been widely publicised was horrified to receive messages purportedly from beyond the grave, authored by an individual with misplaced good intentions. Despite what the dead person might wish, survivors may have mixed feelings about posthumous, algorithmically generated tweets, or pre-scheduled birthday emails from a dead loved one. However much we might miss the person, we seem more comfortable when our loved one's online activity has a clear end point commensurate with the physical death; we are less sanguine when, by accident or design, a posthumously persistent digital self 'acts alive'.

This point of differentiation is illustrated vividly in the 'Be Right Back' episode of the United Kingdom television series *Black Mirror* (Brooker & Harris, 2013). Martha, a young woman bereft by the untimely death of her boyfriend Ash and craving connection with him again, is offered what feels like a lifeline — an online service that creates an artificially intelligent version of the person who died. '[Ash] was a heavy user, he'd be perfect', says her well-meaning friend. 'It's software. It mimics him. You give it someone's name ... It goes back and reads through all the things they've ever said online, their Facebook updates, their Tweets, anything public ... The more it has, the more it's him'. Resistant at first, but desperate to 'relocate' (Parkes & Prigerson, 2010) Ash, Martha eventually takes the plunge, with mixed results.

Tellingly, as long as Martha interacts with the reconstituted Ash only online and over the telephone, she feels comforted. It is only once she subscribes to the premium service — a physical, lifelike animatronic body to house the software — that she falls into the 'uncanny valley' (Mathur & Reichling, 2016). This term describes the negative emotional response — a kind of creepiness — that we experience when we encounter something that is *almost* human, but not quite. The physically reconstituted Ash may be humanoid, but does not feel human enough; his bereaved girlfriend ultimately finds her interaction with his physical clone too unsettling to bear, and stashes it in the attic.

This fictional scenario neatly illustrates how continuing to interact online with posthumous digital reflections, and perhaps wishing to have a persistent digital legacy ourselves, may have very little to do with an actual wish to deny death. As positively as we may respond to complex digital representations of our dead loved ones, and as much as many of them welcome their ongoing influence and persistence in our midst, the demise of the actual biological person is still accepted as irreversible. A sense of presence can be comforting, while intimations of an actual presence may induce horror. To attempt to combat our anxiety about death by utilising technology to raise the dead is a venture that will likely always be doomed to failure. To utilise technology to allow our ancestors' voice and influence to be vital in our own lives, however, is another matter.

Conclusion

While, to our knowledge, no research has been done into the relationship between continuing bonds and death anxiety, we may hesitate the view that there is likely to be a significant impact. Being able to continue a relationship beyond death takes some of the power of death away. There has been evidence from qualitative research that felt presence or continued interaction with the deceased can confirm a belief in an afterlife or lead to such a belief, and this can also be accompanied by a reduction in death anxiety (e.g., Parker, 2005; Steffen & Coyle, 2011). A recent mixed methods study by Cooper (2016) found that those who had reported spontaneous post-death encounters experienced greater levels of hope than those who had not, and the theme of hope for reunion with the deceased loved one was emphasised. Continuing bonds more generally, not just sense of presence experiences, suggest an ongoing existence of the deceased — whether this is in a supernatural realm or on a symbolic level — and this has consequences not only for the way we perceive someone else's death but, by implication, also how we conceive of our own death. Simply put, if those who came before me continue in my life beyond their death, then I might also continue in the lives of those who come after me. More radically put, if my understanding of the self is such that I view myself to be inextricably connected with those I love, then I live on through those I have loved and who have loved me, as I have become a part of them and they have become part of me. In such a perspective, the world of the dead and the world of the living become interwoven on many different levels whereby the physical realm — and thus physical death — is only one aspect of many, and it may not be the most significant aspect when it comes to what it is that is considered to be and experienced as most meaningful.

References

Alter, A. (2017). *Irresistible: Why we can't stop checking, scrolling, clicking and watching*. London, England: The Bodley Head.

Brooker, C. (Writer), & Harris, O. (Director). (2013). *Be right back*. [Television series episode.] In Brooker, C. (Executive Producer), *Black mirror*. London, England: Channel 4.

Chan, C.L., Chow, A.Y., Ho, S.M., Tsui, Y.K., Tin, A.F., Boo, B.W., Boo, E.W. (2005). The experience of Chinese bereaved persons: A preliminary study of meaning making and continuing bonds. *Death Studies, 29*, 923–947.

Cooper, C.E. (2016). Spontaneous post-death experiences and the cognition of hope: An examination of bereavement and recovery (Unpublished doctoral thesis). University of Northampton, United Kingdom.

Cooper, M., & Adams, M. (2005). Death. In Deurzen, E. van, & Arnold-Baker, C. (Eds.), *Existential perspectives on human issues: A handbook for therapeutic practice*. Basingstoke, New York, NY: Palgrave Macmillan.

Davey, H. M. (2011). Life, death, and in-between: Meanings and methods in microbiology. *Applied Environmental Microbiology, 77*, 5571–5576.

Freud, S. (1917). Mourning and melancholia. In J. Strachey (Ed. and Trans.), *The standard edition of the complete psychological works of Sigmund Freud* (Vol. XIV; pp. 252–268). London, England: Hogarth Press.

Goss, R.E., & Klass, D. (2005). *Dead but not lost: Grief narratives in religious traditions*. Walnut Creek, CA: Altamira Press.

Grimby, A. (1998). Hallucinations following the loss of a spouse: Common and normal events among the elderly. *Journal of Clinical Geropsychology, 4*, 65–74.

Gudmundsdottir, M., & Chesla, C.A. (2006). Building a new world: Habits and practices of healing following the death of a child. *Journal of Family Nursing, 12,* 143164.

Heidegger, M. (1962). *Being and time.* Malden, MA: Blackwell Publishing.

Irwin, M. (2017). Mourning 2.0: Continuing bonds between the living and the dead on Facebook: Continuing bonds in cyberspace. In D. Klass & E. M. Steffen (Eds.), *Continuing bonds in bereavement: New directions for research and practice.* New York/London: Routledge.

Kasket, E. (2012). Continuing bonds in the age of social networking. *Bereavement Care, 31*(2), 62–69. doi: 10.1080/02682621.2012.710493

Kim, J. (2001). Phenomenology of digital-being. *Human Studies, 24,* 87–111. doi: 10.1023/A:1010763028785

Kittler, F. (1999). *Gramophone, film, typewriter* (G. Winthrop-Young & Michael Wutz, Trans.). Stanford, CA: Stanford University Press.

Klass, D. (2006). Continuing conversation about continuing bonds. *Death Studies, 30,* 843–858.

Klass, D., Silverman, P.R., & Nickman, S. (1996). *Continuing bonds: New understandings of grief.* New York: Taylor & Francis.

Klass, D., & Steffen, E.M. (Eds.). (2018). *Continuing bonds in bereavement: New directions for research and practice.* New York/London: Routledge.

Lindstrom, T.C. (1995). Experiencing the presence of the dead: Discrepancies in the 'sensing experience' and their psychological concomitants. *Omega: Journal of Death & Dying, 31,* 11–21.

Mathur, M.B., & Reichling, D.B. (2016). Navigating a social world with robot partners: A quantitative cartography of the Uncanny Valley. *Cognition, 146,* 22–32.

May, R. (1958). The origins and significance of the existential movement in psychology. In R. May, E. Angel, & H.F. Ellenberger (Eds.), *Existence* (pp. 3–36). Lanham, MA: Rowman & Littlefield.

Parker, J.S. (2005). Extraordinary experiences of the bereaved and adaptive outcomes of grief. *Omega: Journal of Death and Dying, 51,* 257–283.

Prensky, M. (2001). Digital natives, digital immigrants. *On the Horizon, 9*(5), 1–6. doi: 10.1108/10748120110424816

Prigerson, H.G., & Parkes, C.M. (2010). *Bereavement: Studies of grief in adult life* (4th ed.). London, England: Penguin.

Rees, D. (1971). The hallucinations of widowhood. *British Medical Journal, 4,* 37–41.

Rosenblatt, P.C. (1997). Grief in small-scale societies. In C.M. Parkes, P. Laungani, & B. Young (Eds.), *Death and bereavement across cultures* (pp. 27–51). London, England: Routledge.

Steffen, E., & Coyle, A. (2011). Sense of presence experiences and meaning-making in bereavement: A qualitative analysis. *Death Studies, 35*, 579–609.

Valentine, C. (2018). Identity and continuing bonds in cross-cultural perspective: Britain and Japan. In In D. Klass & E. M. Steffen (Eds.), *Continuing bonds in bereavement: New directions for research and practice*. New York/London: Routledge.

Walter, T. (1999). *On bereavement: The culture of grief.* Milton Keynes, England: Open University Press.

Yalom, I.D. (1980). *Existential psychotherapy.* New York, NY: Basic Books.

Yamamoto, J., Okonogi, K., Iwasaki, T., & Yoshimura, S. (1969). Mourning in Japan. *American Journal of Psychiatry, 125*, 1660–1665.

Chapter 12

Treating low self-esteem: Cognitive behavioural therapies and terror management theory

Peter J. Helm, Jennifer E. Duchschere and Jeff Greenberg

This chapter will briefly describe terror management theory (TMT; Greenberg, Pyszczynski, & Solomon, 1986). Then we will consider how three forms of cognitive behaviour therapy (CBT) could be used to help treat low self-esteem, and ways in which TMT could enhance the application of these therapies to this problem.

Terror management theory

TMT (Greenberg et al., 1986) is based on the writings of cultural anthropologist Ernest Becker (1971, 1973) and proposes that humans, like other animals, are predisposed to try to survive while avoiding death. However, humans have sophisticated cognitive abilities that give rise to self-awareness, which allow us to contemplate our existence and reflect upon past, present, and possible futures (e.g., James, 1890; Kierkegaard, 1844/1957). One consequence of this self-awareness is that humans are acutely aware of their inevitable deaths, which give rise to potentially terrifying anxiety.

According to the theory, humans manage this potential terror by developing and investing in cultural worldviews that imbue life with meaning and standards of value. By sustaining faith in cultural worldviews and living up to cultural standards of value, members are able to attain a sense of enduring personal significance (i.e., self-esteem), which ultimately allow individuals to transcend death either literally (e.g., heaven or reincarnation) or symbolically (e.g., leaving a legacy of achievement). In other words, culture provides the basis for maintaining psychological equanimity even with the knowledge of inevitable mortality.

Self-esteem is generally conceptualised as the extent to which an individual views oneself favorably or unfavorably (e.g., Rosenberg, 1965; Smith & Mackie, 2007). TMT notes that this evaluative orientation toward the self is predicated on standards of value derived from the individual's internalised version of the cultural worldview; it only makes sense to view oneself as of value or not if one has bases for determining what is or is not of value, and the culture provides those bases. Thus, from a TMT perspective, self-esteem is predicated on two elements. The first is faith in a cultural worldview that presents life as meaningful and enduring. The second is the belief that one is a valued contributor to that meaningful reality. Thus, self-esteem is inherently a cultural creation because it is determined by the individual's perception of how well s/he is meeting the standards of value of the individual's internalised worldview. And meeting the standards of value affords the individual a sense of safety, security, and continuance beyond death. Self-esteem therefore functions as a buffer against existential anxiety.

To understand how the need for self-esteem develops and serves a terror management function, it is important to understand the process of socialisation (Becker, 1971). Humans are born helpless and completely dependent upon their parents for protection, warmth, love, and sustenance. Human helplessness, paired with a unique capacity for self-awareness and imagining future possibilities, produces a creature particularly prone to fear and anxiety. Parents function to help soothe these anxieties and fears throughout childhood, providing physical safety and psychological security.

Early in life, children are cared for and loved unconditionally regardless of their behaviour. However, as children grow and develop, parental love and affection becomes increasingly contingent upon 'appropriate' behaviour,

behaviour often contrary to their natural proclivities. For example, children must learn to use the toilet or use table manners. If a child fails to live up to their parent's standards (e.g., they throw their food at the dinner table) they are reprimanded and are met with parental disapproval, which causes negative feelings, anxiety, and insecurity. In contrast, if children succeed in meeting parental standards, they are given praise and encouragement, which causes positive feelings and security. Thus, children begin to equate goodness with security and badness with insecurity and anxiety. In other words, living up to parental standards become the basis for the child's self-esteem. As such, the source of fear and anxiety changes from threats to survival to concerns about worthlessness.

The process of contingent self-esteem and security is eventually transferred from personal relationships to cultural standards as the child continues to grow and develop. This process is generally a smooth transition as parents convey their cultural values to their child from birth. Becker writes that self-esteem is thus 'a natural systemic continuation of the early ego efforts to handle anxiety; it is the durational extension of an effective anxiety-buffer' (Becker, 1971, p. 67). Of course what constitutes appropriate behaviour may vary significantly from one cultural context to the next. For example, American students are often praised for being assertive in class while Japanese students are praised for being undisruptive and passive (e.g., Heine, 2001). Ultimately, self-esteem becomes contingent upon cultural standards of appropriate behaviour. From this perspective, the drive towards self-esteem is a universal phenomenon, but how it is sought and maintained depends upon the individual's internalised cultural oughts' and ideals.

The child's process of negotiating personal desires and parental and societal demands is a struggle, and what emerges from that struggle is a person, a symbolic self who strives to be of value to minimise anxiety (Becker, 1971). Becker (1971, p. 142) writes, 'what we call character is really a series of techniques or a style of living, aimed principally at two things: to secure one's material survival; and to deny the fact that one really has no control over his finitude: mutilation, accident, and death lurk at every breath, and this is what one tries to forget'. The adult that emerges from this process functions with equanimity to the extent that s/he views the self as an object of significance in a meaningful universe.

This TMT analysis led to some core hypotheses that have been supported by research. The first is that self-esteem should buffer anxiety and reduce defensive responses to the threat of death. Accordingly, Greenberg and colleagues (1992) assessed whether raising self-esteem would reduce anxiety in response to threat. In support of this hypothesis, researchers found that boosting self-esteem via false personality feedback led to lower self-reported anxiety after viewing a graphic video of an autopsy compared to those who received moderately positive feedback. In two follow-up studies, researchers used a measure of skin conductance to measure anxiety in anticipation of an electric shock. Those who received positive feedback about the self showed no increase in skin conductance compared to those who those who received mildly positive or no feedback. Likewise, Greenberg and colleagues (1993) found that those with high dispositional self-esteem did not show typical defensiveness after reminders of mortality compared to those with dispositional low self-esteem. Harmon-Jones, Simon, Greenberg, Pyszczynski, and Solomon (1997) found that both elevated and high dispositional self-esteem attenuate defensive reactions after reminders of death. Thus, both experimentally boosted and high dispositional self-esteem has been shown to serve terror management functions (for reviews, see Burke, Martens, & Faucher, 2010; Solomon, Greenberg, & Psyzczynski, 2004).

A second hypothesis was that if self-esteem protects people from concerns about mortality, reminders of mortality should increase efforts to obtain and bolster self-esteem. In support of this hypothesis, Greenberg, Simon, Pyszczynski, Solomon, and Chatel (1992) found that liberals, who value tolerance, respond to reminders of death by favorably evaluating someone who challenges their worldview. This effect was generalised to a broader sample of students only when they were primed with the value of tolerance. Taubman Ben-Ari, Florian, and Mikulincer (1999) found direct behavioural evidence for increased self-esteem striving following death primes. Among participants who valued their driving ability as a basis of self-esteem, reminders of death caused them to increase risky driving behaviour assessed by self-report and on a driving simulator. These studies have been replicated with a wide variety of self-esteem enhancing behaviours (e.g., Hirschberger, Florian, Mikulincer, Goldenberg, & Pyszczynski, 2002; Zestcott, Lifshin, Helm, & Greenberg, 2017). These studies demonstrate that reminders of mortality increase efforts to live up to standards that are both dispositionally ingrained and temporarily made salient.

If self-esteem protects people from mortality concerns, then enhanced self-esteem should reduce the extent to which death thought is accessible, and threats to self-esteem should increase the accessibility of death-related thought (DTA). In support of this third major hypothesis, research shows that elevated self-esteem reduces DTA and threats to self-esteem increase it (for a review of self-esteem and DTA, see Greenberg, Landau, & Arndt, 2013).

Since self-esteem is derived from one's cultural values, bolstering one's worldview can serve a self-esteem and terror management function as well. For example, Jonas and Fischer (2006) found that highly religious individuals were less defensive after threat only if they had an opportunity to affirm their religious beliefs beforehand. In other words, having an opportunity to affirm the basis for one's self-esteem served to mitigate the impact of a threat.

In sum, the terror management theory view of self-esteem has been strongly supported by research, lending credence to its main propositions: that the need for self-esteem emerges out of the socialisation process and serves an anxiety-buffer function, and further, that self-esteem is predicated on the values of the individual's internalised worldview. This conceptualisation has important implications for how to use clinical interventions to counteract problems of low or unstable self-esteem.

This chapter will next briefly review three evidence-based therapeutic approaches and how they view and address self-esteem. It is important to note that these therapies do not explicitly address issues of low self-esteem, but handle them more implicitly. We will begin with CBT, considered a 'second wave' approach (the first wave being strictly behavioural). Then, we will review acceptance and commitment therapy (ACT) and dialectical behaviour therapy (DBT), which build off of the second wave and incorporate elements of mindfulness.[1] TMT's conceptualisation of self-esteem will then be considered in relation to these therapeutic approaches and recommendations for incorporation will be presented.

Cognitive Behaviour Therapy

Dr Aaron Beck developed CBT; CBT has developed and expanded rapidly to reach patients with a wide variety of psychopathologic presentations. CBT is now the most widely tested and used evidence-based practice.

---

[1] It is beyond the scope of this chapter to comprehensively detail each therapeutic approach. Thus, if there is interest in learning more, please refer to the relevant references.

As is described by Judith Beck (2011), CBT is based on a cognitive model, which suggests that psychopathologies share a common thread of dysfunctional thought (although the content and presentation of these thoughts may differ). As people develop and age they attempt to understand their environment, which is influenced by a wide variety of factors and experiences such as genetics, temperament, familial interactions, etc. This understanding leads to the development of 'core beliefs' about the self, and may or may not reflect reality. It is thought that there are three general categories of disordered core beliefs including the belief that one is unlovable, helpless, or worthless (i.e., suffering from low self-esteem).

Core beliefs are ultimately perceived as 'truths' and shape the content of 'intermediate beliefs' which include an individual's assumptions, attitudes, and rules (Beck, 2011). These intermediate beliefs then influence how an individual perceives a given situation and gives rise to 'automatic thoughts', which are thoughts which occur naturally and rapidly (Beck, 2011). Ultimately, how an individual *responds* to a given situation is influenced by these beliefs and thoughts (Beck, 2011). For example, someone may believe they are worthless (core belief: '*I am worthless*'); they then might hold the assumption that '*I fail everything that I try*' (intermediate belief). If this individual is then placed in a situation where they are attempting something for the first time, they may think '*I am too stupid to understand this*' (automatic thought). This thought is likely to influence how they behave (e.g., stop putting effort into the new task).

If the content of these beliefs and thoughts are negatively disposed, psychological disturbances may arise (Beck, 2011). The goal of the therapist is then to affect cognitive change by replacing dysfunctional thoughts and beliefs with functional and realistic alternatives (Beck, 2011). Continuing the above example, a therapist may work with the client to shift the belief '*I fail at everything I try*' to '*I likely won't get something new right the first time*' or '*I might not be good at this, but I succeed at other things*'. This shift in cognition is not easy to accomplish but can be worked toward with various therapeutic techniques. With shifts in cognition, emotional and behavioural changes are assumed to naturally follow (Beck, 2011).

While the foundation of CBT is based on dysfunctional thought, CBT is often implemented differently depending on the presenting psychopathology. Adaptions and manuals thus tend to focus on implementing CBT principles in specific diagnoses (Fennell, 1998). Low self-esteem is not considered a diagnosis by itself, but is commonly experienced in clinical populations (Fennell,

1998; Hall & Tarrier, 2003; McManus, Waite, & Shafran, 2009; Shirk, Burwell, & Harter, 2003; Taylor & Montgomery, 2007). Due to this perception of low self-esteem as a 'symptom' rather than the core of a presenting problem, self-esteem has not been a significant explicit focus in intervention research and applications (Fennell, 1997, 1998; Hall & Tarrier, 2003; Rigby & Waite, 2007; Shirk et al., 2003).

Melanie Fennell appears to be the only researcher who has attempted to specifically apply CBT to the presentation of low self-esteem (1997, 1998, 1999, 2004, 2016). Fennell has described low self-esteem as that which 'lies in a global … negative core belief[s] about the self' (Fennell, 1998, p. 297). These core beliefs are maintained by both biased perceptions and biased interpretations (Fennell, 1998). This means that information received, which is inconsistent with our core beliefs are typically ignored, whereas information received consistent with core beliefs are processed, remembered, and potentially amplified (Fennell, 1998). Thus in treating low self-esteem directly in CBT, the dysfunctional beliefs, attitudes, and thoughts should be shifted to ones more closely reflecting reality and improve daily functioning (as is the goal in forms of CBT for specific diagnoses).[2] As TMT suggests, stable and positive self-esteem results in one's ability to live up to the current cultural standards; thus, these cognition shifts may help reframe these standards and make them more attainable. To our knowledge, Fennell's work has yet to be empirically tested.

Acceptance and commitment therapy

Steven Hayes developed acceptance and commitment therapy (ACT) in 1986. It has rapidly gained popularity and research support in diverse populations and clinical presentations (Harris, 2006). Many therapeutic approaches view psychological suffering as abnormal and problematic, and thus seek to relieve or minimise this distress; ACT challenges this approach as it views psychological suffering as a natural and inevitable part of life (Hayes, Strosahl, & Wilson, 2012).

ACT ultimately proposes that persistent psychological struggles result from 'psychological inflexibility', which manifests in many ways but ultimately narrows one's behaviours to a limited set of options (Hayes et al., 2012). Thus,

---

[2] For further information regarding Fennell's cognitive model of low self-esteem, see her works from 1997 and 1998.

the ultimate goal of intervention would be to shift to 'psychological flexibility' (Hayes et al., 2012). To better understand what these terms entail, we will briefly discuss the six proposed components of psychological inflexibility, as well as the alternative versions reflecting psychological flexibility.

The first component is cognitive fusion, which is when thoughts are equated to reality and are taken seriously (Harris, 2006; Hayes et al., 2012). When a person allows their thoughts this much power, the thoughts strongly influence their behaviours (Harris, 2006). For example, if an individual believes '*I am a bad person*' they may interpret their behaviours as negative or even choose behaviours that would align with this thought, thereby giving it more validity. One can become more flexible with 'defusion', or the ability to observe thoughts nonjudgmentally and not automatically labeling them as true (e.g., '*I notice I am having the thought that I am a bad person*'; Harris, 2006).

The second component is experiential avoidance, which is the attempt to get rid of or avoid unwanted internal experiences (e.g., sadness; Harris, 2006; Hayes et al., 2012). Persistently avoiding these experiences may create additional suffering by spending more time and energy on this rather than on things they value (Harris, 2006). 'Acceptance' is the flexible alternative to experiential avoidance, or 'the voluntary adoption of an intentionally open, receptive, flexible, and nonjudgmental posture with respect to moment-to-moment experience' (Hayes et al., 2012, p. 272). Thus, rather than isolating oneself when feeling anxious (experiential avoidance), the client would learn to be willing to have this experience as it is.

The third component is inflexible attention, which is when an individual focuses on their past or future to the extent that they are unable to notice their current environment (Hayes et al., 2012). This can impact choices for actions or behaviours, as one who is not present-focused may not notice important cues, which would influence their decisions (Hayes et al., 2012). 'Present-moment awareness' can help clients notice their context in a nonjudgmental manner (Hayes et al., 2012). For example, rather than someone ruminating about the past, the therapist may teach the client to notice where they are and how they are feeling right now.

The fourth component is a disruption of chosen values, indicating that someone either does not have clarity regarding what they care about or may be abiding by what others have told them to care about (Hayes et al., 2012). Through 'values clarification/construction', an ACT therapist helps the client discover what it is they care for (Hayes et al., 2012).

The fifth component is inaction, impulsivity, or avoidant persistence, which is when someone rigidly responds (behaviourally) to a given situation (Hayes et al., 2012). To develop flexibility, clients may be asked to perform 'committed action', or behaviours aligned with their values (Hayes et al., 2012).

The last component is an attachment to the conceptualised self, which is when people fuse with certain ideas about themselves based on their histories, roles, or characteristics (Hayes et al., 2012). The content of these ideas do not matter so much as the fact that they limit people from taking into account who they are at the present moment and ultimately limiting their behavioural options (Hayes et al., 2012). For example, if someone believed '*I am an alcoholic because my father was an alcoholic*', there is little room for alternative behavioural options, and inconsistencies with this statement may be perceived as scary. Another example presented by Hayes et al. (2012) is that if a person fused with the belief that they are kind, there is decreased likelihood of directly addressing instances of cruelty or harmful behaviours as it presents inconsistency.

In becoming more psychologically flexible in this component, ACT proposes not to *change* this conceptualisation but to detach from it or lessen its power over behaviours (Hayes et al., 2012). This can be accomplished through increased self-awareness of the present moment but also increased perspective taking in what is labeled 'self-as-context' (Hayes et al., 2012).

Overall, ACT would likely perceive low self-esteem as resulting from fusion (i.e., inflexibility) to persistent (but natural) negative self-evaluations and a conceptualised self. Rather than attempting to get rid of these thoughts or experiences, a clinician would help the client *notice* this fusion and allow them to choose how it is they would like to move forward. This in itself may increase initial experiences of anxiety, as the client is asked to more directly face their unwanted internal experiences and to experience them fully. This anxiety, of course, could include fears of the future and inevitable mortality. In addition, clinicians would ensure that their clients clarified their individual values so as to provide a direction for behaviours rather than abiding to a rigid worldview.

Dialectical behaviour therapy

Using CBT protocols, Marsha Linehan found working with chronically suicidal clients problematic, because clients felt invalidated by change procedures, and it was difficult to teach new skills given the severity and chronicity of the patients' suicidal motivations (Dimeff & Linehan, 2001). Thus, in 1993 Marsha

Linehan released a new protocol known today as dialectical behaviour therapy (DBT; Dimeff & Linehan, 2001; Linehan, 1993a, 1993b). DBT is considered an intensive treatment for individuals with borderline personality disorder (BPD), although it has been adapted for many other disorders that are particularly resistant to treatment or present challenges with emotion regulation (e.g., substance abuse, binge-eating; Dimeff & Linehan, 2001).

The term dialectical refers to a synthesis of seemingly opposite approaches. Dialectics appear in many ways within DBT, although most prominent is that of validation versus change (Pederson, 2015). This suggests that it is important to recognise where a client is and acknowledge that their concerns and feelings are legitimate, while using this acceptance to lead to the possibility for future change (Pederson, 2015).

DBT rests on biosocial theory, which postulates that BPD results from and is maintained by biological and environmental influences (Linehan, 1993a; Lynch, Chapman, Rosenthal, Kuo, & Linehan, 2006; Pederson, 2015; Robins & Chapman, 2004). Typically biological influence refers to emotional dysregulation, or a 'heightened sensitivity and reactivity ... to emotionally evocative stimuli, as well as a delayed return to baseline emotional arousal' (Lynch, et al. 2006, p. 462). While there may be environmental influences, an invalidating context (contexts in which an individual's thoughts and/or feelings are explicitly ignored or labeled as unreasonable) is thought to be most prominent in cases of BPD (Robins & Chapman, 2004). Invalidation, in combination with a vulnerable emotion regulation system, can exacerbate emotional experiences and reactions (Pederson, 2015). Thus, treatment generally focuses on stabilising internal emotional experiences, increasing effective responding in stressful situations, and moving toward self-validation (Pederson, 2015).

Treatment itself occurs in four stages. The first stage targets the safety and stability of the client, focusing on decreasing any suicidal thoughts and behaviours, self-harm, therapy-interfering behaviours (e.g., failure to attend sessions consistently), and quality-of-life interfering behaviours (e.g., substance abuse; Dimeff & Linehan, 2001; Pederson 2015). The second stage targets posttraumatic or other significant stress responses when relevant, as well as a shift to emotional acceptance (Dimeff & Linehan, 2001; Pederson, 2015). Stage three targets problems of daily functioning (which are dependent on the given client; Dimeff & Linehan, 2001; Pederson, 2015). Lastly, stage four focuses on moving toward self-fulfillment and actualisation' (Dimeff & Linehan, 2001; Pederson, 2015).

As currently conceptualised by the *Diagnostic and statistical manual of mental disorders* (5th ed.; DSM-5; American Psychiatric Association, pp. 2–13), BPD is characterised by a 'pervasive pattern of instability of interpersonal relationships, self-image, and affects, and marked by impulsivity' (American Psychiatric Association, 2013, p. 663). One of the criteria worth noting here is that of 'identity disturbance' or unstable sense of self (American Psychiatric Association, 2013). Research has suggested that individuals diagnosed with BPD may have clinically significant low self-esteem (e.g., Lynum, Wilberg, & Katerud, 2008), although also note that those with BPD rapidly shift in their sense of self and thus may also experience frequent changes in their self-evaluations (e.g., Hedrick & Berlin, 2012). While not explicity DSM-5 criteria, this pattern of responses may also present in individuals experiencing distress from substance abuse, posttraumatic stress disorder (PTSD), or eating disorders.

Individuals may have both explicit and implicit attitudes toward themselves; when they differ, discrepant forms of self-esteem may arise (Greenwald & Banaji, 1995). Some researchers have suggested that these discrepant forms are more problematic in the case of BPD, such as Vater, Schröder-Abé, Schütz, Lammers, & Roepke (2010) who suggest that two forms of problematic self-esteem can be found in those with BPD: damaged self-esteem (low explicit self-esteem, high implicit self-esteem) and fragile self-esteem (high explicit self-esteem, low implicit self-esteem).

It is clear that those diagnosed with BPD struggle with an inconsistent sense of self and worth. DBT does not *directly* aim to increase self-esteem, although elements of treatment may do so such as validation of thoughts and feelings. If it is true that BPD develops in part from an invalidating context, individuals in this context may experience an inability to live up to given standards from their caregivers and later on their culture. Thus, shifting to validation may help them to recognise that their thoughts and feelings about their environments are real and that living up to forced standards may not be realistic.

Many studies measure self-esteem alongside other outcomes (e.g., Safer, Telch, & Agras, 2001; Telch, Agras, & Linehan, 2000), but few focus on self-esteem as a primary outcome. However, one study measured self-esteem facets and self-concept clarity in a traditional DBT program and found significantly increased scores of global self-esteem and social self-esteem (Roepke et al., 2010). However, more research is needed to better understand the relationship between self-esteem, BPD, and DBT.

Terror management theory and cognitive behavioural therapies

TMT offers an existential perspective on self-esteem. The most basic point it brings to the fore is that in the big picture of reality in this universe, none of us have any ultimate worth. We are just organisms that come and go, like the many billions before us. As Solomon, Greenberg, and Psyzczynski (1991, p. 96) put it, humans 'could not function with equanimity if they believed that they were not more significant and enduring than apes, lizards, or lima beans'. So we build self-esteem on an internalised, fictional, and largely culturally derived view of reality in which there is meaning, purpose, and values, and we humans can have enduring significance by serving those purposes and living up to those values. From this perspective, low self-esteem results from either failing to sustain such a meaningful view of reality or not believing sufficiently that one is serving the purposes and living up to the values prescribed by that worldview. TMT suggests that, regardless of the specific approach, therapists would benefit from explicitly recognising: (a) that clients bring with them such an internalised worldview; (b) that low and unstable self-esteem contribute to many mental health problems and rectifying these deficits are worthy goals of therapy; (c) that improving self-esteem likely requires consideration of the client's worldview and may require guiding the client toward changes in aspects of that worldview.

These recommendations would not be difficult to incorporate in the three described cognitive behavioural therapies because each therapeutic approach is broadly consistent with TMT's conceptualisation of the human creature. TMT's conceptualisation of the process of developing self-esteem mirrors CBT's conceptualisation of developing core beliefs. Like CBT and DBT, TMT would argue that how an individual responds to a given situation is a function of their core beliefs. Likewise, ACT's construal of psychological inflexibility likely arises out of an individual's attempt at negotiating the external world and turning anxiety into safety, and psychological rigidity is analogous to investment in rigid cultural worldviews (e.g., Greenberg & Arndt, 2012). Given these commonalities, one contribution TMT offers is a broader perspective for the therapist about the existential functions of living up to cultural worldviews that the client brings with them. In other words, TMT could help to position any given set of thoughts/behaviours/emotions into a broader framework of human attempts to be a valued contributor to a meaningful worldview.

The three therapies tend to focus on individual experience and phenomenology by working to replace dysfunctional thoughts (CBT), accept their cognitions and move towards flexibility (ACT), or to specifically target problematic behaviours and move a client towards safety (DBT). In each case, as with many clinical interventions, self-esteem is not directly addressed, but rather seen as a symptom of other underlying problems. For example, lower self-esteem may be associated with experiential avoidance (ACT), but is not viewed as the problem itself.

TMT suggests low or unstable self-esteem often is the core problem, because it leaves the individual riddled with anxiety, which is a problem in itself but also is often then coped with in maladaptive ways like drug abuse or compulsive behaviour. So these approaches would be well-served to be more explicit about addressing self-esteem deficits and how they do so. And to do so, therapists must carefully attend to the two components upon which self-esteem is predicated: faith in a cultural worldview and maintaining a sense of value within that worldview. These goals can be accomplished via either general maintenance (e.g., exposure to cultural artifacts, consuming media, living up to cultural standards, achieving cultural success — such as wealth or fame), or by defensively responding to threat (e.g., activating self-serving biases, derogating alternative worldviews). Specifically, defensive reactions tend to arise when personal or cultural value is undermined (e.g., one fails the bar exam).

Cognitive behavioural therapies may benefit from taking TMT's nuanced view of self-esteem into account. The tenets of the above approaches fail to acknowledge that the client arrives with needs for meaning and significance, a deeply ingrained cultural worldview, and specific ways they are trying to attain and sustain self-esteem within the context of that worldview. Restoring self-esteem requires understanding the client's worldview and the routes to self-esteem the client is trying to take (but failing to succeed at). Since self-worth is predicated on an internalised worldview and our sense of value within it, as worldviews expand and shift, so do our strivings to sustain our self-worth (Greenberg, Vail, & Pyszczynski, 2014). Which ways to bolster our self-esteem or worldviews are chosen depend upon an individual's worldview and self-esteem investments, as well as the salience or accessibility of particular aspects of that person's worldview. As mentioned previously, cultural worldviews can vary drastically (e.g., there are numerous subcultures within the broader American worldview), and within any worldview, there can be various paths toward perceiving oneself as having enduring value. Thus, from the therapist's perspective, there may be numerous avenues to achieve this goal.

In terms of CBT, TMT would focus on how a person's dysfunctional thoughts relate to their cultural standards and how they facilitate (or fail to facilitate) personal significance, or, how those thoughts create obstacles to living up to cultural standards. For example, TMT would suggest moving beyond a given core or immediate belief as dysfunctional for a specific task or situation, but how these beliefs are dysfunctional in the broader cultural framework. TMT suggests that sometimes the worldview has to be modified and sometimes the routes within the worldview a person has chosen are the wrong ones for the person, and other times the routes are right but the way the person is trying to be a good parent, doctor, etc. are misguided or not suited to the individual's talents and temperament.

Similar to CBT, TMT would suggest that ACT therapists help the client not only focus on their own values or goals, but incorporate these into some larger set of cultural values and goals. Self-esteem ultimately has to be socially validated, so personal values and goals have to be compatible with some larger collective worldview. However, TMT would remind us that sometimes the client values can also be a problem if they are inconsistent with possible means for that individual to achieve sustainable self-worth. Furthermore, the problematic behaviours themselves could be a result of failing to live up to internalised values. In other words, low self-esteem (as defined by TMT) could be the cause of dysfunction. And finally, although learning to be mindful of ones thoughts can protect the individual from damage to self-esteem, ultimately people cannot simply accept some thoughts and function well, and that they have no value is prominent among those.

Lastly, DBT focuses on individuals who tend to be resistant to therapy and may be chronically suicidal. Of course the primary concern should be to target safety and stability of the client rather than integrating personal goals with cultural frameworks. TMT insights may be most useful when considering the causes of damaged, fragile, and unstable self-worth. These problems may reflect unstable faith in a meaningful worldview. They could also result from unattainable, excessively high standards of value internalised over the course of the socialisation process. Moving the individual toward a sense of stable, validated self-worth may require some dis-assembling and re-assembling of the ways BPD individuals view the world, other people, themselves, and appropriate standards by which to judge themselves of value. Once this is accomplished, such individuals could more effectively move toward implementing stage four — self-fulfillment and actualisation. And when a therapist seeks to help a client achieve self-fulfillment, they should work towards fulfillment via a cultural path that offers enduring significance.

In sum, all three approaches implicitly target low and/or unstable self-esteem and would benefit by making this a more explicit part of the process. TMT demonstrates that self-esteem is a critically valuable anxiety-buffer that derives from the underlying cultural worldviews of the client. Each approach attempts to move clients toward a more positive view of themselves and their significance in the world. Thus, TMT insights can complement the therapeutic process by grounding growth in a culturally prescribed manner, which should allow the individual to feel as though they are able to be a being of significance in a world of meaning.

References

American Psychiatric Association. (2013). *Diagnostic and statistical manual of mental disorders* (5th ed.). Washington, DC: Author.

Beck, J.S. (2011). *Cognitive behavior therapy: Basics and beyond* (2nd ed.). New York, NY: Guilford Press.

Becker, E. (1971). *The birth and death of meaning* (2nd ed.). New York, NY: The Free Press.

Becker, E. (1973). *The denial of death.* New York, NY: The Free Press.

Burke, B.L., Martens, A., & Faucher, E.H. (2010). Two decades of terror management theory: A meta-analysis of mortality salience research. *Personality and Social Psychology Review, 14,* 155-–195. doi: 10.1177/1088868309352321

Dimeff, L. & Linehan, M.M. (2001). Dialectical behavior therapy in a nutshell. *The California Psychologist, 34,* 10–13.

Fennell, M.J.V. (1997). Low self-esteem: A cognitive perspective. *Behavioral and Cognitive Psychotherapy, 25,* 1–25.

Fennell, M.J.V (1998). Cognitive therapy in the treatment of low self-esteem. *Advances in Psychiatric Treatment, 4,* 296–304.

Fennell, M.J.V. (1999). *Overcoming low-self-esteem: A self-help guide using cognitive behavioral techniques.* London, England: Little, Brown Group.

Fennell, M.J.V. (2004). Depression, low self-esteem and mindfulness. *Behaviour Research and Therapy, 42,* 1053–1067. doi: 10.1016/j.brat.2004.03.002

Fennell, M.J.V. (2016). *Overcoming low self-esteem: A self-help guide using cognitive behavioral techniques.* London, England: Little, Brown Group.

Greenberg, J., Landau, M., & Arndt, J. (2013). Mortal cognition: Viewing self and the world from the precipice. In D. Carlston (Ed.), *The Oxford handbook of social cognition* (pp. 680–701). New York, NY: Oxford University Press.

Greenberg, J., Pyszczynski, T., & Solomon, S. (1986). The causes and consequences if the need for self-esteem: a terror management theory. In R.F. Baumeister (Ed.), *Public and private self* (pp. 189–212). New York, NY: Springer-Verlag.

Greenberg, J., Pyszczynski, T., Solomon, S., Pinel, E., Simon, L., & Jordan, K. (1993). Effects of self-esteem on vulnerability-denying defensive distortions: Further evidence of an anxiety-buffering function of self-esteem. *Journal of Experimental Social Psychology, 29,* 229–251.

Greenberg, J., Simon, L., Pyszczynski, T., Solomon, S., & Chatel, D. (1992). Terror management and tolerance: Does mortality salience always intensify negative reactions to others who threaten one's worldview? *Journal of Personality and Social Psychology, 63,* 212–220.

Greenberg, J., Solomon, S., Pyszczynski, T., Rosenblatt, A., Burling, J., Lyon, D., … Simon, L. (1992). Assessing the terror management analysis of self-esteem: Converging evidence of an anxiety-buffering function. *Journal of Personality and Social Psychology, 63,* 913–922.

Greenberg, J., Vail, K., & Pyszczynski, T. (2014). Chapter three: Terror management theory and research: How the desire for death transcendence drives our strivings for meaning and significance. *Advances in Motivation Science, 1,* 85–134. doi: http://dx.doi.org/10.1016/bs.adms.2014.08.003

Greenwald, A.G. & Banaji, M.R. (1995). Implicit social cognition: Attitudes, self-esteem, and stereotypes. *Psychological Review, 102*(1), 4–27.

Hall, P.L., & Tarrier, N. (2003). The cognitive-behavioural treatment of low self-esteem in psychotic patients: A pilot study. *Behaviour Research and Therapy, 41,* 317–332. doi: 10.1016/S0005-7967(02)00013-X

Harmon-Jones, E., Simon, L., Greenberg, J., Pyszczynski, T., & Solomon, S. (1997). Terror management theory and self-esteem: evidence that self-esteem attenuates mortality salience effects. *Journal of Personality and Social Psychology, 72,* 24–36.

Harris, R. (2006). Embracing your demons: An overview of acceptance and commitment therapy. *Psychotherapy in Australia, 12*(4), 2–8.

Hayes, S.C., Strosahl, K.D., & Wilson, K.G. (2012). *Acceptance and commitment therapy: The process and practice of mindful change* (2nd ed.). New York, NY: Guilford Press.

Hedrick, A.N. & Berlin, H.A. (2012). Implicit self-esteem in borderline personality and depersonalization disorder. *Frontiers in Psychology, 3*(91), 18. doi: 10.3389/fpsyg.2012.00091

Heine, S.J. (2001). Self as cultural product: An examination of East Asian and North American selves. *Journal of Personality, 69*, 881–905. doi: 10.1111/1467-6494.696168

Hirschberger, G., Florian, V., Mikulincer, M., Goldenberg, J.L., & Pyszczynski, T. (2002). Gender differences in the willingness to engage in risky behavior: A terror management perspective. *Death Studies, 26*, 117–141.

James, W. (1890). *Principles of psychology* (1–2). New York, NY: Holt.

Jonas, E., & Fischer, P. (2006). Terror management and religion: evidence through intrinsic religiousness, mitigated worldview defense after mortality salience. *Journal of Personality Social Psychology, 91*, 553–567.

Kierkegaard, S. (1957). *The concept of dread* (Walter Lowrie, Trans.). Princeton, NJ: Princeton University Press. (Original work published 1844, *Begrebet Angest* [The concept of anxiety])

Linehan, M.M. (1993a). *Cognitive-behavioral treatment of borderline personality disorder.* New York, NY: Guilford Press.

Linehan, M.M. (1993b). *Skills training manual for treating Borderline Personality Disorder.* New York, NY: Guilford Press.

Lynch, T.R., Chapman, A.L., Rosenthal, M.Z., Kuo, J.R., & Linehan, M.M. (2006). Mechanisms of change in dialectical behavior therapy: Theoretical and empirical observations. *Journal of Clinical Psychology, 62*(4), 459–480. doi: 10.1002/jclp. 20243

Lynum, L.I., Wilber, T., & Karterud, S. (2008). Self-esteem in patients with borderline and avoidant personality disorders. *Scandinavian Journal of Psychology, 49*, 469–477. doi: 10.1111/j.1467-9450.2008.00655.x

McManus, F., Waite, P., & Shafran, R. (2009). Cognitive–behavior therapy for low self-esteem: A case example. *Cognitive and Behavioral Practice, 16*, 266–275. doi: 10.1016/j.cbpra.2008.12.007

Pederson, L.D. (2015). *Dialectical behavior therapy: A contemporary guide for practitioners.* Chicester, England: Wiley-Blackwell.

Rigby, L.,W., & Waite, S. (2007). Group therapy for self-esteem, using creative approaches and metaphor as clinical tools. *Behavioral and Cognitive Psychotherapy, 35*, 361–364.

Robins, C.J. & Chapman, A.L. (2004). Dialectical behavior therapy: Current status, recent developments, and future directions. *Journal of Personality Disorders, 18*(1), 73–89.

Roepke, S., Schröder-Abé, M., Schütz, A., Jacob, G., Dams, A., Vater, A., … Lammers, C.H. (2010). Dialectic behavioural therapy has an impact on self-concept clarity and facets of self-esteem in women with borderline personality disorder. *Clinical Psychology and Psychotherapy, 18*, 145–158. doi: 10.1002/cpp. 684

Rosenberg, M. (1965). Society and the adolescent self-image. Princeton, NJ: Princeton University Press.

Safer, D.L., Telch, C.F., & Agras, W.A. (2001). Dialectical behavior therapy for bulimia nervosa. *American Journal of Psychiatry, 154*(4), 632–635. doi: 10.1176/appi.ajp. 158.4.632

Shirk, S., Burwell, R., & Harter, S. (2003). Strategies to modify low self-esteem in adolescents. In M.A. Reinecke, F.M. Dattilio, & A. Freeman (Eds.), *Cognitive therapy with children and adolescents: A casebook for clinical practice* (2nd ed.). New York, NY: Guilford.

Smith, E.R., & Mackie, D.M. (2007) Intergroup emotions. In M. Lewis, J. Haviland-Jones & L. Feldman Barrett (Eds.), *Handbook of emotions* (3rd ed.). New York, NY: Guilford.

Solomon, S., Greenberg, J., & Pyszczynski, T. (1991). A terror management theory of social behavior: On the psychological functions of self-esteem and cultural worldviews. *Advances in experimental social psychology, 24*, 93–159.

Solomon, S., Pyszczynski, T., & Greenberg, J. (2004). Willful determinism: Exploring the possibilities of freedom. In R.A. Wright, J. Greenberg, & S. Brehm (Eds.), *Motivational analyses of social behavior: Building on the contributions of Jack Brehm.* New York, NY: Erlbaum.

Taubman Ben-Ari, O., Florian, V., & Mikulincer, M. (1999). The impact of mortality salience on reckless drivingA test of terror management mechanisms. *Journal of Personality and Social Psychology, 76*, 35–45.

Taylor, T.L. & Montgomery, P. (2007). Can cognitive-behavioral therapy increase self-esteem among depressed adolescents? A systematic review. *Children and Youth Services Review, 29*, 823–839. doi: 10.1016/j.childyouth.2007.01.010

Telch, C.F., Agras, W.S., & Linehan, M.M. (2000). Group dialectical behavior therapy for binge-eating disorder: A preliminary, uncontrolled trial. *Behavior Therapy, 31*(3), 569–582. doi: 10.1016/S0005-7894(00)80031-3

Vater, A., Schröder-Abé, M., Schütz, A., Lammers, C.H., & Roepke, S. (2010). Discrepancies between explicit and implicit self-esteem are linked to symptom severity in borderline personality disorder. *Journal of Behavior Therapy and Experimental Psychiatry*, 357–364. doi: 10.1016/j.jbtep.2010.03.007

Zestcott, C.A., Lifshin, U., Helm, P.J., & Greenberg, J. (2017). He dies, he scores: Evidence that reminders of death motivate improved performance in basketball. *Journal of Sports and Exercise Psychology, 38*, 470–480. doi: http://dx.doi.org/10.1123/jsep.2016-0025

Chapter 13

Therapeutic interventions for the dread of death: Personal and clinical reflections

Thomas Heidenreich and Alexander Noyon

> Do not go gentle into that good night,
> Old age should burn and rave at close of day;
> Rage, rage against the dying of the light.
> — Dylan Thomas

> So set your restless heart at ease
> Take a lesson from these autumn leaves
> They waste no time waiting for the snow.
> — Leonard Cohen

> Save our last goodbye
> Embedded in my mind, your face will never leave me
> Save our last goodbye
> It's killing me that I won't get to hear your laughter anymore.
> — Disturbed

All three of the quotes above deal with emotions evoked by death in different circumstances: a Welsh poet who addresses his dying father and urges him to fight death, a singer-songwriter who uses the metaphor of falling leaves to ease the fear of death (apparently opposite of Dylan Thomas's poetic urging) and finally a contemporary heavy metal band mourning the death of someone who is not specified in detail in the song, (although at the beginning we hear a male voice leaving a positive message about his treatment at the hospital on an answering machine). When the present authors started our training in behaviour therapy nearly 25 years ago, we would not have thought that we would be able to incorporate material like this into a professional psychotherapeutic book chapter. But sometimes, both in life and in science, things that have been separate for a long time start coming together.

A wide separation has existed (and still does exist) between existential philosophy and psychotherapy on the one hand, and behaviour therapy on the other hand. However, for the past 10 years, we have started bringing behaviour therapy and existential issues together (Noyon & Heidenreich, 2007, 2011, 2012, 2017; Heidenreich & Noyon, 2011). While this practice attracted some interest from the German cognitive behaviour therapy (CBT) community (as well as scepticism), and initiated rich discussions with colleagues like Florian Gebler, we experienced our endeavour as rather local (Germany being the home of many existential philosophers of the 20th century) and limited in scope, with the rest of the CBT world more interested in behavioural and cognitive mechanisms than in the existential issues that are so central to our understanding of psychotherapy. Yet, as a turning point, during the 8th World Congress of Behavioural and Cognitive Therapies (WCBCT) in Melbourne in 2016, Ross Menzies (who was Congress President) convened a symposium on existential issues that one of us (T.H.) attended. One year later, Mehmet Sungur, President and Convenor of the 47th Congress of the European Association for Behavioural and Cognitive Therapies (EABCT) in Ljubljana (who also had invited Irvin Yalom, one of the most prominent existential psychotherapists, to Istanbul many years ago), invited both Rachel Menzies and Thomas Heidenreich to give plenary addresses on the fear of death (Menzies) and existential issues in CBT (Heidenreich). So — and probably becoming more apparent in the next decade — this may be a time of convergence between two traditions that were quite separate for a long time (and mostly on opposite sides of the fence of therapy schools).

Chapter 13 Therapeutic interventions for the dread of death: Personal and clinical reflections

Writing a chapter on death anxiety, especially if it is to be practical rather than empirical, is both a professional and a personal challenge; professionally, we all deal with patients that may have problems we are also struggling with (such as anxiety or depression, ageing parents and the like), but very often the problems that our patients are facing are quite removed from our own personal experiences. When dealing with death and dying, we all face an issue that either has affected us (by experiencing the death of loved ones), or that will affect us in the future (in our own deaths or in the death of loved ones). This personal involvement with death has important implications. First, we think that it is helpful (and necessary) to find one's own position towards death and dying as a therapist in order to be able to help patients confront their death-related anxieties. Second, depending on the current impact death has on our own lives, we may be more or less prepared to assist patients in dealing with their death anxieties. On a more personal level, having experienced the terminal illness and death of both our fathers during the past two years, we discovered that talking with patients about their death-related anxieties suddenly had taken on another meaning. We experienced strong emotions such as sadness while talking to our patients and struggled with whether it would be wise to tell our patients about our current life situation. We also experienced first-hand the importance of teaching practitioners from all relevant fields of expertise how to communicate with people who are confronted with a dying family member. The chief physician of the intensive care unit where my (A.N.) father passed away was totally unable to cope with his grieving relatives (my mother, sister and I) and was obviously naive about the appropriate counselling techniques to use in this type of situation and about establishing empathetic contact with those affected — and this deficit is especially disturbing because she experiences this situation at least weekly, if not almost on a daily basis in her field of work. In contrast, the hospice where my (T.H.) father died — and where my sister-in-law works as a nurse — was well prepared to make the last weeks of life as liveable as possible, providing my father, relatives and friends a dignified atmosphere to 'say our last farewells' while continually acknowledging that death was looming on the doorstep.

After reading these last few paragraphs it will probably come as no surprise that we prefer a rather personal and direct approach to dealing with the fear of death: thus, while the content of this chapter is rooted in (sometimes our subjective) experience as practicing psychotherapists, some of it is not (or only in very small proportions) evidence-based. Yet we are convinced that the body of empirical research will grow in this highly relevant area over the coming decades.

Case example

Manuela S., aged 34, started therapy due to a major depressive episode. During assessment, it became clear that the probable diagnosis was a dual depression, with long-standing (but never diagnosed) dysthymia that had started during adolescence. Manuela described experiencing her life as dull and meaningless — her work as a secretary did not satisfy her and she had little social contact, few friends and had not been involved in a romantic relationship with the exception of a brief relationship with a co-worker that had ended abruptly (the end of the relationship was, in fact, the start of the major depressive episode that led to her seeking treatment). Therapy with Manuela lasted for a duration of 9 months with mostly weekly sessions and was highly successful: after exploring and scheduling meaningful activities (such as joining a local sports club and approaching possible friends and partners) and working on her social skills, Manuela made a few friends and met a man with whom she became intimate. Although we had discussed ending therapy, Manuela came for one of her last sessions in tears and full of despair; her gynaecologist had detected a lump in her breast and had scheduled a mammography followed up by a biopsy. The biopsy revealed a malignant tumour in her left breast with further testing showing that the lymph nodes were also affected. Further treatment was planned (chemotherapy, radiation therapy) and more assessments were scheduled (e.g., PET to detect possible metastasis in other areas of the body). In the therapy session, Manuela was crying and angry at the same time, accusing herself of 'not having lived my life fuller when I still had it'. She said she felt 'cheated by life' and was horrified by the thought that 'now that I have finally started living a more meaningful life it will probably be over'. This news was shocking for me (T.H.) as well, with no solution at hand.

Fear of death and dying can arise within psychotherapeutic treatments in completely different ways — unexpectedly in patients who are in therapy for other issues, as in this case example, but also as the starting point and primary target of therapy (e.g., for a person who is physically healthy but sees oneself confronted with one's own ultimate mortality through other ways like the death of a loved one or a pet). Conceptualising the role that the fear of death plays for a patient in his or her current life situation is crucial for developing a therapeutic strategy. As in Manuela's case, being confronted with a potentially life-threatening illness is highly likely to activate the fear of death that has not been manifested before. Yet even though the situation of a life-threatening and potentially terminal illness is unarguably exceptional, we are all going to die sooner or later. This remark should not be understood as an attempt to trivialise the suffering of people with life-threatening illnesses but rather show that we all have our defence mechanisms that operate to keep this fear at bay (see Chapters 3, 4, 6, 8 and 12 in the present volume).

Religious and philosophical approaches

When seeking guidance to develop effective therapeutic strategies, psychotherapists usually consult the theories of their respective therapeutic traditions. Of course, this will also be the case when dealing with patients who are afraid of death. For example, psychodynamic traditions will emphasise the role of psychodynamic mechanisms (e.g., Yalom) while behaviour therapists will be more inclined to analyse the potential role of avoidance and catastrophic thinking. With regard to the fear of death, the situation is quite different; besides therapeutic traditions, uncountable numbers of religions and philosophies have dealt with this central fact of life and its inescapability. Rachel Menzies (see Chapter 1 in the present volume) has summarised ways in which people from different cultures have conceptualised and dealt with the fear of death over the centuries. Psychotherapists are well advised to open their perspectives to these traditions as they may provide insights and inspire strategies for therapy.

It is beyond the scope of this chapter to even give a brief overview of religious and philosophical traditions relevant in this field. Examples that may appear strange in our modern times are the 'dances of death' (artistic representations that vividly portray the power of death over life) that were popular in the Europe of the late Middle Ages (Wunderlich, 2001) or meditations in the presence of dead bodies in the Buddhist tradition (Satipatthana Sutra, or the *Four foundations of mindfulness*, Silananda, 2002, p. 70) where the practitioners envision decay, decomposition and finally the elimination of the own body. For behaviourally oriented therapists, who consider exposure to be one of their most important therapeutic techniques, the intensity of the moment of exposure to death and its related anxieties inherent in these traditions can be overwhelming.

Existential philosophy (see Chapters 3 and 8 in the present volume) is especially rich in providing inspirations for therapy. Existentialist thinkers have repeatedly emphasised that considering death as an event that follows 'after' life and terminates life, while not wrong in itself, is at least in part misleading. Indeed, it may motivate people to keep the thought (and potentially the anxiety) of death away from life as long as possible, thus excluding it from one's own existence (see further Chapter 12 in the present volume). As a prominent example, Martin Heidegger rejected this separation of life and death; in his typical idiosyncratic language, he called this stance 'ordinary being towards death ..., which, as a decaying one, is a continuous flight from it' (Heidegger, 1972). This attitude is in constant danger to lead to an 'improper life' because the attitude towards one's own life is distorted by the role which is attributed to death — namely none. An alternative stance (termed 'actual being towards death') is characterised by the individual acknowledging death and realising that death is always with us, from the beginning of our lives until the end. This 'actual way of existence' enables humans to fully draw on their potential, to turn themselves towards shaping the present and thereby living a more meaningful life. They stop postponing their life, for instance, by distracting themselves from the reality of their own deaths (e.g., 'I have lots of time, I can also do that tomorrow or the day after tomorrow') and thus are able to live more fully.

Therapeutic interventions to deal with the fear of death

Potentially, a large number of psychotherapeutic techniques can be useful when dealing with the fear of death. However, before setting out to devise a psychotherapeutic approach, we have to decide whether psychotherapy is the intervention of choice at all. Searching for methods that enable therapists to deal with the fear of death is understandable, however, it can also be a type of avoidance. That is, confronted with death and dying, there will be no way to 'fix the unfixable' or, more concretely, there is no 'solution' to be found. Despite the fact that in many areas of psychotherapy manuals provide security and invaluable skills for therapists, this may not be appropriate when dealing with death and dying. Therefore, the ideas presented in this chapter should rather be understood as basic guidelines that might offer some orientation on a journey that remains fundamentally unpredictable and, therefore, can only be planned partially.

Is psychotherapy the appropriate tool?
The role of the patient's Weltanschauung (worldview)

While therapy in many instances can be completed successfully without a deeper knowledge of the patient's religious and/or philosophical convictions, this is hardly possible when dealing with the fear of death. Some patients fear their ultimate mortality and anticipated meaninglessness associated with it (expecting life to be over at the time of death), while others may be afraid of what awaits them after they have died (especially if they did not adhere to their religious beliefs). Thus, we strongly encourage therapists to explore the meaning of death and dying in the individual *Weltanschauung* of each patient. It can be expected that the stance towards death for a believing Christian or Muslim, who await the judgement of God or Allah, is probably highly different than that of an atheist or agnostic. Questions such as 'What does dying mean for you?', 'Do you consider yourself to be a religious person?' or 'Do you believe in life after death?' may help explore the worldview of the patient and its implications. Becoming familiar with the individual belief system of the patient also means that we have to determine in which domains we can work and if we should offer therapy at all. Some questions (e.g., involving guilt and forgiveness) may be much better addressed by a religious leader of the patient's belief system than by a psychotherapist. Looking at the case example of Manuela, she described her outlook on life as 'not too strongly religious'. Having been raised in a Christian tradition with parents that attended church 'twice a year', the Christian faith did not carry much importance for her at this point in time. 'I don't expect to go to either heaven or hell if I don't survive this' was how she summarised her outlook on life after death. Clearly, her belief system did not provide a resource outside of therapy to deal with her situation.

Case formulation for death anxiety

Death anxiety can present clinically in different situations (e.g., when confronted with a severe illness, 'out of the blue' fear of issues associated with dying, fear of the end of life), and it is important to first describe the exact nature of the fears. In this chapter, we will restrict our analysis to the fear of death that is at least partially consciously accessible to the patient while at the same time acknowledging the broader view of death anxiety espoused by Yalom (1980) who argues that the primary source of all psychopathology is a poorly processed fear of death.

Exploration of the patient's anxiety should initially focus on the content of the fears: Is the patient afraid of death in the sense of life's finitude or is s/he rather afraid of the suffering that may go along with dying (i.e., fear of dying rather than fear of death). In our case example of Manuela, her initially strong reaction to the diagnosis of metastatic breast cancer is hardly pathological. Most of the readers (and ourselves) have had the experience of loved ones (friend or family) being diagnosed with a life-threatening illness and may remember their own intense reactions. Rather than pathologising normal and intense emotions and reactions (in some cultures women pull out their hair in mourning), we assume that pathological developments are characterised by the fear of death paralysing patients and thereby hindering their attempts to live their lives.

It will usually be helpful to first analyse the patient's reaction in the physiological, cognitive, emotional and behavioural domains and then explore long-lasting basic assumptions of the patients. In Manuela's case, it soon became evident that her feeling of 'not having lived her life' was overwhelming and threatened to throw her back into depressed passivity. She was also afraid of the medical procedures awaiting her, but she trusted her physicians to manage her pain and other symptoms. Therefore, the most distressing experience for Manuela was her overwhelming feeling of having led an 'unlived life'.

Therapeutic stance
The first (and probably the most important) intervention for death anxiety is validation: (1) Yes, it is hard to receive a diagnosis like this; (2) No, you don't have to be in control of your confusing emotions at this time; and (3) Yes, life can be unfair. Manuela, for example, felt understood when I (T.H.) validated all these conflicting responses and did not attempt to change them in any way but rather respected an event that profoundly altered all experiences that had occurred. (One is reminded of another popular poem titled 'Funeral Blues' by W.H. Auden: 'Stop all the clocks, cut off the telephone, prevent the dog from barking with a juicy bone'). One of my (A.N.) patients had completed chemotherapy successfully after an initial onset of cancer but suffered a severe anxiety relapse afterwards, and it irritated him that nobody — not his family, not his friends — wanted to hear anything about his fears. ('Therapy was successful, come on, just be happy!'). He became so angry with the situation that he was on the brink of reacting violently, so his wife led him to therapy. He was very relieved when I validated his fears, and after this he was able to hear me also validating the avoidance behaviour of his family ('It is natural that your wife can't stand hearing your fears of dying and leaving her alone with two

kids'). Following this, the contact to his loved ones increased substantially. Unfortunately, his fears were justified, and he is currently suffering with cancer for a second time.

Validating the fear of death requires experience along with a certain amount of courage and the willingness for self-disclosure on the side of the therapist. We assume that taking a therapeutic stance that is characterised by openness and courage in the face of death is more important than any other individual strategy or technique. There may be no easy way for acquiring this therapeutic stance: Some therapists will have had similar experiences in their lives and work and will use this knowledge while others may have not had that 'privilege'. We agree with Yalom (2009) that adhering to the usual therapist role may be problematic because it can be a sign of avoidance of the topic. For example, insisting that the thought 'It is horrible that I might die soon' is an overgeneralisation involving catastrophising, and then offering means of cognitively exploring and restructuring this thought, may make some sense in theory but clearly will not be helpful to the client initially. Rather, honestly sharing one's own thoughts and feelings may be the most appropriate way — even if this includes unwanted emotions such as helplessness, sadness and shock. Having said this, we also assume that while we stay in contact with the patient's suffering, we have to somehow 'keep our heads above the water' ourselves. It is very important to accept — as a therapist — that there is nothing that we can *really* do when someone is dying or suffering from loss. That is, often what the person *really* wants is to stay alive or to have their lost person back. If the therapeutic stance taken in such a situation is like the one portrayed here, then the therapist is capable to allow what Shakespeare suggested over 400 years ago. In our view, it remains the best way to deal with the mental pain of loss, (noting that these words of wisdom are uttered by Malcolm after being told that his castle had been attacked and his wife and children slaughtered):

> Give sorrow words. The grief that does not speak
>
> Whispers the o'erfraught heart and bids it break.
>
> *Shakespeare, Macbeth (Act 4, Scene 3)*

Therapy as human company

One of the aspects of death that patients are afraid of is that the process of dying is a lonely endeavour. Yalom (2009) has stressed the importance of 'offering mere presence' as opposed to providing therapeutic strategies. As in all therapy, we have to be real and present with the patient and help her or him to establish meaningful relations with other people. Of course, therapy itself can be a very important meaningful relationship, even until the final day or days of the patient's life. From our experience, the nearer the moment of death of a patient, the more the relationship becomes a 'normal' relationship, with fewer characteristics of the 'professional', therapeutic relationship. It can be challenging for therapists to balance the required closeness and the necessary separation at the same time. In Manuela's case, although suffering from a life-threatening condition, she was not close to death in the sense described in this paragraph. Nevertheless, she later stated that 'having you by my side during this horrible time' was very valuable for her.

Distinguishing problems and facts

In the face of death, it is highly important not to confuse problems and facts. Dying patients often wish that they would have 'more time', but therapists are unable to provide this and of course should not aim to do so. In this sense, therapy cannot be solution focused because there may not be a solution — and neither is there a problem (since these are usually characterised by the possibility of solutions), because death is a fact of life. Nevertheless, besides these existential aspects of death, dying is also accompanied by a large number of tasks that have to be accomplished, such as taking care of one's financial affairs, providing relatives with important passwords and account information, and so on. Sometimes therapists recoil from these bureaucratic issues, but in our experience patients are very grateful when therapists address these questions carefully and with respect. Returning to what we mentioned in the last paragraph when speaking about the balance between being too close or too distant from a patient, working with people who are confronted with death and dying challenges therapists with many situations where they have to find equilibrium between the two extremes.

Dealing with the finitude of life

Some patients suffer from the notion that life loses its meaning through death. In this case, we can explore this thought more thoroughly (although not all patients will experience relief). One thought experiment that may be helpful is exploring the option of endless living: while many patients are open to this thought at first, it usually becomes obvious that there would be a high price to pay (as exemplified by Count Fosca in Simone de Beauvoir's 1992 story, *All men are mortal*). Living eternally would mean that we do not have to make choices right now (after all, we could still do the activity at hand a century later). Furthermore, if the rest of mankind remained mortal (as in de Beauvoir's thought experiment), the immortal person would experience the death of many loved ones — potentially culminating in the opinion that it is safest not to form meaningful human relationships at all. What all these reflections suggest is that while we may die at a point where important aspects of life are not 'finished' (i.e., children raised, professional work completed), the only way forward is to stop wishful thinking ('If I only had another year …') and live the life that is still remaining — no matter how long or short this might be. For Manuela, the part of therapy dealing with these matters was long and sometimes painful. During the months of medical treatment in which I (T.H.) visited her in the oncology ward, she experienced moments of serenity 'just living' while sometimes she was simply too weak to gather a single thought together during chemotherapy. Yet, after months of invasive therapy when her doctors proclaimed that 'all that can be done is done' and she had returned to work and moved into a shared flat with her partner, she felt increasingly confident that she could continue to live meaningfully regardless of whether her life would last for some months (which, at least at this point, seemed unlikely), years (which seemed probable) or decades (which seemed at least possible). In one of the last sessions of her therapy, she told me 'that she learned a lesson the hard way — postponing life is a dangerous thing, as is grieving things that should have been done years ago'. She described herself as having become 'more courageous' in life, asking herself 'will I probably get another chance?' when possibilities opened up and she felt afraid.

Leaving traces in the world

For some patients, it is helpful to explore what will remain of them after they are gone. While we may not survive individually, we will leave traces of ourselves in the world. This may include one's own children and the memories these children have, and/or personal and professional impacts. This thought is beautifully described by Yalom (2009) using the metaphor of a stone in a pond that forms ever larger ripples. This notion was neither comforting nor important for Manuela, she told me — for her, it was enough to have meaningful relationships in life.

The role of consciousness

Another intervention that Yalom (2009) borrowed from Epicurus is the reflection on what death really brings — in fact, when we are dead we cannot be sad or angry about this. Where we are death is not, and where death is we are not. This is even more obvious when we become aware of the fact that we did not live for eons before our birth (as we will not live for eons after death). To enlighten a patient about this, a useful contemplation is that almost everyone who is frightened about not being here until the end of time did not think about the fact that they have not been here since the beginning of the universe, but only entered existence at their birth.

Dealing with anxiety of dying

As stated above, it is useful to distinguish between fear of death and fear of dying. For people who have already entered the dying phase and are affected by it (e.g., experiencing intense pain), psychotherapeutic interventions play a secondary role, with medical interventions and palliative care being centre stage. Only when these have succeeded in stabilising the physical condition will it be possible to deal with the mental reality of dying. As people become closer to death, fewer therapeutic options remain available to treat them. As described above, simply 'being there' is important and helps clients to deal with their anxiety and other feelings, thus comforting them. Usually, this role will be taken by friends and family; however, some patients are so isolated that this can become a very important role for therapists to fill.

Alongside these philosophical arguments, there is another dimension to fear of death and dying: the fear of pain, loss of capabilities and other suffering, for instance, feeling threatened by being unable to breathe. A sometimes shockingly honest description of the physiological course of dying is provided by Nuland (1995). Given the often unbearable pain in the terminal phase of cancer, reflections on mortality and existential issues seem a bit of a 'luxury' problem — longstanding illness as the cause of dying will most likely be associated with the body being in the front row of experience. Fortunately, modern palliative medicine is able to abate almost all symptoms of dying, with the most powerful intervention of terminal sedation, if nothing else, effective for the treatment of pain. Therefore, from our point of view it is essential to counsel dying patients very thoroughly on the capabilities of modern palliative care to dispel their irrational fears of the process of dying as much as possible.

But also people who are not ill can be possessed by this fear. One experience that is especially difficult is the isolation that sometimes comes with death: Melanie Lockett (2009), who has repeatedly worked with terminally ill patients and who also underwent radiation therapy herself describes her feelings of utter loneliness on the table when undergoing radiation therapy.

Bibliotherapy and art

When dealing with the fear of death, bibliotherapy as well as using therapeutic tools of other media such as movies and music can be very helpful. Gaining a reflected position on death together with the client equates to entering an existential search process together with the client rather than trying to provide solutions. The aim of this process is achieved when the client gains a position where mortality is not just accepted in a resigned way but rather enriches the experience of living. Once more we want to emphasise that mortality is not a problem that can be solved — thus, the aim of all therapy and counselling must be to help clients overcome a perspective that is blocking their view on life and death.

In therapy, we regularly recommend books to patients and ask them to mark passages that are relevant for them. Albom (2002), Pausch (2008) and Yalom (2009) have authored books that we have found helpful in this existential search process. *Tuesdays with Morrie* (Albom, 2002) tells the story of Mitch, an American sports journalist, whose former teacher Morrie Schwartz suffers from ALS. Mitch visits Morrie on Tuesdays to discuss matters of life and death, and the written notes that the author has kept of these talks are enormously fruitful from our point of view. *The last lecture* takes this American tradition literally — Randy Pausch, an information technology professor at Carnegie Mellon, received the diagnosis of incurable pancreatic cancer and prepared and presented his final lecture on 'Really achieving your childhood dreams' shortly before his death in 2008 at the age of 46 years. *Staring at the sun: Overcoming the terror of death* by Irvin Yalom (2009) is a very popular book by one of the most influential existential therapists of our times. From a Buddhist perspective, but pertinent for most people is *Living in the light of death* by Larry Rosenberg (2000). People with a Christian background can benefit from reading the Bible (e.g., the Psalms). Using bibliotherapy in this way requires the familiarity of therapists with both the books they recommend and with the topic of mortality. Some patients can also benefit from reading academic literature on death and dying such as Frankl's (1986) *The doctor and the soul: From psychotherapy to logotherapy*.

There is a wide variety of music that can be included, from the last choral in Bach's *Matthäus Passion* (i.e., *We are sitting down in tears*) to popular music (e.g., *Save our last goodbye* by the Chicago-based heavy metal band, Disturbed). Of course, the choice of music has to fit the patient's musical preferences and general outlook on life — for us, it is amazing that feelings and thoughts of comparable depth can be found in such different musical traditions.

Closing remarks

It should be clear to the reader that there is no really convincing possibility to *solve* the dilemma of our existence (i.e., that we all will die one day) because it is a fact rather than a problem. While the interventions described above may be helpful for some patients, in the end everyone has to find their own answer. Therefore, we have outlined various ways of dealing with one of the 'biggest' questions that humans face from a therapeutic standpoint in which we strongly encourage therapists to confront their own anxieties related to death. In our view, this is necessary to have a therapeutic stance that enables the therapist to honestly encounter the patient in therapy. This therapeutic stance is much more important than any particular therapeutic technique. Put another way, dealing with death is not as simple as following the guidelines outlined in therapy manuals. However, the various approaches discussed here might prove helpful for therapists treating patients confronted with the issues of death and dying.

References

Albom, M. (2002). *Tuesdays with Morrie: An old man, a young man, and life's greatest lesson.* New York, NY: Broadway Books

De Beauvoir, S. (1992). *All men are mortal.* New York, NY: Norton.

Frankl, V.E. (1986). *The doctor and the soul: From psychotherapy to logotherapy.* New York, NY: Vintage.

Heidegger, M. (1972). *Sein und Zeit* [Being and time], 12. Auflage. Tübingen, Germany: Max Niemeyer.

Heidenreich, T. & Noyon, A. (2011). Existenzielle Therapieansätze: Entwicklungen und Potenzial für die Kognitive Verhaltenstherapie [Existential approaches: Development and potential for cognitive behaviour therapy]. *Verhaltenstherapie und Psychosoziale Praxis, 43*(3), 571–581.

Lockett, M. (2009). Reflections on cancer counselling. In Laura Barnett (Ed.). *When death enters the therapeutic space. Existential perspectives in psychotherapy and counselling* (pp. 45–56). London, England: Routledge.

Noyon, A. & Heidenreich, T. (2007). Die existenzielle Perspektive in der Verhaltenstherapie [The existential perspective in behavior therapy] *Verhaltenstherapie, 17*, 122–128.

Noyon, A. & Heidenreich, T. (2011). Umgang mit Tod und Sterben in Psychotherapie und Beratung. [Dealing with death and dying in psychotherapy and counselling]. *Verhaltenstherapie und Psychosoziale Praxis, 43*(3), 605–620.

Noyon, A. & Heidenreich, T. (2012). *Existenzielle Ansätze in Beratung und Therapie.* [Existential approaches in counselling and therapy]. Weinheim, Germany: Beltz.

Noyon, A. & Heidenreich, T. (2017). Existenzielle Ansätze. Ein Plädoyer für Realitätsorientierung und Menschlichsein. [Existential issues. A plea for reality orientation and humanity]. In D. Bertold, J. Gramm, M. Gaspar, & U. Sibelius (Hrsg), *Psychotherapeutische Perspektiven am Lebensende* (S. 121–136). Göttingen, Germany: Vandenhoeck & Ruprecht.

Nuland, S.B. (1995). *How we die: reflections on life's final chapter.* New York, NY. Vintage.

Pausch, R. (2008). *The last lecture.* New York, NY: Hyperion.

Rosenberg, L. (2000). *Living in the light of death. On the art of being truly alive.* Boston, MA: Shambhala.

Silananda, V.U. (2002). *The four foundations of mindfulness.* Boston, MA: Wisdom Publications.

Yalom, I.D. (1980). *Existential psychotherapy.* New York, NY: Basic Books.

Yalom, I.D. (2009). *Staring at the sun: Overcoming the terror of death.* New York, NY: Wiley.

www.ingramcontent.com/pod-product-compliance
Lightning Source LLC
Chambersburg PA
CBHW070321240426
43671CB00013BA/2324